N. Murray

MEMOIRS

OF THE

REV. NICHOLAS MURRAY, D.D.

(KIRWAN.)

BY

SAMUEL IRENÆUS PRIME,

AUTHOR OF

"TRAVELS IN EUROPE AND THE EAST," "THE POWER OF PRAYER," "THE OLD WHITE MEETING-HOUSE," "LETTERS FROM SWITZERLAND," &c., &c.

NEW YORK:
HARPER & BROTHERS, PUBLISHERS,
FRANKLIN SQUARE.
1862.

TO KIRWAN'S FRIEND

AND MINE,

THE REV. WILLIAM BUEL SPRAGUE, D.D.,

THIS VOLUME

Is Affectionately Inscribed.

INTRODUCTORY NOTE.

THE author of this volume thinks it proper to state that with him its preparation has been solely a labor of love, performed at the solicitation of the surviving family of his lamented friend, to whom all the avails of the work exclusively belong.

The rich materials furnished in the manuscripts of Dr. Murray, and in the reminiscences by his friends, have made a memorial of rare interest and value, to which the biographer could add little or nothing. The strange and romantic incidents in the childhood and youth of the subject of these memoirs, his early and wonderful rescue from the wiles of a false religion, his rapid mental and moral development, his brilliant career and well-earned fame, and, above all, his vast usefulness as a pastor, preacher, and author, make him an illustrious example worthy of record for the encouragement of the young, the edification of the Church, and the praise of Divine Grace.

CONTENTS.

CHAPTER I.

CHAPTER II.

CHAPTER III.

CHAPTER IV.

CHAPTER V.

CHAPTER VI.

CHAPTER VII.

CHAPTER VIII.

CHAPTER IX.

CHAPTER X.

CHAPTER XI.

CHAPTER XII.

CHAPTER XIII.

CHAPTER XIV.

CHAPTER XV.

CHAPTER XVI.

CHAPTER XVII.

CHAPTER XVIII.

CHAPTER XIX.

CHAPTER XX.

CHAPTER XXI.

MEMOIRS

OF THE

REV. DR. MURRAY.

CHAPTER I.

Birth, Parentage, and Early Associations.—Hardships of his Childhood and Youth.—Comes to this Country.—Enters the Harpers' Printing Establishment.—Religious Awakening.—What he saw of Popery when a Boy.—How he was disgusted with the System.

Coming to America. The future.

THE ship Martha, from Dublin, about forty-five years ago, brought a crowd of Irish emigrants to our shores. Among them was a lad seventeen years old, who had come alone to seek his fortune in the western world. In the month of July, 1818, he set his foot in the streets of New York, with little money in his pocket, and no place to call his home. It would have been presumption to predict that this friendless, wandering Roman Catholic boy would become a distinguished Protestant divine, a champion of the faith, and win a name to go back on the wings of fame to the green isle he had left.

Such a lad was Nicholas Murray; such was his introduction to this country, and such was his future career.

He was born in Ballynaskea, in the County of Westmeath, Ireland, December 25, 1802. He was the son of Nicholas and Judith Mangum Murray, both of them being Irish Roman Catholics, though their Christian names are indicative of a different parentage. His father was a farmer of some property, and exerted considerable influence in the civil affairs of the neighborhood in which he lived. He died when his son Nicholas was only three years old.

The son remained at home under the care of his mother till he was about nine years old, when he went to live with an aunt, the sister of his mother, some ten or twelve miles distant, where he went to school till he reached the age of twelve. Now he was old enough to begin to earn something, and he was apprenticed as a merchant's clerk in a store in Grannard, near Edgeworthtown, where he remained three years. These were eventful years in his mental and moral history, as we shall see when he comes to speak of the first influences that the practices of the Roman Catholic Church made upon his mind.

He was sadly and badly used by his employer, but he bore it as well as he could for three long dreadful years, and then fled from the oppression to his mother's house. But his mother disapproved of this step, and entreated him to return to the service from which he had escaped. He steadily refused, and chose to embark on the wide world, and seek his fortune beyond the seas, in the land of the West. He told his brother that he would relinquish all right to any property that might hereafter be his from the estate of his father if he would give him ready money enough to take him to America. His brother gave him the necessary aid, and he left his native land.

His mother was a woman of strong feelings, and bitterly opposed to his going away. She was grievously offended with him for leaving the store, and even more for going abroad, and in the spirit of her Church had him cursed from the altar. A few years afterward, when she heard that he had become a Protestant, she had masses said for the repose of his soul, and regarded him as dead. She died without, so far as he ever knew, breathing a word of forgiveness or regard for the boy who lived to be the crown of her house, and a rich blessing to the world.

The curses of a priest that followed the lad as he went to Dublin to embark for America did him no harm.

He had about twelve dollars in money when he came to New York. Finding lodgings, he began to search for business, going from place to place in the city, willing to work, and resolved to do any thing that was honest for the sake of support. It was a kind Providence that directed him to the printing-house of the Messrs. Harper, who were then in business in Pearl Street.

Unlike many employers, these men felt a deep responsibility for those whom they employed, and the most of their apprentices at that time were boarded and lodged under their own roof. Young Murray was thus immediately introduced into a Protestant Christian family, into associations with young men of his own age who had been religiously educated; and the influences were eminently favorable to his own moral improvement.

Few, if any, boys ever came into the establishment of the Harpers with less promise in their appearance and manner than Murray. His education and associations in the old country had not fitted him to fill any position that required culture; but he was ready to turn his hand to any thing useful. He worked at the printing business and at the press with a steady cheerfulness that won for him the favor of all around him. Even at this period in his history, a vein of humor, technically called Irish humor, ran through his conversation, making him a lively, genial companion.

The Harpers were and are members of the Methodist Episcopal Church. The partners were then the brothers James and John. Two younger brothers, Wesley and Fletcher Harper, who are now with them in the firm of Harper & Brothers, were then working at the business with Murray and others. They were also his companions by night and day, occupying the same room with him in their mother's house. This mother of the Harpers was a mother indeed: a woman full of faith and the Holy Spirit, a living witness and example of the power of that religion which she loved, and commended to all in her house. Dr. Murray has often said that the first misgivings that he felt after coming to this country as to the reality of the religion in which he was born and taught were caused by the holy life and conversation of this venerable and pious woman. She was then making an impression upon the mind of one who was afterward to make his mark upon the mind of the world.

One of his fellow-apprentices is now the Rev. P. C. Oakley, of the Methodist Episcopal Church. He also lodged in the same room with him and the younger Harpers. Mr. Oakley says,

"I remember his fine ruddy countenance and hair as black as a raven. His voice and appearance clearly indicated that he came from the Emerald Isle. Being myself a Protestant, and associating with him constantly, we had frequent and earnest controversies on the subject of religion. He often became greatly excited. On one occasion, after I had gone to bed, he became so out of patience with me in one of our doctrinal controversies that he exclaimed, 'I would not be a Methodist or a Presbyterian if I knew they were right!' Of course that silenced me for that time. He, however, became modified in his views and feelings, and ultimately became first a Methodist, and then a Presbyterian. There was at this time a gracious revival of religion in progress in the John Street Methodist Church, then under the pastoral care of the Rev. Tobias Spicer. Young Murray attended the meetings, became deeply interested, and professed to be converted to God."

From the moment that his mind was awakened by the religious exercises in this Christian household, and by the discussions he had with the young men around him, he determined to look for himself into the truth of the system in which he had been trained in his childhood. He went to the Bible, not doubting that he should find it all there. But he was so ignorant of the Bible, though eighteen years of age, that he did not know the difference between the Old and the New Testaments; he could not tell whether Moses was or was not one of the apostles, or Paul one of the ancient prophets! His education had been in the rites and ceremonies of the Roman Catholic Church, but not in the word and doctrine of the Bible. In after years, when setting forth the reasons that induced him to leave the Church of Rome, he gives an account of his own personal experience that will be read with even intenser interest in this connection:

"I was born of Roman Catholic parents, and received my early education in the full faith of that Church. I was baptized by a priest—I was confirmed by a bishop—I often went to confession—I have worn my amulets, and I have said my Pater Nosters and my Hail Marys more times than I can now enumerate. When a youth, none excelled me in my attention to Mass, nor in the performance of the penances enjoined by the father confessor; and, whatever were my occasional mental misgivings, I remained a true son of the Church until I had at least outgrown my boyhood. Then, on as full an examination of the subject as I could give it, I came to the conclusion that I could not remain a Roman Catholic. I first became an infidel. Knowing nothing of religion but that which was taught me by parents and priests, and thinking that that was the sum of it, when that was rejected, infidelity became my only alternative. Could it be otherwise? Subsequently, by the reading of the Bible and by the grace of God, I was led to embrace the religion of the Gospel.

"Although the son of intelligent parents, and educated from my youth for the mercantile profession, the miraculous power of the priest is yet associated with my earliest recollections of him. Two things greatly shook my faith in the possession of this power. There resided not far from my parental residence a priest, whose fame as a miracle-worker was known all over the county in which he resided. The road to his house (called in that country a bridle-road) went by our door. I frequently saw, in the morning, individuals riding by, with a little keg resting before them on the saddle, or a jug hanging by the horse's side. I often asked who they were, and where they were going. I was told that they were going to Father C——'s to get some of their sick cured. I asked what was in the keg or jug. I was told that it was Irish whisky to pay the priest for his cures. I asked why they went so early in the morning. I was answered that unless they went early they would not find him sober. The tabernacle of poor Father C—— was made of dry clay, and needed a daily wetting.

"In one of the large interior towns of Ireland where I resided, the bishop of the diocese met his priests, or a part of them, once a year. Their meeting was always held in the house where I resided, and over the store in which I was then a clerk. Among the priests that always met the bishop was the rollicking Father B——, whose fame as a miracle-worker was extensive.

He had also a reputation for learning and eloquence, and, because of his connection with an old and wealthy family, exerted a wide social influence. He always staid with us when he came to town. About ten o'clock one night, after one of those meetings of bishop and priests, I went out to shut up the store windows, and, hearing a singular noise in the gutter, I went forward and assisted a man out of the mire. I soon recognized him to be Father B——, the miracle-worker. Running in, I announced, with some excitement, to the lady of the house, that Father B—— was drunk in the street. I received for my pains a stunning slap on the side of the face, with this admonition, 'Never say again that a priest is drunk.' This was a very impressive argument, and which, for some time, rung in my ears. I staggered under the blow. I assisted in cleaning off his reverence. I gave him his brandy next morning; and, young as I was, my faith in miracle-working priests was effectually shaken. Although fearing to draw the conclusion, I felt it, that God would not bestow miraculous power upon those who lived a life, not of occasional, but of habitual intemperance.

"The doctrine of Purgatory is one of the peculiar and most cherished doctrines of the Roman Catholic Church. In Ireland the custom of the priest is, at a certain point in the service of the Mass, to turn his back to the altar and his face to the people, and to read a long list of the names of deceased persons whose souls are in Purgatory, and to offer up a prayer for their deliverance from it. This is done, or used to be done, in our chapel on every Sabbath. To obtain the name of a deceased relative on that magic list, the priest must be paid so much a year, varying, I believe, with the ability of the friends to pay. If the yearly payment is not made when due, the name of the person is erased from the list. A respectable man in our parish died in midlife, leaving a widow and a large family of children to mourn his loss. True to her religious principles and to her generous instincts, the widow had her husband's name placed on that list, and heard, with pious gratitude, his name read over from Sabbath to Sabbath, with a prayer offered for the deliverance of his soul from Purgatory. After the lapse of two or three years, on a certain Sabbath the name of her husband was omitted from the list. The fact filled her with mingled joy and fear—joy, thinking that her husband had escaped from Purgatory; and fear, lest she had done something to offend the priest; and they are very easily offended when money is in question. On timid inquiry, she learned that his soul was yet in Purgatory, but that she had forgotten to send in the yearly tax at the time it was due. The tax was promptly paid, and the name was restored on the next Sabbath. That widow was my own mother, who sought the release of the soul of my father from Purgatory. This incident made a deep impression upon my youthful mind, and shook my faith in the whole system. And, as far as memory serves me, Father M—— was an amiable man, and above the ordinary level of the men of his calling.

"Another fact which early impressed me in reference to Purgatory was this. The Romish Church makes a distinction between mortal and venial sinners. The former go to hell forever; the latter go to Purgatory, 'whence they are taken by the prayers and alms offered for them, and principally by the holy sacrifice of the Mass.' Now I always saw that the *most mortal* sinners, that every body would say went to hell, could always have masses said for them as if they went to Purgatory, provided their friends could pay; and that *less mortal* sinners, that people would say went to Purgatory, were sent to hell if their friends could not pay for masses for them; and their souls were kept in Purgatory for a long while when their friends paid promptly every year, but their souls were soon prayed out whose friends could not pay long for them. Facts like these very early impressed my mind, and shook my faith in the religion of my parents and priests; and when, in maturer years, I could more fully consider them, they led me to reject religion as a fable cunningly devised by priests.

"Again: to pray to angels and saints is a doctrine of the Romish Church. In our parish chapel there were a great many pictures of saints, with very little pretension to art, and which reflected but little credit on painter or engraver. Whose pictures they were I do not remember; but on Sabbath morning, an hour before Mass, I have often seen the poor people, and even some more wealthy and refined, going on their knees from the one picture to the other, and counting their beads, and bowing before them with external acts of the most profound and sincere worship. Although then I thought differently, I have not now a doubt but that it was idolatry. But the idea that struck me was this: Here are some praying to Peter, or Paul, or John, or Mary; the same pictures are hung up in ten thousand chapels all over the world, and in all these chapels persons are praying to them. Can these good saints hear but in one place, or can they hear all every where praying to them? If they can hear all, then they are omnipresent; if omnipresent, they are gods. Thus we have as many gods as saints. But if they hear but in one place, then nine thousand nine hundred and ninety-nine out of the ten thousand are praying to an absent saint! This one thought very early in life impressed my mind, and was not the least powerful among the causes which led me, eventually, to reject the authority of the Roman Catholic Church.

"The doctrine of confession is one of the primary doctrines of the Romish Church. It requires every good papist to confess his sins to a priest at least once a year. If any sins are concealed, none are forgiven. This doctrine makes the bosom of the priest the repository of all the sins of all the sinners of his parish who make a conscience of confession. Hence the common saying in Ireland, 'You carry as much sin about you as the priest's horse.' And this is one of the sources of the fearful power which the priests have over the people; and with this doctrine of confession is connected the power of the father confessor to grant absolution to the confessing penitent.

"Father M—— held frequently his confessions at the

house in which I was clerk. He sat in a dark room up stairs, with one or more candles on a table before him. Those going to confession followed each other on their knees from the front door, through the hall, up the stairs, and to the door of the room. When one came out of the confessing-room, another entered. My turn came. I entered the room, from which the light of day was excluded, and bowed myself before the priest. He made over me the sign of the cross, and after praying something in Latin, he ordered me to commence the detail of my sins. Such was my fright that my memory soon failed in bringing up past delinquencies. He would prompt me, and ask, Did you do this thing or that thing? I would answer yes or no. And when I could say no more, he would wave his hand over me, and again utter some words in Latin, and dismiss me. Through this process I often went, and never without feeling that my sins were forgiven. Sins that burdened me before were now disregarded. The load of guilt was gone; and I often felt, when prompted to sin, that I could commit it with impunity, as I could soon confess it and secure its pardon.

"The questions, however, often came up, Why does the priest go into a dark room in the daytime? Why not pray for me in English, and not in Latin? How can he forgive sin? What if my sins, after all, are not forgiven? And I always found that I could play my pranks better after confession than before, for I could go at them with a lighter heart. Very early in life my confidence in this doctrine of confession was shaken, and at a later period I came to the conclusion that it was a priestly device to insnare the conscience and to enslave men.

"Another thing which made early a deep impression on my mind was this. On my first remembered journey to Dublin, we passed by a place called, unless I mistake, St. John's Well. It is one of the 'holy wells' of Ireland. There was a vast crowd of poor-looking and diseased people around it. Some were praying, some shouting; many were up in the trees which surrounded it. All these trees were laden, in all their branches, with shreds of cloth of every possible variety and color. I inquired what all this meant. I was told, 'This is St. John's Well, and these people come here to get cured.' But what do those rags mean, hanging on the trees? I was told that the people who were not immediately cured tied a piece of their garments on some limb of the trees, to keep the good saint of the well in mind of their application; and, judging from the number of pieces tied on the trees, I inferred that the number that went away cured were very few. I had previously read some travels in Africa describing some of the religious rites of the sable sons of that continent, and the thought that those performed around St. John's Well were just like them occurred to me. I have no doubt but that the rites witnessed in my youth are performed there yet; that the rags of diseased persons are now streaming from those trees to remind the saint of the requests of those who suspended them. There was always a priest present to hear confessions, and to receive the pennies of the poor pil-

B

grims; and the impression then made upon my mind was, that it was a piece of paganism.

"I well remember yet another of these impostures. When a boy, I often heard that on the morning of Easter Sunday the sun might be seen dancing in the heavens and in the chapels, to express its joy on the anniversary of the resurrection of Christ, and I often wished to be where I could witness the phenomenon. It took place in a certain chapel, and in the presence of many pious and admiring beholders. An unbeliever in priestly miracles was present, who traced up the dancing of the sunbeams through the chapel to an individual managing concealed mirrors so as to produce the wonderful effect! Of this I heard; and although it seemed incredible, yet it made an impression on my mind. The probability of the imposture can not be doubted by those who know that the earth which covers the grave of Father Sheely (who was convicted of treason, and hung in the county of Tipperary), when boiled in milk, cures a variety of diseases.

"For years together I sat daily at table with a Catholic priest, who was a member of the family, and the curate of the parish, and I never saw a Bible used in the family. I never heard at table, or in the morning, or in the evening, a religious service. The numbers of the Douay Bible, published by subscription in folio, were taken in the family, but never read. And not only so, but I never heard a sermon preached in a Catholic chapel in Ireland, nor a word of explanation on a single Christian topic, doctrine, or duty. The thing nearest to a sermon that I heard was a scold from the altar because some person sent for the priest at midnight to confess and anoint a dying person. And before I was sixteen years of age I never read a chapter in the Word of God, while in other respects my education was not neglected. I often asked the meaning of this thing and the other, but there was no explanation.

"On reaching the years of maturity my mind was a perfect blank as to all religious knowledge. While my mind was filled with superstitious notions concerning meats and penances, and external observances and legends, it was utterly ignorant of the Bible. With my Missal I was somewhat familiar: I said the Catechism when I was confirmed, at the age of nine or ten, and that was the amount of my religious education. At the age of eighteen years the Catechism was forgotten and the Missal was neglected; and as my conscience was uneducated, and my mind unfurnished with religious principles, the only test of truth left me was my common sense. I then became the associate of companions of Protestant education, who would sometimes ask me my reason for this and that observance, and not being able to give any, as none were ever given me, I was frequently put to the blush.

"From my youth up I was taught to abstain from all meats on Fridays and Saturdays. Why on these days more than any other I was never told. And if, by mistake, I was involved in the violation of this law, I felt a burden upon my conscience of which confession could only relieve me. Circumstances led me to inquire into this matter. I saw good papists eating eggs, and fish, and getting drunk on these days, but this was no violation of the law of the Church! Yet, if these persons should eat meat of any kind, or use gravy in any way, their consciences were troubled, and they must perform penance! This led me to ask, Is this reasonable? If I may eat meat on Thursday, why not on Friday? Can God, in things of this kind, make that to be a sin on one day which is not on another? I saw, also, persons for whose moral worth I had the highest regard eating meats on those days, and without any injury, and I came to the conclusion that the regulations upon this matter were unreasonable, and rejected them. And, as far as I now remember, this was my first step toward light and freedom.

"Devoted to reading at this period of my life, I perused, without discrimination, every thing that came in my way. Some book or tract, now forgotten, gave rise to some inquiries as to the Mass. I asked, What does it mean? I could not tell, though for years a regular attendant upon it. Why does the priest dress so? What book does he read from when carried now to his right and now to his left? What mean those candles burning at noonday? Why do I say prayers in Latin which I understand not? Should I not know what I am saying when addressing my Maker? Why bow down, and strike my breast, when the little bell rings? What does it all mean? The darkness of Egypt rested upon these questions. I thus reasoned with myself: God is a spiritual and intelligent being, and He requires an intelligent worship. What worship I render Him in the Mass I know not. My intelligent worship only is acceptable to Him, and is beneficial to me. I am a rational being, and I degrade my nature and insult my Maker by offering to Him a worship in which neither my reason nor *His* intelligence is consulted. Having come to this conclusion, I gave up the Mass as a superstitious form, well enough fitted for an idol, but unfitted to be rendered by a rational being to the infinitely intelligent Jehovah. I have never been to Mass since, save out of curiosity to see how an ignorant people can be edified by what seems to me the most unmeaning and farcical of all the rites that ever man has devised.

"When I came to this conclusion on the subject of the Mass, I experienced no great difficulty as to other matters which passed rapidly in review before me. Must I go to confession? My prejudices said Yes; my reason said No; and my logic was simply as follows: If I truly repent of my sins, God will forgive me; if I do not, the priest can not absolve me; and I spurned as unreasonable, and as an insult to my common sense, the terrible doctrine that 'every Christian is bound, *under pain of damnation*, to confess to a priest all his mortal sins, which, after diligent examination, he can possibly remember; yea, even his most secret sins—his very thoughts; yea, and all the circumstances of them which are of any moment.'

"With yet greater abhorrence I gave up the doctrine of transubstantiation. As explained by Dr. Challoner in his 'Catholic Christian Instructed,' it means 'that the bread and wine are changed by the consecration into the body and blood of Christ; and are so changed that Christ himself, true God and true man, is truly, really, and substantially present in the sacrament.' With this doctrine in view, I went to witness the administration of the Eucharist. I went to St. Peter's, in Barclay Street. The communicants drew around tho altar upon their knees. With a little box in his hand, the priest passed from one to the other, taking a wafer, smaller than that used in sealing a letter, from the box, and placing it upon the extended tongue of the communicant. I was always taught that the teeth must not touch the wafer—that it must melt upon the tongue. This I find to be the law of the Church. I witnessed the ceremony, as I had often done before. I retired from the scene asking these questions: Is that little wafer the real body and blood of Christ? Does the priest, in that little box, not as large as a snuff-box, carry two or three hundred real bodics of Christ? Do these communicants, each in their turn, eat the real body and blood of Christ? I can not express the violence with which my mind rejected the absurdity. Look at it in what light you may, it is abhorrent to our common reason: it gives the lie to every sense with which God has endowed us. It is a wicked imposition. It is an impious priestly hoax, which, if practiced by a juggler, would subject him to the penalties of the law against blasphemy.

"Having gone through this process, not with a light and trifling, but with a serious mind, my prejudices rising in stormy rebellion against my convictions, I raised my eyes, and behold, my religion was gone! The priest was a juggler, and his religion a fable! Every thing that I had ever learned from parent and priest to esteem as religion was now rejected as false; and not knowing but that this was all of religion that was in the world, I had no alternative but infidelity. I had no test of truth but my reason, and when I brought the Roman Catholic system to that, I was compelled to reject it, not only as false, but as a monstrous absurdity, and with it all religion."

CHAPTER II.

Hears Rev. Dr. Mason. — Conversion. — Joins the Brick Presbyterian Church.— His first Prayer in Public.— Letter from Rev. Mr. Steele.—Meets Rev. Dr. Proudfit.—Letter from him.—Encouraged to study for the Ministry.—Goes to Amherst Academy.—Writes to Rev. Dr. Griffin.—Letter from him.

In the perplexity and darkness which beset him when compelled to abandon the miserable religion he brought with him from Ireland, Mr. Murray was kindly and rapidly guided into the way of light and truth. During the months of his conflict, and while he was actually persuading himself that the conflict was over, and all religions were alike impostures unworthy of his belief, he was led one day to hear a sermon by the Rev. Dr. John M. Mason, and another and another. One from that distinguished preacher on the First Epistle of Peter shattered his poor fabric of infidelity into fragments. He awoke to the consciousness of his condition as a sinner in need of salvation. The way of life by Christ Jesus was opened to him by the Spirit. He was received as a member on probation in the Methodist Church, and so remained for a year or more.

About this time he was thrown into association with some of the young men who belonged to the Brick Presbyterian Church, of which the Rev. Dr. Spring was pastor. He had sought religious counsel and instruction from Dr. Mason, whose reception did not encourage him to repeat his visit. But his young companions soon brought him into communion with Dr. Spring, and when his religious views became more settled, and he had had time to give the subject serious study and reflection, he made a public profession of religion in this church.

In the autumn of the year 1820 young Murray, still in the employment of the Harpers, became a boarder in the house of Mr. Kirk, in Liberty Street. Mr. Kirk was a worthy and well-known member of the Church of the Rev. Dr. Mason, and one of the straitest of the denomination that held fast to the forms and faith of the Kirk of Scotland. Equally did he hold in abhorrence the practice of *reading* sermons in the pulpit and the use of Watts' hymns. Dr. Mason, with others of the Church which he adorned, had established a school for the instruction of young men in theology, and the families of the Church were in the habit of "taking student boarders," thus giving them important assistance in making their way through their divinity course. Among the students to whom this kindness was extended was one who is now the Rev. J. B. Steele, of the Reformed Dutch Church. He gives me his recollections of that winter with Nicholas Murray:

"In the winter of 1820, I resided with Mr. George Kirk in Liberty Street, and was a student in my senior year, in Dr. Mason's Seminary, receiving the instruction of Dr. Alexander M'Leod, Dr. Alexander M'Clelland, and Dr. John Knox. Mr. Kirk was a

Scotchman of the old school, very intelligent, pious, orthodox, and a great hater of Dr. Watts' Psalms and Hymns. He was a member of Dr. Mason's Church. There was also in the family a maiden lady of great intelligence and piety, Margerie M'Leod. She was a prim lady, wore a high turban, was very dignified in her manners, and a very kind-hearted woman. She still lives, and is over ninety years of age. She had a select school of young ladies from the best families in the city, the second school of the kind in New York after Mrs. Graham's. She had with her in her school her niece, an educated young lady. Into this family came young Murray in the fall of 1821; he was seventeen or eighteen years of age. At that time he was a stout, thick-set, clumsy-looking boy. He was singularly dressed; had a round, open, generous face; was full of Irish wit, humor, joke, and blunder. His manners, though awkward, were soon overlooked, and he became the favorite of the whole family. At every meal we anticipated his good humor; and, while we all enjoyed his pleasantries, it was not long before we discovered that he possessed real native talent, and the high-turbaned lady was the first to say, 'That young man should be educated.' Mr. Kirk kept a store, which prevented him frequently from attending morning prayers, and sitting with his family at meals; and it usually fell to my lot to conduct the devotions of the family, ask a blessing and return thanks, according to the good old custom, when people had time to eat and thank the Lord. Murray at this time had made a profession of religion, and appeared to be a genuine Christian. He was always willing to listen to pious discourse, and much pains were taken to cultivate his grace and lead him to exercise some spiritual gifts. I had much conversation with him on subjects of this nature, and said to him on one occasion, 'Murray, I will ask you some day to return thanks at the table, and you must not refuse; you must serve the Lord openly, and now is a good time to commence.' A few days after, at the table, when we had just had considerable amusement, I turned to Murray and said, 'Return thanks.' The company were astonished, Murray was confounded, and raising up both hands, he said:

"'Come Holy Spirit, heavenly dove,
With all thy quickening powers;
Come shed abroad a Savior's love
In these cold hearts of ours. Amen.'

"The ludicrous scene was indescribable. The high-turbaned lady and the whole company were in a roar of laughter as Murray left the room and ran to his bed-chamber. I followed, and found him in a perfect state of confusion, and said, 'Why, Murray, what have you been doing? When I ask you to return thanks, you should not repeat Watts' hymns; besides, if Mr. Kirk should hear you repeat *Watts*, he would turn you out of the house.' The only reply he gave was, 'You took me by surprise, but I will try and do better next time,' and so he did. After preparing the family for his second effort, he expressed himself with great propriety. In less than a month he took his regular turn, and before the end of the second month he engaged in turn in conducting family worship, and at the end of three months he held forth in prayer and exhortation at the social meetings in Dr. Spring's church. Many a merry laugh Dr. Murray has had with me in relation to his early religious services. I have never been acquainted with any young Christian who advanced so rapidly in religious graces and gifts. And I have often said to myself, when hearing the distinguished Dr. Murray in the pulpit or on the platform, 'Is this the Irish boy who commenced his public performances by repeating as a thanksgiving at the table a verse of a hymn?' His manners and appearance improved every week, and before the month of June he was almost a new man. At this time he was engaged in a printing establishment in Pearl Street. His evenings were unoccupied, and he was almost constantly in my room. In the way of self-defense, and also for his good, I furnished him with reading, which he eagerly devoured. I had discovered in him talent, and acting on the hint of Miss M'Leod, that he should receive an education, I said one evening, 'Murray, would you like to learn a little Latin this winter?' 'Ind*ade* I would,' and his eyes sparkled with delight. Latin books were procured, and he commenced his studies with vigor. After a few weeks he brought a companion with him from the same office, and it was arranged that I should give them an hour three evenings in a week, and before the first of June Murray was translating Virgil, and had a good knowledge of Greek grammar. *I never saw a man take so much delight in his studies, or advance so rapidly.* Often during the winter I impressed it upon his mind that he should seek a liberal education, and should set his heart upon the ministry; and he has often said that the start which I gave him in his studies that winter influenced him to go forward in his preparations to become a minister of the Gospel.

"I was licensed in the beginning of 1822. Young Murray left Mr. Kirk's family about the same time, and I heard nothing from him until he had entered college. I have watched his progress through life with much interest; have frequently visited him at Elizabethtown, and shared his hospitality and pleasant conversation; and he has often told me that the winter which he spent in Mr. Kirk's family was one of the brightest spots in his memory, and that he looked back upon that time as the turning-point in his history. He was my good friend, and when he died I found another link broken which binds me to this world."

By this communication from Mr. Steele we are carried back to the first attempt of our young friend to open his lips in the performance of a religious service in the presence of others. That he was embarrassed, confused, and made a ridiculous failure; that he speedily recovered, resolved at once to do better, and carried out his resolution with decision and success, are interesting facts to record in the early history of this remarkable man. Had he been weak and irresolute, the first failure would have been the last effort. But he rose from his fall the stronger in heart, and in the course of a few weeks this youth, who could not find words to use in thanking God for his daily bread, is leading the devotions of the Church, and offering words of exhortation to the people, in meetings for conference and prayer, in one of the most prominent congregations in the City of New York. This was the man, though yet in his youth. Here was the self-reliance that had already enabled him to embark on the world alone, and now it was shown in the earnest, hopeful spirit with which he assumed the new responsibilities of the Christian life.

In the course of the winter of 1820 and 1821 he came under the notice, and at once received the kind, paternal attentions of the Rev. Alexander Proudfit, D.D., of Salem, Washington County, N. Y., who was delivering a course of lectures in the City of New York in the place of Dr. Mason, who had been compelled by ill health to retire from the theological chair.

The encouragement which Dr. Proudfit gave him was the means of bringing him into the ministry, as he himself most feelingly and gratefully affirms in after years. Among Dr. Proudfit's letters, the following letter from young Mr. Murray was found:

"New York, May 18th, 1821.

"Rev. Sir,—I have been anxiously waiting for your return to New York, on your way to Synod, for some time past; but having learned from the Rev. Mr. Boyd, who stopped here on his way to Philadelphia, that you were unable to attend your appointment by reason of your indisposition, I propose writing you these few lines, at the same time begging your pardon for the trouble they may put you to.

"Under a sense of my own unworthiness and of my own nothingness, I would be humbled under the mighty hand of Jehovah, seeing that He is exceeding all my hopes and disappointing all my fears, and that His everlasting loving-kindness has thus far followed and preserved me. I would cast myself and all my concerns for this life, and for that which is to come, upon Him, under a full assurance that He, on whose arm creation hangs, is able to support and sustain me.

"Reverend sir, I am conscious of the trouble I have given you during the last winter, but the day may not be far distant when, by the help of God, I may be enabled to render you some recompense of reward for your trouble.

"A few days ago I had an interview with the Rev. Dr. Spring. I was mentioning to him the great object I had in view; I also represented to him my circumstances, and my incapability of obtaining the desired object of myself. I also told him of my intercourse with you during the last winter, and how I was kept back from attending your lectures—all which I suppose you will remember. He told me, if I would obtain a few recommendatory lines from you, then he thinks he would be able to obtain by subscription enough money to support me and carry me through my studies. My object in writing to you at this time is to obtain information from you what to do under these circumstances. If you think that it is best for me to accept of the offer, I will be under infinite obligations to you for a few lines to that effect, supposing that you are satisfied as to my intentions and the purity of my motives. If you think it best for me not to accept the offer, you will please let me know.

"Under a sense of my obligations to you for the pains you have taken by me, I wish to be guided and directed solely by you in reference to the object in view. Fearing that you were making some provision for me, I would enter into no engagement until I hear from you. I still remain at Mr. Harper's, and board at Mr. Kirk's. It is my prayer to the Almighty God that your useful labors may be long spared to His Church and to His people, and when the Lord of the harvest shall call you to render an account of your stewardship, that you may be found having your wedding garment on, with your lamp trimmed and brightly burning, ready to enter into the joy of our Lord. Amen. Believe me to be your prayerful servant,

"NICHOLAS MURRAY."

The result of this application is evident in the fact that Mr. Murray was soon enabled to proceed with his studies under the auspices of benevolent individuals in the Brick Church. His success in the performance of religious exercises had already attracted their attention, and convinced them that he ought to be prepared for the sacred ministry. Two of the elders, Mr. Peter Hawes and Mr. Cunningham, communicated to him the wishes of his friends and their willingness to bear the expenses of his education.

Many long years afterward, in the year 1860, when the 50th anniversary of Dr. Spring's settlement in the Brick Church was celebrated, Dr. Murray was one of the distinguished speakers, and he then gave utterance to his own feelings in remembrance of his early relations to the venerable pastor and the people who were the friends of his youth. The whole speech is intensely interesting in this very place:

"MR. CHAIRMAN,—We may have a great many teachers, but we can have but one Father; so says the Sacred Record. We may be connected with many churches, but after all there is one church to which our affections always return, as the needle, which has been drawn from its true direction, trembles back to the pole. I have been, in the course of my ministry, acquainted with many ministers; but there is one minister who is associated with every thing that is precious in my youthful years. I have been connected with many churches, but there is one church, in the aisle of which I stood when I devoted myself to God, and that church is ever before me. I came to this city, a mere boy, in the year 1818. I was, through the providence of God, cast into a Presbyterian family that worshiped in the Murray Street Church, under the pastoral care of Rev. Dr. Mason, and I went there occasionally to church. Dr. Mason was soon removed to the presidency of Dickinson College; and on his removal, having no particular attachment there, save to hear the Gospel from the lips of that eloquent man, I passed over the Park to the old Brick Church. There I became acquainted with a few young men, one of whom still lives, a pillar of a church in Liverpool. We went into the Sabbath-school together. I was not then a professor of religion, but my mind became deeply interested, and I had a private conversation with Dr. Spring in reference to my state of mind, which was then in a very doubting state—indeed, it was wavering as to the truth of Christianity itself; and he talked with me in the kindest manner. I called again; and I attended the lectures in that old white lecture-room in the evenings. At that time this beloved man, who has just been carried out to the lecture-room (Mr. Holden*), was an elder. One evening Dr. Spring was unwell, and that man arose and read a sermon which I remember well. That sermon was from the text, 'His feet stand on slippery places; and in due time they shall slide'—a sermon in one of the volumes of the great Jonathan Edwards. It riveted my mind, and very deeply impressed my soul. I went again to see the pastor of the Church, and he invited me to meet with the Session, as it was my duty to become a communicant of the Church. I went on a certain evening to meet with the Session, and laid my hand upon the latch of the door in order to enter. But my heart failed me, and I turned away. And for three months I staid away. A notice was given again; I went to the same door and laid my finger upon the latch, but faltered, and was turning upon my heel to go away again, when that old and sainted man, Father Cunningham, came behind me, laid his hand upon the latch, opened the door, and said, 'Walk in, young man;' and, almost against my will, I was ushered into

* Alluding to the fact of Mr. Holden having fainted during the exercises.

the room, where I went through such an examination as was usually there given with a very faint heart. The following Sabbath I was received into the Church. I was baptized by Rev. Dr. Spring in the name of the Father, Son, and Holy Ghost. By him I was led, in the private interviews to which I have alluded, to Christ; under his ministry I devoted myself to God; and by his hand I was baptized and received into the Church. I went about my business. Six or eight months had passed away, when, on a certain afternoon, two individuals came into the office in which I was employed: one was Father Cunningham, and the other was another sainted elder of this Church, years ago gone to rest—Peter Hawes. They asked me, after a little introduction, if I thought of devoting myself to the ministry. I told them, No; that the thought had not entered my mind, and that there were other courses marked out before me. They told me to consider the subject, and that they would call to see me again. They saw me again: on a certain evening I had another conversation with them in the lecture-room, and the result was that in a few months more I was in a course of preparation for the ministry, under the care of this Church, and by advice of its pastor; and from that day unto this day, the Lord has kept me. Therefore I ought and must feel a great veneration for this beloved man, and a great veneration for the old Brick Church. I look around me this evening, and I find that many whose names have been read by our beloved Holden are absent. John Adams is gone; and Mr. Lockwood, and Peter Hawes, and Mr. Cunningham, and Mr. Phelps, and Mr. De Forest—all gone! Mr. Fisher is yet living; Mr. Havens is gone; Mr. Couch yet lives; Mr. Holden has been here to-night; Halsey, too, is gone. Those men I knew as a boy; they were pillars of the Church—of the old house; they have fallen, but the main pillar remains.

"It is one thing, Mr. Chairman, to be a minister *in* New York, and quite another thing to be a minister *of* New York. Almost any body, with ordinary talent, could be a minister in New York: John Smith could be a minister in New York—why, I myself could be that; but it is a very different thing to be a minister *of* New York. A minister *in* New York may be a very small minister indeed, and his ministrations may be very limited; but a minister *of* New York must be every inch a man. And this venerable man has been a minister *of* New York; his hand for fifty years has been upon every thing that has been good here. What great and good enterprise has arisen here in this city for fifty years with which his name has not been connected? Is it the Bible Society? Is it the American Tract Society? Is it any of our great missionary societies? And if we go from our Church to our national societies, is it the American Board? Is it our own Presbyterian Board? Pray tell me what it is that has arisen within the last fifty years in this city or in this land to bless the world, with which this beloved man has not been connected? He has been a minister, not only in and of New York, but he has been a minister of the world. His name is known in Ireland, and in Scotland, and in England, almost as well as it is known in the city of New York. His works praise him in the gate, and in every gate in the world. He has been a minister here, and a minister at the same time to our common humanity. Hence we should honor and imitate him. Not merely in the way that his venerable classmate (Dr. Humphrey) has stated, has he been a blessing, but in many other ways. He has been here for fifty years; the winds have beaten about him, and the floods have come up around him, but he has been as a pillar unmoved. Why? Because, as a minister of Christ, as a preacher of the Gospel, he has been founded on the Rock. Others have fallen and have been swept away, but he has remained strong and immovable as the mountains that surrounded Jerusalem. He has stood firm. Changes have passed over other churches and other men; clouds have passed over the characters of others, but the sun of this brother has shone clearly, summer and winter, for the last fifty years, and has been growing brighter, and brighter, and brighter, even unto the perfect day. Fifty years have passed over him, and where in this city, or where in this land, is the individual that can rise up and accuse him of saying any thing or doing any thing unworthy of his position as a Presbyterian minister of the Gospel? Why, sir, in the presence of such a man I feel very much as one feels in one of those old cathedrals—Westminster, for instance—going around that old chapel of Henry VII.; or, standing under the shadow of those old trees in Hyde Park. I venerate those things; I look upon them with veneration; and we must venerate still more the man who, for fifty years, has gone on among the same people, preaching to them the truth, breaking to them the bread of life—without a stain upon his character, and going down, quietly, the hill of life amid the admiration of those to whom he has so long ministered. Surely we must venerate such a man as that. But not in this way alone has he been a minister of New York. He has been a constant preacher, and, as I heard John Breckinridge say himself, one of the most impressive and eloquent men of his day (and I repeat it now in his own presence), the 'prince of preachers.' He has been not only a constant preacher, but he has been an industrious, laborious, and active man. He has made the most diligent preparation for the pulpit. He has brought out of his treasures things new and old, and has never drawn from the top of his mind, as a great many individuals do whose minds, unlike milk, make no cream. He gave them beaten oil from the sanctuary; and in this respect, as well as in every other, he stands up before the youthful ministry of this land as a man every way worthy of their imitation. If I, on a future occasion, should have any thing to say in reference to this man when his work is ended, I should hold him up to the ministry of this country as every way worthy of their respect and admiration. The course which he has pursued has made a man of him; and it would have made a man of an individual far less endowed by nature than he is. But the evening is becoming late. I feel that, as a son of this Church, I could not have said less than I have said.

"There is one thing, however, that fills our hearts

with mourning this evening, and that is, that the partner of his life should be absent from this ovation. But she has gone to a better and a higher world; and when her venerable partner goes the way which she has trod before him, if we live we shall strive to follow him to his resting-place, good men shall carry him to his burial, and long after his sun shall have set in the west will its heavenly light shine on the high places of our Zion."

Returning to our narrative, we find that Mr. Murray was not reluctant to avail himself of the aid proposed. It was just what he desired, as it gave him the opportunity of obtaining an education, and he seized upon it with avidity. Even while as yet the way was not open, he was improving every leisure hour in the acquisition of classical learning, hoping against hope that he might yet find his way into the pulpit. In the circle of young Christians with whom he was now brought into contact there were some who have since been distinguished in various public and private walks of life. His associations were the happiest and most useful. With them he mingled in the regular meetings for prayer in the church; and for their own improvement, as well as to do good to others, they joined in private prayer-meetings among the poor. One of these meetings he describes:

MEETING AT AUNT BETSY'S.

"It was my first visit to the prayer-meeting at Fulton Street, where God has so signally manifested His presence. The room on the first story was full, and I made my way up to that on the second. I found a seat in the middle of the room, from which I had a good view of the persons around the pulpit, and could look out of the windows in its rear. And as I glanced upon the high brick stores in Ann Street, the memories of other days rushed in upon me. Where those brick stores now rise, upward of thirty years ago there stood some wooden buildings of very lowly pretensions. In an upper room of one of them there dwelt an old colored woman, then widely known as Aunt Betsy, or Sarah—which, I now forget. She was very old, and very feeble, and remarkably pious. To what church she belonged I do not remember, nor is it necessary to my present purpose to know. She was dependent upon the hand of charity for her daily bread; nor was she neglected. Some ladies, not now unknown in the religious circles of New York, were sent to her room by their parents on their first errands of mercy to the poor. And some young men, mostly from the Presbyterian and Methodist Churches, held a prayer-meeting in her room on each Sabbath afternoon, as she was too infirm to attend on any of the public means of grace. She lay on her lowly bed during these meetings of prayer; and, as we retired, she took each of us by the hand, and gave us her parting blessing.

"That meeting in the upper room of that poor disciple had passed away from my recollection, although it was in it I offered the first prayer I ever uttered in the hearing of man. But now, in a meeting for prayer, and in sight of the very place, it came up in all its freshness before me. The old buildings took the place of the lofty stores. I could go round the room of Aunt Betsy, and count its chairs, and almost talk with the young men that sat on them. I could hear them pray, and see them retire, each receiving in his turn the blessings of the 'aged disciple.' And as I was busy with my own thoughts, scarcely hearing the singing and praying that occupied all in the room, I was waked from my revery by a voice from behind me. It was that of a merchant exhorting his brother merchants to a deeper interest and a warmer zeal in the salvation of men. As the voice seemed familiar, I turned round to see who was the fervid and fluent speaker. He is now one of the princely merchants of New York, but in his youth he was one of the young men who met for prayer in the room of Aunt Betsy, and his wife was one of the little girls who, as the ravens did to Elijah, carried to her daily food!

"Those young men were not the sons of wealth; if not poor, they supplied their own resources by their daily employment, and all of them were too young to have made for themselves position or character. They were Sabbath-school teachers, most of them were communicants of churches, and all of them professed to love the Bible, and the place where prayer was wont to be made. And what has become of the young men that met weekly in the room of Aunt Betsy? Of the subsequent history of some of them I have no knowledge. It is to be hoped that, having commenced aright, they held on the even tenor of their way—that

C

they have finished their course with joy, or yet live to be useful. But as to others of them my knowledge is distinct and full.

"One of them rose to eminence as an accomplished writer and editor. He became an honorable politician, and for years has served his country and the cause of Protestantism with distinction as a minister at a foreign court.

"Another of them is an ex-mayor of the city of New York, whose hand has never been withheld from any work of religion or philanthropy.

"Another is the honored partner of one of the largest publishing houses of the city of his residence.

"Another of them has held on the even tenor of his way; has risen to eminence as a merchant, has acquired a large fortune, and is a pillar in one of the most important congregations and one of the best known in the British Isles.

"Another was the merchant behind me in the room of prayer, so affectionately addressing the audience, and now the head of one of the largest mercantile houses of the Union.

"Another is also a well-known merchant of New York, who has a heart for every good work, and who has never withdrawn his hand from the plow.

"Another is a useful minister in the Western States, whose labors have been eminently blessed in turning many to righteousness.

"Two others, who gave fair promise of usefulness in the more secluded walks of life, were early removed to their home in heaven. I was myself among the youngest of the company, and, when I was first invited to join the circle in the room of Aunt Betsy, was not a communicant of the Church.

"On a subsequent day I made the above statement at the prayer-meeting in Fulton Street, and based upon it an appeal to young men to make the religion of Christ the law and the rule of their life; and as they valued their prosperity in this life and the life to come, not to neglect the place of prayer.

"When I sat down, a man rose in another part of the room, his tremulous accents showing the feelings that were within him. 'I have,' said he, 'recently visited the prison at Sing Sing. As I went from cell to cell, I met with an old man who told me a very different story from that just narrated. He said that when young he was one of a company of young men who formed an infidel club, and who met once a week for talking infidelity, gambling, and drinking, not very far from the upper room of Aunt Betsy; and I was shocked as he told me of the end to which his companions came. One, said he, died by his own hand; another by the hand of violence; some in state prison; some of *delirium tremens;* and, as far as I know, I am the only one of them surviving; and here am I in the garb, and daily at the work of a felon.' And he also ended his narrative with a most striking and touching appeal to young men to remember their Creator in the days of their youth.

"The contrast which the two narratives presented was most striking. All felt it to be so. No doubt the room of Aunt Betsy and the gambling-hell were very differently furnished. The companies that met in each were very different in character, and in their governing objects and principles. And their end was very different. Religion has the promise of the life which now is and of that which is to come. Nor are there any youth more likely to become men than those who first seek the kingdom of heaven and its righteousness. Even now do I feel the warm pressure of the hand of Aunt Betsy, although for thirty or more years she has been with her Lord; and it may be that the blessings which have followed those who met for prayer in her room have been in answer to her benedictions and prayers. True religion, early embraced, is a great element of success, even as to the life that now is."

He was still an apprentice to the Harpers, and his time and services were now more valuable to them than they had been while he was learning the business. But when he sought their counsel and aid in reference to a change in his whole plan of life, they cheerfully gave him the remainder of his time, and bid him God-speed in his new career. They stood in the relation of parents or elder brothers to him—who had come to them when he was without friends or home—and the friendship then formed with the boy continued, without abatement, so long as he lived. They became, in subsequent years, the publishers of his works, and the intercourse between him and them was always the most genial and delightful.

Under the auspices of the kind friends in the Brick Church who had offered to sustain him in his studies, he went in the fall of 1821 to Amherst Academy, in Massachusetts, where he pursued his studies in preparation for college under the instruction of Gerard Halleck, Esq., afterward the distinguished editor of the *Journal of Commerce*, in New York.

Of his brief residence here we have little or no knowledge beyond the obvious fact that he made rapid, indeed astonishing progress in his preparatory studies. He was also engaged in the advancement of the cause of his Master, and extending his views to the distant and destitute in heathen lands. Among his old letters is one from Levi Chamberlain, for the Treasurer of the American Board of Foreign Missions, written to Mr. Nicholas Murray, as one of a committee of students who were engaged in raising money to educate a heathen boy in Ceylon by the name of Gerard Halleck, which was the name of the principal of the academy.

He remained at Amherst but three fourths of a year, and then we find him writing to Rev. Dr. Griffin, the president of Williams College, and making inquiries as to the probabilities of his being admitted with his present amount of classical knowledge. To these inquiries the president replies:

"Williams College, August 10, 1822.

"Dear Sir,—I received your letter of July 22d, but various causes have prevented me from answering it before. I think you may venture to come to Williamstown at Commencement, or as soon as you please, with a view to enter the next Freshman class, and to make up your deficiencies in the fall and winter vacations. The expenses will not exceed what was mentioned in my letter to Dr. Spring.

"Affectionately yours,

"E. D. GRIFFIN.

"Mr. Nicholas Murray, Amherst, Massachusetts."

CHAPTER III.

He enters Williams College, Mass.—Letter to Rev. Dr. Proudfit.—His Answer.—Rapid mental Progress.—College Exercises.—Writing for the Newspapers.—Oration on July 4th.—Dr. Griffin predicts that he will be a distinguished Man.—Letter from Professor Albert Hopkins.—Letter from Chester Dewey, LL.D.

In the autumn of 1822 he entered the Freshman class of Williams College, in Williamstown, Massachusetts. The Rev. Dr. Griffin was then its president, and in the zenith of his power and fame as the prince of American preachers; a man to make the deepest impress of his own characteristics upon the young men who sat at his feet. Unrivaled as a pulpit orator, severe as a critic, and punctilious in all the details of manner that mark the Christian gentleman, Dr. Griffin was just the man into whose hands it was eminently desirable that Mr. Murray should fall. Thus far we have noticed that each step of the young man's course has been guided by peculiarly kind providences, but none were more favorable than that which threw him under the social, religious, and intellectual training of the Rev. Dr. Griffin.

In his Sophomore year he writes to his friend and counselor, the Rev. Dr. Proudfit, the following letter:

"Williams College, December 7th.

"Rev. and dear Sir,—Notwithstanding the time that has elapsed since I have had the pleasure of seeing you, the recollection of the favors you so generously conferred upon me, and of the direction and impulse you gave to my hopes and desires when I had none to direct me, recall you to my mind with that affection and tenderness with which a son reviews the favors of a kind father. How can I but dwell with grateful recollections on the memory of him who is my chief benefactor; who has, by his counsel and influence, thus far enabled me to pursue my literary course in preparation for the Gospel ministry? If the world shall ever gain any thing by my labors—if the glory of the Church shall ever be enhanced through my instrumentality—if I ever shall be the humble instrument of bringing a son or daughter of Adam home to glory, from their heavenly habitation they will doubtless look upon you as the great first cause of their exaltation. Since, therefore, I owe all that I am in my present pursuits to your kindness and Christian philanthropy, how can I but look upon you as a father and friend? As such, sir, I cherish your memory; as such I shall always consider you.

"Since the fall of 1822 I have been pursuing my studies under the care of Dr. Spring's Session, and I am at present a member of the Sophomore class in this college. I have long desired to see you, that I might make known to you my feelings and desires respecting the course I am to pursue in after life. The time is yet distant, it is true, when I shall be prepared to go forth into the vineyard, but, notwithstanding, I want to determine on some course, and to have my eye fixed on that through all my research. It is my desire to become a missionary; but whether it is my duty to spend my life among those that gave me existence, and whom I can call, as Paul did the Hebrews, my kinsmen according to the flesh, or devote my life to foreign missions among the heathen, I have not as yet determined. On this point, together with some others which I will not now mention, I want to consult you. I know that I can make my feelings known to you better than I can to any other person; and you, knowing better than any other person the history of my past life, are best calculated to judge of my views and motives.

"I have thought, during the term which is now nearly at a close, that, as I should have nothing to do next vacation, which is six weeks long, and as Salem is but forty miles from this place, I would call to see you, to ask your counsel on these interesting topics; but, fearing I might be disappointed in not finding you at home, I have taken the liberty of writing to you. If, sir, you would let me know what part of the vacation I would find you at home and at leisure, I will gladly avail myself of the opportunity of calling on you.

"Your ever obliged friend and servant,

"NICHOLAS MURRAY.

"N.B.—Vacation commences 1st of January.

"Rev. Dr. Alex. Proudfit."

Reply from the Rev. Dr. Proudfit.

"Salem, December 13th, 1823.

"MY TRULY ESTEEMED YOUNG FRIEND,—I received yours dated 7th instant, and rejoice that the Lord has so far prospered you in your exertions for obtaining an education for the important work of the ministry. Set up your Ebenezer, saying, 'Hitherto hath the Lord helped me,' and remember that His arm is not at all shortened, nor His ear heavy, nor His fullness diminished, nor His compassion to our wants lessened. He is the same yesterday, and to-day, and forever; always ready to guide us in darkness, and support us in difficulty, and supply us in want, and sympathize with us in our distresses and disappointments. In short, He is infinitely able to do in us and for us exceedingly abundantly beyond what we can ask or conceive, and, glory to His name, He is as able as He is willing. Trust, then, in the Lord forever; trust Him for bringing you into His vineyard, and trust Him for directing you what work in the vineyard He wishes you to perform; whether to improve some uncultivated region, or whether to 'dig around,' and prune, and cultivate those trees of righteousness which His own right hand hath planted. If my feeble counsels have been in the least degree conducive to your encouragement in the prosecution of study for the sacred ministry, give God the glory, and be assured that it will afford unfeigned delight to be a farther instrument of consolation to you. Therefore, come immediately to my house, and it will afford me real pleasure to see and entertain you. If I should be absent, make yourself known unto Mrs. Proudfit, and remain with her until I may return. My house is always open to receive fellow-pilgrims in their journey toward Zion, and especially for the entertainment of those whose attention is directed to the delightful employment of winning souls unto Christ. In expectation of seeing you shortly, and with earnest prayer for your prosperity in your important pursuit, I remain your brother in the faith of the divinely loving and lovely Savior,

"ALEXR. PROUDFIT.

"Mr. N. Murray."

One who was a fellow-student with him then, writes of him now:

"Schaghticoke, N. Y., April 28, 1862.

"It is now nearly forty years since I first met him, yet I have a very distinct recollection of the circumstances of our meeting—of his personal appearance, and the impression he made upon my mind. I occupied my room at Williams a few days before the opening of the term in the autumn of 1822. One evening, I think the one before the term opened, a stranger called at my room and introduced himself as Nicholas Murray, from New York. I was probably the first person in college upon whom he called; he had come to join the class to which I had been previously admitted. I was enabled to render him some assistance in making necessary arrangements for commencing study. I know of no other reason than the simple fact just alluded to that could have led him to cherish such an interest in my behalf, as he always manifested both while in college and in all subsequent life.

"His first appearance was very prepossessing, and made a marked impression upon me. His countenance was fresh and ruddy, his hair jet black, his manners easy and winning; his whole bearing was that of a Christian gentleman who had mingled with the world more than most of his age, and had profited by the advantages enjoyed. His knowledge of men and things generally was greater than that of most of our classmates. He was gifted also in an uncommon degree with conversational powers.

"He had not enjoyed as full advantages as most of his classmates in the studies preparatory to entering college. This was a disadvantage to him throughout the whole course, yet in scholarship he always ranked well. In some respects he had few, if any superiors, especially as a writer and debater.

"From the first he was a model of diligence and close application to study. He always acquitted himself well. Seldom, if ever, did the hour of recitation find him unprepared. Several times during our course he was selected to represent the class on public occasions. In our Sophomore year he delivered the annual oration before the college on the anniversary of our National Independence.

"When our college life ended I think all the class felt that one so gifted by Nature as he was, and one who loved study as he did, would surely make his mark in the world. His subsequent life never disappointed the expectations thus early entertained in reference to him.

"It has ever been a source of pleasure to me to reflect that I was permitted for so long a time to be on terms of intimacy, and daily associated in study with one of such genial feelings, and who proved himself such a model of diligence and successful effort in the Master's service.

"Very respectfully yours, J. H. NOBLE."

The rapid progress of Mr. Murray's mind has been revealed in his religious exercises before entering upon a course of study; but the rush which he made toward the highest standard of excellence the moment that he began to devote his energies to the pursuit of a classical education is scarcely credible. Among his books and papers we have found a manuscript volume, entitled "A Commonplace Book of Original Pieces: N. Murray, 1824," sealed up with an indorsement in these words: "The pages here inclosed are old college scribblings, of no use to any body, and never to be used for any public purpose. June, 1840." But these scribblings *are* of great use and interest to his friends and to the public, for they are the evidences of the attainments which he had already made at a period in his history when most young men have scarcely begun to develop their intellectual powers.

In the second year of his college life he was elected to be the orator of the day for the 4th of July, and his oration is among the "scribblings" here preserved. The lofty spirit of patriotism it breathes shows how thoroughly he had become an American as well as a Protestant; and the whole address is remarkable as illustrating his clear apprehension of the nature of our political institutions, and his own ability to defend them. "The UNION of our States," he says, "forms our only safety; it protects and defends us; it has raised the American name to an honorable elevation among the nations, and affords its invisible and omnipotent shield to every citizen. Every where it may be felt surrounding us with its magic influence, till we have almost lost the perception of its favors in the flow of its varied blessings. Give an absolute independence to each of our states, and the promise of our youth is blasted, and the world's best hopes laid low."

In the year 1824, when he was entering his Junior year, the Pittsfield Sun of Sept. 30th published a communication from his pen under the signature of "Mopsus," in which he opposes with great vigor and ability the charter of Amherst College, in Massachusetts, which would naturally rival the institution with which he was connected. One passage in this essay is so *like* him in his after author life that it must be cited:

"The revival of religion which took place in the spring of last year is again and again adduced as evidence of the favor of God toward the institution. I was rejoiced to hear of that revival. I could and did pray for its extension. But when I saw and heard of the manner in which it was made use of—when I saw it posted in every gazette, under the staring capitals, A REVIVAL IN AMHERST COLLEGE; when I heard of its being brought forward in the Legislature as a reason why Amherst should have a charter, and made use of on a great many occasions to collect funds and to conciliate the favor of the pious, I could not but exclaim, 'Lord, forgive them, for they know not what they do!' A revival was going on at the same time among the convicts of the state prison. I would ask the Amherst gentlemen whether the Lord sent that as a token that He was well pleased with the polity of that institution? According to their mode of reasoning, he certainly did."

This characteristic allusion to the prison revival brings the adage readily to mind, "The boy is father of the man." It is scarcely worth referring to, as Amherst College was chartered, became a great and blessed institution, and the local jealousies and rivalries between Williams and Amherst, that marked its early history, have long since given place to mutual respect and harmonious co-operation in religion and education.

For the Junior exhibition in May, 1825, he wrote a dialogue called "The Hostile Brothers; or, 'Free and Equal Born are all Mankind.'" The scene is laid in Ireland, in 1801, the year after the union of the Irish and English Parliaments. It is written in blank verse, and was spoken by himself, George W. Francis, and Jonathan H. Noble. It is remarkable only as another indication of the strides the young author was making in the power of expression; the various illustrations and allusions reveal something of the extent of his reading and the culture of his intellect. It is evident, even at this early period, that he was laying the foundation for future eminence. And in immediate connection with the rhetorical performance of this dialogue we have a pleasing proof of the expectations he had already excited in the mind of his distinguished president. He had not come under the immediate teachings of Dr. Griffin, but that great man had marked the progress he was making, and ventured to give expression to his hopes. Having learned that Murray was thinking of hastening into the ministry without going through the regular college course, Dr. Griffin writes the following letter:

"Williams College, May 17, 1825.

"To the Benefactors of Nicholas Murray in the City of New York:

"GENTLEMEN,—It has come to my knowledge of late that Murray was contemplating leaving college after this (his Junior) year, to enter upon his theological studies; and upon inquiring into the matter, I find that he has an impression that this is expected by some of you. I beg leave to represent to you that such a measure, in my opinion, will greatly interfere with his education, and materially limit his future usefulness. I hope his benefactors will take the same view of the subject, and dissuade him from the measure, and continue their kindness, so as to enable him to complete his education.

"Murray has an excellent mind, and bids fair to make a distinguished and very useful preacher. He has a high standing as a scholar, and is correct and exemplary, so far as I can know, in all his Christian conduct. At the Junior exhibition this day he acted a part in a dialogue which he had written, and which was of the first character. And his acting showed that he will be able to express with great force and effect by his elocution what his pen has written. I hope your kindness will be continued to him, and that he will reward you by a course of distinguished usefulness. E. D. GRIFFIN."

These wise suggestions were heeded, and the student remained to finish his literary course at Williams. His Senior year brought him under the immediate instructions of Dr. Griffin. This was his most profitable year in college. He needed just such a critic as Dr. Griffin to take him down and build him up. An incident will illustrate the manner of Dr. Griffin in dealing with his pupils and its influence.

Dr. Murray, when a young man, and even down to the day of his last illness, wrote a free, round, and beautiful hand; and on one occasion his exercise, which was to undergo the scrutiny of his venerated preceptor, had been prepared with uncommon neatness and accuracy. Dr. Griffin was accustomed to use a quill pen with a *very broad nib.*

Introduced into his august presence, young Murray, with becoming diffidence, presented his elegantly written piece for the ordeal. The discerning eye of the president passed quickly over the first sentence, and with a benignant look he turned to his pupil and said, in a peculiar way,

"*Murray, what do you mean by this first sentence?*"

Murray answered blushingly, "I mean so and so, sir."

"Then *say so*, Murray;" and at the same time drew his heavy pen through line after line, striking out about one third of it.

Having carefully read the next sentence, the venerable critic again inquired,

"*Murray, what do you mean by this?*"

He tremblingly replied, "Doctor, I mean so and so."

"Please just to *say so*," striking out again about one half of the beautifully written page.

In this way, with his broad nib (which made no mean mark), he proceeded to deface the nice clean paper of the young collegian, so that at the close of the exercises the erasures nearly equaled all that remained of the carefully prepared manuscript.

This trying scene was not lost upon young Murray. He considered it one of the most important events of his college course. It taught him to think and write concisely; and when he had any thing to say, to say it in a simple, direct, and intelligible manner.

Indeed, much that distinguished him as one of our most vigorous and pointed writers may be attributed to that early lesson, "SAY so, Murray."

He cherished the liveliest and most grateful reverence and affection for Dr. Griffin, of whom he narrates some tender and affecting reminiscences in a letter to Dr. Sprague:

"Early in the spring of 1824, if my memory serves me, there were glowing appearances of a most extensive revival in college. Indeed, not only the college, but the town was greatly shaken. Dr. Griffin was all fervor and zeal. The excitement continued four or five weeks; a few individuals seemed converted. A wicked fellow, by the name of R——, began to exhort us with great power and effect. But the excitement subsided as suddenly as it sprang up; and after all feeling had passed over, there was but one in town or college that gave evidence of true conversion, and that was William Hervey, whose bones repose in India, where he went as a missionary under the American Board. He was one of the best men I ever knew. In a few weeks R—— was found drunk. In reference to all this matter, I heard Dr. Griffin say afterward: 'To save one immortal soul the Lord will shake a whole Church, a whole town, and, if nothing less will save it, He will shake a whole continent.' And to illustrate this position, he would narrate, with melting pathos, the story of Hervey's conversion.

"If I recollect dates aright, in the spring of 1825 there was a truly powerful and genuine revival in town and college. In this work Dr. Griffin was the prime instrument. Some of the most touching moral scenes that I ever saw or heard of occurred during its progress. Guilty of the sin of David, we numbered the converted and the unconverted. The report went out one morning, and reached Dr. G., that all college was converted but eighteen. There was to be a prayer-meeting that night, and he sent over word that he would meet with us. Although the evening was dark and stormy, and the ground exceedingly muddy, there was not probably a student of college absent from the meeting. He came, and the lecture-room was so crowded that he stood in the door while giving his hat to one and his cloak and lantern to others. He stood for a moment gazing through his tears on the crowd before him; then clasping his hands, and lifting up his face to heaven, he uttered, in the most moving accents, these words: 'Or those eighteen upon whom the tower of Siloam fell, think ye that they were sinners above all men that dwelt in Jerusalem?' The effect was overpowering. For minutes he could not utter another word, and the room was filled with weeping. It was one of those inimitable touches which he could occasionally give, beyond all men that I have ever known. I narrated the incident to him a few weeks previous to his death. He wept aloud on its recital, but had forgotten all about it.

"In my repeated interviews with him previous to his death, I found nothing to interest him so much as little incidents in reference to revivals in college, and intelligence in respect to the usefulness of students converted through his instrumentality. In my last interview with him I told him the story of the conversion, in 1825, of a Mr. H——, now a highly useful minister, but then a profane and worthless profligate. The doctor was in the habit of frequently closing his sermons with "Hallelujah, amen," and always repeated the words in a peculiarly varied and musical tone. His tones were caught and repeated with laughable accuracy by H——. Just at the commencement of the revival he was often heard repeating these words, and with great force, and wit, and sarcasm, exhorting his fellow-students to get converted, swearing that he himself would get converted the very first one. He was seen on a fast-day morning coming into the prayer-meeting, as we all thought, to make sport; but before the meeting ended he arose, and such an appeal to the students as he made, and such an effect as it produced, I never witnessed; and, to the close of the revival, he was as useful as any among us. The story affected the doctor to such a degree that, for a time, he was entirely overcome."

At the feet of such a man as this Nicholas Murray sat four years. With him they were formative years.

The Rev. Albert Hopkins, now a distinguished professor in Williams College, and brother of the president, furnishes the following recollections of Dr. Murray in college:

"DEAR SIR,—You ask me to furnish some college reminiscences of my former classmate and friend, Rev. Dr. Murray. I retain a very lively impression of him as he appeared when a student, now nearly forty years since, and can easily present a correct portrait to those who knew him late in life. We naturally think of the youth in college, unknown to fame and struggling with difficulties, and the venerable clergyman, the able debater, and author of world-wide reputation, as two very different things. Those, however, who knew Dr. Murray in the former relation, found no difficulty in identifying him when his pen and voice had rendered him widely known.

"Owing, in part at least, to his active life and previous business habits, Murray had acquired, before entering college, that essential prerequisite to success—a sound constitution and vigorous health. His frame was well knit and athletic. The gymnasium, in those days, was unknown; but the students used to practice various athletic exercises, both for the sake of amusement and for better health. One of these, I remember, was that of throwing, or, as we used to say, *heaving* the axe. It was in connection with this exercise that I first found out the physical vigor of my classmate. Standing with the feet firmly fixed, I was able to excel him; but he had a knack of whirling his body round two or three times, and thus giving a part of its momentum to the axe. Allowing this to *be fair* (which I was not disposed to do), I was obliged to give in to him. I might multiply incidents in this line, some of them rather amusing, but the grave purpose of the memoir prompts me to refrain.

"The social qualities of Dr. Murray were quite remarkable. He had genuine humor, some wit, relished a good story, and knew how to tell one better than most. This was true in his early as well as in his later years. Add to this that, having seen more of life than most persons of his age, he had a fund of topics and incidents which enabled him both to amuse and interest beyond what is common in college circles.

"As a speaker and debater Murray stood high. In college meetings, and on occasions which called forth ability in these directions, he was prominent. One of these will doubtless be remembered by surviving contemporaries; I refer to the celebration commemorative of the completion of the great New York Canal. It may be thought singular that in New England a day should have been set apart for such a purpose; but some of the students, and Murray, I believe, among the most prominent of them, were aware that President Griffin was a particular admirer, as well as personal friend, of De Witt Clinton. Although the opening of the New York Canal, therefore, was not an event celebrated in the *United States* generally, they made bold to appear before the doctor and request the day. This, somewhat to the astonishment of the college, was granted. The celebration, accordingly, proceeded in due form; a number of speeches were made, of which I retain no distinct recollection except that of Murray, in which, after happily setting forth the marriage of the Atlantic with the Lakes, he told us, going on to speak of Clinton, 'that there were many brilliant stars above the horizon, but one, or, to give his characteristic brogue, but *waun* in the zenith!'

"During our Senior year a remarkable revival of religion occurred in the college. Professors of religion, as well as others, shared largely in the work. Dr. Griffin renewed the zeal and activity, and displayed much of the power which characterized his best days in the ministry. The effect of the work on the subject of this sketch was salutary. It chastened somewhat the exuberance of his spirits, rendered him more devoted, though not less cheerful, and prepared him, no doubt, to give himself with more earnestness to the sacred work on which his eye had been fixed from the commencement of his course.

"Since graduating, there have been several meetings of our class. At one of the last of these, thirty years, I think, since we parted on Commencement day, Dr. Murray was present. He appeared in perfect health, and retained the sprightliness and freshness of former years, though his gray hair contrasted strikingly with the jet black and somewhat curly locks he used to wear when a student. On leaving the meeting, some one remarked, 'How perfectly Murray retains his identity!' Though a riper experience had given more elevation to his character, yet his manners and modes of expression, the peculiarities of his mind, heart, and temperament were singularly preserved; in a word, the whole man was again before us.

"I need not add that his loss was deeply felt by the class, as, indeed, it was by the college, with whose Board of Trust he was this year to have taken his seat for the first time."

Letter from Rev. Chester Dewey, LL.D.

"Nicholas Murray was graduated at Williams College in 1826, and received the high honorary degree of Doctor of Divinity from his Alma Mater in 1843. I had no acquaintance with him until he became a member of the college; but, coming as a young Irishman who had been converted from Catholicism, and who seemed to have adopted the Protestant faith with strong convictions of its truth and living power, he excited no little interest in my mind. As he came into my department in the Junior year, I saw his active and earnest application to his studies, and his warm-hearted and genial temperament, as well as his winning playfulness of spirit and language. He stood on high ground in the view of his friends, and all were attached to him that knew him. The embryo of that peculiar elasticity of feeling, and felicity of thought and diction, for which he was so highly distinguished in the latter years of his life, seems to me to have been greatly developed as he was called to act in a more important position, and enjoyed more intimate fellowship with highly-gifted and cultivated minds. His warm, benevolent feelings and deep Christian sympathies led him strongly to desire the enlightenment of his countrymen who were still enshrouded in that darkness which the Sun of righteousness had dispelled from his own mind and heart. As I had known him when this sympathy was young in his mind, I rejoiced to see it acting with impressive power as his useful and influential age was increasing. . . .

"What a reward came to his friends and teachers who, without an effort, enabled a meritorious youth to accomplish his heart's desire! Many of them lived to see his honorable and high career of ministerial usefulness. His gratitude was often expressed, when I had the privilege of meeting and rejoicing with him, in all the blessings our God and Savior had bestowed upon him in his course. He was a good young man. Fine talents. The future, already finished on earth, was the realization, under the good providence of God, of what his youth had foreshadowed."

D

CHAPTER IV.

Out of College and at Work.—Becomes an Agent of the American Tract Society.—Travels in Washington County, N. Y.—The Men he met.—His Diary.—Fruits of his Labors.

SCARCELY was he out of college walls before he was in a field of useful and active labor. He graduated in September, and was to enter the Theological Seminary at Princeton in November. This brief interval he employed in an agency for the American Tract Society. Leaving the city of New York on the morning of Friday, September 22d, 1826, he had a disagreeable passage up the Hudson River on the Olive Branch. Riding in the stage-coach from Albany to Troy, he was attacked with a pain in his neck so severely as to call out the sympathies of a stranger, Mr. Tracy, who took him to his home, and entertained him kindly and hospitably. In the evening Dr. Robbins bled him, and he was confined two days to the house. Rev. Dr. Beman gave him a cordial welcome when he called on his recovery, and encouraged him greatly in his work. September 27th he left Troy, and, passing through Lansingburg, he journeyed to Washington County, the field to which he was sent. Arriving at Salem, he was made at home in the house of the Rev. Alexander Proudfit, D.D. This distinguished servant of God received him with great kindness, and entered heartily into the work. Together they rode into the neighboring towns, made appointments for public meetings, delivered lectures and addresses, and formed auxiliary societies. At Granville the Rev. John Whiton was his guide and support, and here his labors were very successful. At Sandy Hill the Rev. Ravaud K. Rogers took him warmly by the hand, and made his labors delightful and fruitful. At Cambridge he stopped at the house of Rev. Mr. Prime, who went with him to other places and cheered him in his work. In his journal he writes: "Nowhere have I met with more efficiency, nor found an individual more hearty in the cause than Nathaniel S. Prime." His sketches of the scenery and the characters of the men he met with in this town are exceedingly graphic and truthful. The following are

Extracts from Journal of an Agency for the A. T. Society.

"Whitehall is situated in a narrow defile, between high, rocky, and bleak mountains. Nature seems to have fortified it on every side with walls of adamant. When the breeze is so light that it scarcely causes a leaf to flutter on the mountain top, the rush of winds through its narrow passage is deafening. Its proximity to Lake Champlain, and its situation at the head of navigation, together with its being the thoroughfare to the Canadas, and at the entrance of the Champlain Canal into the lake, point it out as a place of commercial and religious importance. Hitherto its wickedness has been proverbial. Being the landing-place in the United States of those European emigrants who come by the way of the Canadas, and these being generally of the lowest order, they settle down here and stagnate, like a filthy marsh, polluting even the very atmosphere. Until very lately the Sabbath was openly profaned, the streets exhibiting the same degree of bustle and business as any other day in the week. But society begins now to assume a different aspect; a neat little Presbyterian church is seen to lift its sparkling dome to the sunbeams, and from the exertions of the pious, and the influence they possess in the village, we may soon expect to see Whitehall, like the peaceful bosom of the lake on the borders of which it is situated, reflect the image of heaven."

"To Fort Ann is nothing but Wood Creek widened. A more sterile, cold, and rocky country I think I never passed through. A wide waste of marshy land, with here and there a blue pool of stagnant water, and in the distance, which is not generally far removed, white limestone rock, partly covered with stunted trees, are the scenes which continually meet the eye. Houses in ruins, and naked and starved-looking women and children are seen in numbers along the road. The business continually going on through the canal gives to the dreariness of the place a little variety, but you never see any thing more pleasing than a sluggish boat 'dragging its slow length along,' or hear any thing more musical than the voice of the driver, echoed back by the mountains, heaping blessings and curses alternately upon the consumptive nag as it quickens or slackens its pace. About two o'clock P. M. we arrived at Fort Ann."

"In company with some ladies, I took a walk to the

celebrated Glenn Falls, rendered classic by the pen of Cooper. The village is in the county of Warren, and in the town of Queensbury. It is indeed a most romantic spot. Every thing sublime and awful in the ragged rock, and in the headlong thundering torrent, present themselves to view. Looking downward on the confused and tumultuous waters as they pursue their angry and headlong course through the channels they have worn in the everlasting rocks, you are amazed. Here, century after century, they have been roaring and tumbling. They have sung their dirge over the last of the brave men that once wandered free on their borders, and will continue to sing when the persecutors of those brave men shall have perished forever. The water was so low that you go all over the immense rocks around which the waters are roaring. In some places you find holes twelve feet deep, completely circular, and as smooth as if made with an auger, and all over their surface you find indentations similar to those which can be made by pressing the finger on mortar. Nor are the rocks solid. They are all disjointed masses, in some places thrown promiscuously together, and in others laid with great regularity, as if by some Titanic power. I went into the cave where Uncas and black-eyed Cora, together with their songster, Gamut, passed the terrible night when the infernal Magua was in their pursuit. It looked not as if it would make a bed 'soft as downy pillows are.' It is formed by the meeting together of two rocks which Nature's chisel seems to have converted into an alcove. It is admirably calculated for the protection of innocence from Indian ferocity. The tree now exists not on which Hawkeye shot his pursuer, nor can we find many of the prominent situations and cliffs described by Cooper. They are fast passing away; even the adamantine rocks decay before the withering march of Time."

In this agency he visited and performed valuable service for the American Tract Society in Troy, Lansingburg, Salem, Greenwich, Hebron, Granville, Whitehall, Fort Ann, Kingsbury, Sandy Hill, Glenn's Falls, Hartford, Fort Miller, Union Village, Argyle, Easton, Buskirk's Bridge, Cambridge, and several congregations in other places. Some of these places he visited two and three times, being obliged to go first and make arrangements for public meetings, and then return to address them and attend to the business of the society. In most of them he found auxiliary tract societies, and in some towns that are large, including several villages, he organized one in each settlement. Every where he was kindly received, and his pleasing address and popular manners gave him access to all houses and hearts.

In this journal of his first service in the cause of Christ we find an account of his expenses for the six weeks in which he was employed, including every thing he spent, from the blank-book in which his journal is written, twelve and a half cents, to his fare from Albany to New York, four dollars, on his return. It is worthy of being recorded as an evidence of his economy and systematic habits, that the entire expenses of this trip, involving daily travel from place to place, often by stage and hired conveyance, but more frequently by the kindness of friends who helped him on his way, amounted in the whole but to fourteen dollars sixty-two and a half cents! And half of that was spent in getting to and from the city of Albany by steam-boat.

His services were appreciated by the Society, and a larger compensation awarded to him than had been promised. The available talent of the young agent, his remarkable facility for adapting himself to every situation into which he was thrown, his tact for getting along with all sorts of men, his easy familiarity with the people whose favor it was important to conciliate, marked him as a young man destined to uncommon usefulness.

Thus the little interval between the close of his collegiate course and his entrance on his theological studies was improved with an industry, energy, and efficiency that distinguished his whole career.

The minutes of the American Tract Society's Executive Committee furnish the following testimonials:

"At a meeting of the Committee of the American Tract Society, New York, Sept. 23, 1826,

"*Resolved*, That Mr. Nicholas Murray, a graduate of Williams College, and about to join the Theological Seminary, Princeton, be commissioned to labor seven weeks in Washington County and vicinity, New York, to have his expenses borne, and to receive after the rate of $20 for six weeks as compensation."

"At a meeting of the Committee of the American Tract Society, Nov. 11, 1826, a letter was read from Mr.

N. Murray, the Society's agent in Washington County, New York, and vicinity, respecting his agency for six and a half weeks, during which time he assisted in forming seventeen auxiliaries, and collected $236. Whereupon, *Resolved*, That $8 per week be allowed him as compensation for his services."

In a letter to Dr. Halleck, dated Princeton Theological Seminary, Nov. 25, 1826, in which he speaks of the allowance of $52 for his services, he says:

"I must say now what I told you at the time, that my compensation was unexpected, though not unearned. Were I to receive nothing more than the approbation you bestowed on me, I would feel myself liberally paid. I commenced my agency with the determination to accept of nothing for my labors unless I accomplished something worthy of the object in which I was engaged. I labored incessantly; the Lord blessed my exertion. * * *

"I am here pursuing my studies, and under expense, without any earthly prospect of being able to pay my expenses. What some of my friends in the city will do for me I know not, but even if they fulfill my highest expectations, I will not receive enough to pay half my expenses. I must, therefore, do something or other to meet my just debts and to supply my pressing necessities. I have thought of leaving the Seminary for the present, for the purpose of earning some money by teaching a school; but my friends are utterly opposed to it. If I remain in this place I would wish to know, sir, if I could spend my May and October vacations in the employment of your Society as an agent. Be assured I feel most warmly your kindness." * * *

CHAPTER V.

Diary in Princeton Theological Seminary.—Formation of Character. —Ambition.—Goes to Philadelphia.—An Agent again.—Travels. —Self-discipline.—Labors in the City.—Called to Account by his Presbytery.—Remarkable Letter in Self-defense.—Letter from Rev. Dr. Aydelotte.—Letter from Rev. Joshua N. Danforth, D.D. —Private Letters.

Extracts from his Diary.

"THIS is the first Sabbath that I have ever spent within the walls of a theological seminary—the first Sabbath that I have ever spent under the character of a student of theology. Although the ministerial character is that which has been for years the object of my pursuit, I have frequently lost sight of it, and in the ambitious pursuit of pre-eminence in scientific attainments have forgotten its importance. I have viewed it as the sinner does the day of his account, afar off. Oh! how many hours have I spent in the circles of mental dissipation which might be spent in the acquirement of knowledge of which I am now completely destitute. Of my attainments in science, considering my advantages, although they might be vastly greater than they are, I have no reason to complain; but in the pursuit of these attainments I have neglected my Bible and my God.

"Ambition was my controlling principle while in college. It was my polar star by night, my compass and canvas by day. As it will bring every individual, it brought me sometimes into shoal water, and among rocks and quicksands; but thus far the Lord has saved me from shipwreck. Sometimes it has endangered my bark among storms and tempests, but the waves have not as yet overwhelmed me, nor has the storm destroyed me. Seeing that I am now beyond the periphery of ambitious influence, at least as far as a separation from college carries me beyond it, I am determined, instead of encouraging it as I have hitherto done, to war in the strength of the Lord against it. Ambition will do very well in the heart of an Alexander or a Bonaparte, for their aim was earthly honor and earthly dominion; it will do very well in the bosom of a Burke or a Fox, for their aim was to stand at the head of their party; but in the bosom of a student of Christian theology, whose supreme object ought to be to know God and to do His will, to break the slavery of sinners to the devil, and to extend the boundaries of Christ's kingdom, it is not only out of place, but it is absolutely sinful. People may say what they please about ambition in the abstract—that it is only a desire to be great in any particular profession; but it is not only a desire to be great, but it is a desire to be the *greatest*, and that, too, at the expense of every body else. To the ambitious man no obstacle is insurmountable, no task too arduous. To him mountains become plains, and seas rivers. To him the remote parts of the earth become contiguous. He will even dare to scale the heavens; while on the field of vision an object or an individual more prominent than himself exists, he is restless and unhappy. He must be, consequently, a man of jealousy and envy, unhappy himself, and rendering those around him so. Like sulphuric acid, wherever he goes he causes fermentation. Nor is such a being happy in heaven. While God, the perfection of the world, holds His throne, and stands far ahead of the realm of intelligence to which He has given existence, the ambitious spirit, which lives only on conquest, and succeeds only by taking the highest rank, can not possess itself in peace. If such is the true character of an ambitious spirit, can it with propriety be cherished by a theological student?

"With these ideas and views of ambition, I here most solemnly and sincerely protest against it in every form. It is an unholy principle in all its operations. Instead of this cankering principle, let a holy emulation possess my bosom; let me be emulous of gaining exalted ideas of God, debasing ideas of myself; emulous of making those acquisitions and manners which have a tendency to render men useful to the Church and to the world, so that, unlike the mass of men, I may not go off the stage leaving no impression on the world behind me.

"*Jan.* 1, 1829, found me in Princeton, among my books and classmates. Oh, how refreshing the reflection of the happiness there enjoyed. Shut out from life's busy cares, how sweet to study the workmanship of God! The hours spent at Princeton will be ever dear to me. Even now their memory comes over me, recalling many a holy hour of prayer and brotherly communion. Some of my companions—where are they? Oh, how has one short year dispersed the little band that loved and lived together! The John of the sweet band is gone to isles where Hall, and Young, and Whiting, and Janeway, and Baird no more, unless in thought, shall bow with him to ask sweet gifts from heaven. May the South Sea Isles forever feel thy influence, dear Gulick! Oh, may you see her idols deserted, her ignorance enlightened, her pollution washed away by the atoning and cleansing blood of Christ. And when the sun, which never makes a night, shall gird the isles of the South Sea with one broad zone of *light*, may you, and those saved through you, meet with those you have left behind, never, never more to part. Oh, then we'll think of Princeton, and bless the day we met in its revered halls.

"On the second week of April last I joined the New York Presbytery. Would that for such a solemn relation I had been more prepared in heart. Dod, and Hunter, and Gray joined with me. A good examination. Would that I could with as much ease and honor acquit myself before the bar of Heaven. But in Thy merits, Jesus, let me stand acquitted. The examination in classics nothing but form; on experimental piety little else. If ever permitted to be a presbyter, oh, let me regard the office I sustain, if not myself.

"On the 17th May, engaged as agent for the American Tract Society, to spend six weeks in Pennsylvania. Came by accident to Philadelphia, where I commenced labor with a poor prospect of success. Succeeded far beyond the expectations of my friends. At the end of six weeks, could not return to Princeton on account of the importance of my labors to sustain the cause commenced. Was prevailed on to remain, at least, during the summer months. During the summer, visited Baltimore, Gettysburg, Carlisle, Harrisburg, and through Lancaster to Philadelphia.

"About the 1st of November was prevailed on to remain for one year from that time. And now the commencement of the new year finds me in this city, where, at the commencement of the last, I had no more expectation of being than in the moon. Thus we are constantly led by a path which we know not. How vain the labor, at which man so frequently toils, of planning ways and means to guide his future life! Oh, how hard the lesson to walk by faith and not by sight!

"For the mercies of the last year I ought to be thankful. General health has been meted out to me; no sickness which detained me a single day to my bed. Prosperity has been my lot. The agency under my control has been prospered beyond measure. The Tract Society has introduced a new era into Pennsylvania exertion. I have formed friends and friendships which will be dear to me through life. Among the pious and intelligent I have found a name. Of many of them I have made particular friends; of many more, pleasing acquaintances. For this, to God be all the glory. Oh, let me never forget the hole of the pit from which I was digged.

"I have been permitted to take an active part in many objects, some unnecessary to mention. The tract has been my leading. May I not be a castaway, while I am devoting my time, and money, and talents to the general cause of benevolence.

"Sabbath evening, January 6th, 1828.

"This has been the first Sabbath of the new year. Shall I see its last? Perhaps I may; perhaps not; but the preponderating probabilities are that I shall not. I have passed my 25th year; 30 years make the mean proportion of men's lives: 25 chances, then, are gone! Oh that I might see this subject in the light of eternity!

"I heard Dr. Rice, of Virginia, preach this morning, in Dr. Skinner's Church, on the subject of the Sacrament. In the former part of the exercises my feelings seemed desirous to get out of their wonted slow, dull mood, and rise to fervent and holy communion; but flesh so domineers over spirit, and *reason* over *faith* with me, that, before the close of the sermon, I sunk to my dull, prosing mood again. Oh that I could walk more by faith, and depend less on sight! I seem like the ancient mariners, sailing only in shoal waters, where my short line can find soundings—without the bold, Christian intrepidity which enables its possessor to launch forth into the broad ocean of a Savior's love, without that faith which entereth into that within the veil, whither the forerunner has gone.

"This was Dr. Skinner's communion Sabbath. I had the privilege of sitting at the table set in the wilderness. Oh that its dainties might be more palatable to me! I sat as at a table of carnal, common food; I partook as without appetite or relish. The emblems had, for me, none of the flavor of the honey or the honeycomb. How long shall I be thus feeding upon husks, while there are dainties enough in my father's house, and to spare? One reason for this barrenness I find in the neglect of self-examination and prayer. O Lord, may I with greater humility seek the light of thy reconciled countenance.

"In the afternoon, commenced instructing the first Bible-class that was ever under my direction, in the Rev. Mr. Kennedy's Church. What a delightful employment, to be imbuing young minds in sacred truths; and how high the trust, to be permitted to make impressions on minds which neither time nor cares can obliterate! Oh that the Lord would give me the souls of some of my class for my hire, and make me true to my trust, and to weep between the porch and the altar for their conversion! Heard Mr. Kennedy lecture on the first eleven verses of the 4th of Matthew. Was gratified with his exegesis. Some of his thoughts practical and original. I have many opportunities of learning, and hearing the Gospel ably and faithfully expounded: would that I had a heart more to profit by it! My heart, how hard and cold it is!

"Nothing of special moment has transpired during the past week to disturb my happiness, or quicken or retard my usefulness. Had the pleasure of a short interview with Mr. Nettleton, the revival reformer. I long for a greater knowledge of him.

"Oh that, as my years, months, and Sabbaths are rolling away, I might have a more realizing sense of the obligations which rest on me; and that, as I increase in years, I may also in the knowledge of myself, and of my Lord and Savior Jesus Christ!"

"Sabbath evening, January 13th, 1828.

"Another week and Sabbath have fled forever! How quick and ceaseless is the flight of time! Unlike the bird which flies through the air, it never wearies, never needs any rest; but, like the stone rolling down an endless declivity, it seems, and really does, acquire new strength as it proceeds. For, to all the world besides immortal man, time is nothing, is of no value. In youth, the glow of health and buoyancy of youthful feeling resists the influence of Time's withering touch; but far otherwise in manhood and yet riper years: Time's footsteps we can trace; he leaves his marks behind him. The whitened locks, the wrinkled brow, the tottering step, the frigid feeling, all proclaim Time's march, and add great strength to that whose only tendency is to corruption. The man of twenty lives one year in five; the man of sixty lives five years in one. How precious, then, are youthful years! If years are precious, so are months, and weeks, and days, and hours, and minutes. Oh that I, at twenty-five, may spend my days as sober sixty may approve!

"How sweet the Sabbath, how adapted to man's condition! How sweet to tread the Lord's most sacred courts after six days' labor! Oh that these opportunities of enjoying the smiles of God may be more appreciated by me!

"During the week have felt well in the discharge of duty. Duties have been numerous; increased very much by my duties as Secretary of the City Bible Association; but the Lord has given me strength to discharge them all with acceptance. To God be all the glory for my opportunities of getting and doing good. That the Lord would keep me from placing any dependence upon good works or any thing else, unless upon the all-sufficient merits of Jesus Christ my Lord!

"This morning heard Dr. Janeway on the text, 'Train up a child in the way in which he should go:' it was *good* and *practical.* After all, for the man who wishes to render up his account with acceptance to the Mediator of the new covenant, practical preaching is the stuff. Theories may please, but seldom profit; essays may gratify, but rarely do good; learning may enlighten, but rarely impresses. Good, practical preaching reaches and affects head and heart. If am permitted ever to enter the ministry, may I show by my conduct and preaching that I fully believe these positions.

"In the afternoon heard my Bible-class, and Mr. Kennedy preach. There is much of a self-denying spirit necessary to constitute a good teacher of youth. There is so much restlessness, inattention, stupidity, and vagrancy, that men of more than ordinary polarity of feeling are required to get along with them.

"Mr. Kennedy's sermon was on *Temptation.* He is generally *good* and *sensible.* 'The man,' he said, 'who parleys with temptation is *gone.*' This he proved by a reference to Eve. Oh that I may be enabled to resist the devil, and he will flee from me. May I never parley with the enemy, but at every assault command him, with holy authority, 'Get thee behind me, *Satan*.'"

"Sabbath evening, January 20th, 1828.

"During the past week I have been privileged to do something in the way of sending the Bible to the destitute of the city, and of doing good in other ways as God has given me opportunity. Have not that sweet, intimate communion with God which I have formerly felt. Oh for a greater and still greater hungering and thirsting after righteousness! that as the hart pants after the water-brooks, so may I pant after Thee, O my God!

"This evening heard the Rev. Mr. Livingston on Intemperance: never did I see a house more crowded or more attentive; it was a good sermon, and did good. I am another week nearer the grave—another nearer my last solemn trial. Oh, when my hour of departure has come, may I be found ready, and not subject to the awful reflections of weeks, and Sabbaths, and other opportunities all misspent and misapplied! During the two past weeks some circumstances of considerable bearing on my life and destiny have transpired. Oh for the divine direction in all things pertaining to my usefulness and happiness. May I not be left to myself, to choose my own ways or to guide my own footsteps. Oh that I might continually feel that I am a pilgrim in a barren land."

"Sabbath evening, Feb. 3d, 1828.

"Through the tender mercy of a loving God, I have been spared since the last entry I have made. If for the sustaining power of God for one hour I ought to be thankful, how much more when that power is continued for weeks, months, and years! Oh God, give me a heart to love and serve Thee, and a willing disposition to do Thy will. Subdue my proud imaginations, and humble my haughty heart, and give me the docile spirit of a child; may I continually feel and acknowledge my dependence.

"At this time the Rev. Mr. F—— is the great topic of conversation. To his preaching and measures I feel in some degree hostile; may I be kept from fighting against God. The dread of this sin has, no doubt, caused many of the friends of true religion to permit measures to pass unnoticed which their better judgments condemned, and which, on the whole, ought to have been suppressed. On measures for the promotion of the kingdom of Christ, as well as upon every thing else spiritual and temporal, men ought to exercise their deliberate judgment, and act according to its decisions. There is, to be sure, a great difficulty in forming such a judgment, but yet it should be formed, and difficulties conquered. We are creatures of passions and prejudices; and oh! how much of their unhallowed leaven is mixed with all our actions and judgments; how great the amount of fermentation they cause in a life lengthened out to threescore and ten!

"There is great danger of intermixing passion and feeling (carnal, I mean) with the subject of religion; and there is great danger of going to the opposite extreme. The difficulty nowadays is, that some run to one extreme and some to the other. The coldness of what is called the orthodox party has driven the other into the fire; and so pleased are they with their temperature, they wish others to enjoy it also. The excesses of this party have driven the other still farther poleward, where a satisfaction similar to the other is engendered. While the one glows with feeling, the other is chilled with intellect; the one addresses the passions, the other the reason; the one aims at creating fear, the other convincing the understanding; the one drives, the other persuades; the one thunders the law, the other whispers the mild entreaties of the Gospel. This creates a difference in their actions also; the profession of the one is bold and decided, of the other quiet and distrustful; the dependence of the one rests much on their feeling, of the other more upon God; the one looks at God as a sovereign, the other as a moral governor.

"To neither of these extremes do I wish to incline; and, as Dr. Beecher says in his Missionary Sermon, the man who takes a central position is liable to the fire from both sides. A complete dependence, Lord, may I have upon Thee, and a heart give Thou to me to act as if the salvation of the world depended on my efforts; but against feeling engendered by natural causes may I ever guard. Such unholy fire may I never offer as incense to my God.

"Yesterday the mortal remains of the venerable Joseph Eastburn were committed to the grave—for many years the seaman's friend. Such a public manifestation to private worth I never witnessed. Although raining heavily, at an early hour the streets all the way from his house to his grave were crowded with anxious spectators. The hour of three came. The streets, for miles in all directions, were impassable. The oaken coffin was taken from the house into the street—a thrill ran through the multitude from one extremity to the other. The veteran seamen, for whose salvation he spent many of his days, were formed into a procession, and the mortal remains of their friend committed to them to be carried to the grave. They approached it, and sighed. They raised the bier, on which rested the coffin, to their shoulders, and wept. It was an affecting sight. To see faces hardened by the severities of the ocean wet with tears was truly affecting. With solemn step they commenced their march to his last home. A select companion carried a flag before them. It was the Bethel flag, which often summoned them to hear the prayers of him who never bent his knee before his Father's throne without remembering them *who went to the sea in ships.* They seemed to vie with each other for opportunities to be honored with bearing his remains. They placed him in the grave; and as the cold clods of earth resounded on his coffin, signifying that dust was given to dust, they turned away with a heavy heart, and many of them, no doubt, retired to their vessels to give vent to their manly, honest grief.

"In his procession were the most respectable and intelligent citizens—ministers, lawyers, doctors, masters of vessels, seamen and their wives, individuals of all religious denominations; for, although a Presbyterian, he was no sectarian. All pulpits and places were open to him while alive, and all hearts mourned for him when dead. To say that ten thousand witnessed his burial would, in my estimation, be saying less than the truth. He is gone to his home. A common question of his to the pious friends that visited him was, 'Have you any commands to your friends in glory? If so, I will deliver them.'

"What triumphant faith! For years previous to his decease, which was accomplished in his eightieth year, his last enemy was vanquished. Let me die the death of the righteous; let my last end be like his! Amen and Amen."

Mr. Murray's absence from the Seminary was not agreeable to the Presbytery of New York, under whose care he was studying as a candidate for the ministry. He had neglected to inform them of the reasons that, in his judgment, made it necessary. He had not deemed it his duty to ask their advice or consent in the matter. Perhaps he was not bound by any statute to obtain their sanction before deciding to interrupt his course of study; but it was certainly becoming in him to do so; and the Presbytery, taking that view of the case, directed the Moderator to write him a letter of inquiry and caution. That letter was written, and received by Mr. Murray. It is not to be found among his papers, but its substance and tenor may be easily inferred from the following reply, which the grieved young man was roused to return:

"Philadelphia, Feb. 25th, 1828.

"To the Moderator of the New York Presbytery:

"REV. AND DEAR SIR,—I herewith transmit to you the letter of the Moderator, written by order of Presbytery, admonishing me for leaving my studies, and for practicing what he calls '*field preaching*,' together with the letter of the Executive Committee of the Tract Society in answer to the first accusation, and the testimony of some of our ministers in answer to the other. It is hoped these documents will place my conduct, in both particulars, in a proper light. If it is a deviation from the civil and Christian statute for a culprit to vindicate himself after condemnation, in this case the fault is not mine. I thought I had a right to be heard in self-defense before condemnation, but it seems I was mistaken.

"My 'lay preaching' in general has been but seldom; and never did I indulge in this conduct, which has such a tendency 'to blast, if not destroy future usefulness,' but at the earnest request of settled ministers. Frequently, as general agent of the Tract Society, I have been necessitated to make public addresses, but as there is no specification under this head, I suppose excuse is unnecessary. I should like to know if I must refrain from this 'until I receive the sanction of that body under whose care I have placed myself!'

"I may have erred in not making known to Presbytery at its last session that 'I had relinquished my studies at Princeton for a time, and engaged myself in some agency in Philadelphia.' If there is a law on that subject, of its existence I was then, and am now, totally ignorant. Consequently, where there is no law there is no transgression.

"How long I shall remain in my present situation I know not. My intention now is to resume my studies in Princeton next November. Of this movement I am not absolutely certain. Dependent as I am at present on my own resources, I must, in a great measure, be governed by circumstances. I am now making what progress my arduous duties will admit in a regular course of didactic theology.

"I would not have troubled Presbytery with this letter and these arguments if the letter of —— could be silently borne. I have shown it to many individuals, and in no single instance has its manner or spirit been approved.

"I have another reason for troubling Presbytery with them. I have shown the letter to some individuals of the New York Presbytery, who palliate the matter by saying that toward the close of the Session some vague report of my misconduct was communicated, and that the pressure of business caused the Presbytery to refer the matter to the 'Moderator.' To this method of placing the feelings and peace of a young man in the hands of an individual I object. It may sometimes happen that authority be delegated to one who will not use it with moderation. If, in cases like mine, counsel is not given with Christian kindness, it ought to come in such a form as at least to make it respected. When I offend against the rules of Presbytery, or against the 'law of love,' I hope the Lord will give me a heart to repent of it. But for the offense alleged in the present instance I can not manifest any feelings of regret, because none exist.

"I am, reverend sir, yours most respectfully,

"N. MURRAY."

Having sent this letter to the Presbytery, he continued his labors in Pennsylvania, with what ability and success we may learn from the following letter from the Rev. Dr. Aydelotte, of Cincinnati:

"Cincinnati, March 26th, 1861.

"REV. AND DEAR SIR,—I have seen a notice that the Life of our beloved departed brother, Rev. Nicholas Murray, D.D., was about to appear, and a request that all who could would promptly send to you letters, reminiscences, etc., of the deceased. Believing that such a work must form a precious legacy to the Church and the world, and supposing that what I am about to say may throw light upon the early developments of so remarkable a life and character, I have felt impelled to send you the following very brief record of facts and reflections.

"In the year 1826, I being then rector of Grace Church, Philadelphia, the Pennsylvania Branch of the American Tract Society was formed. I took part, by request, in all the meetings for organization, and was put into the Board of Directors. The field of the new society's operations was necessarily very large, and of difficult cultivation. It embraced all Pennsylvania and Delaware, and extended to the West indefinitely. Whether the institution would prove a failure or a success depended largely upon the character of him who might at the outset be intrusted with the superintendence of its concerns.

"At that critical period, Mr. Nicholas Murray, then a student in the Theological Seminary at Princeton, presented himself before us as a candidate for the office of general agent of the new society. He was apparently about twenty-two years of age, firmly built, of ruddy countenance, and of very frank, pleasing manners. His testimonials, and the impression made by him personally, were such as secured his immediate appointment.

"As one of the executive committee, I was obliged to visit the Depository almost daily, and the newly-appointed agent continually consulted with me upon his plans and operations, and upon all the trials and difficulties which beset his path.

"The result of this constant supervision and conference was an ever-deepening conviction on my part that Providence had favored us with just the man we needed for a post so important.

"He was indefatigable in application to the duties of his office, perfectly methodical, of rare prudence, always kind, and yet ever firm and faithful to his convictions and the interests of the Society. Besides attending to all the business of the Depository, and keeping the accounts, he received and answered all the letters of the numerous agents and colporteurs, and directed all their operations. He attended also the meetings of the executive committee, gave a minute report of all that had been done since the last session, of the state and prospects of the work, and recommended new appointments of laborers, and such new measures as he deemed called for. None but a man of extraordinary business talent, and, I may add, of rare constitutional energy and endurance, could have accomplished what he did. The labors of the Board were thus exceedingly lightened; indeed, he left them little to do beyond approving his proceedings and measures.

"Let me here note the early manifestation of that peculiar bent of mind which was afterward so remarkably developed in our friend. I mean his signal ability and disposition to controvert Popery. Doubtless this was owing in some measure to his being a Romanist by birth, his thorough practical acquaintance with the influence and workings of that system, and his subsequent conversion. This course of providential training evidently fitted him for the great work which he subsequently accomplished. Not long after entering upon the tract agency his peculiar bent showed itself. At his earnest recommendation, the Board published "The History of Andrew Dunn," a narrative, the distribution of which in Ireland, as he stated, had been so blessed to the conversion of Romanists that the priests were compelled to denounce it from the pulpit.

"When I removed from Philadelphia in 1828 to take charge of a church in this city, I left Mr. Murray still in the Tract Depository. We parted with mutual kindness and regret. I felt confident that if God spared his life he would do a great work for his Master, and achieve an enviable name for himself. I therefore, from this, my Western post, watched his future movements with deep interest. I rejoiced in the accounts I heard from time to time of his labors and success at Wilkesbarre, and at the still greater measure of usefulness and honor accorded to him at Elizabethtown.

"The different productions of his pen, whether in separate volumes or in the columns of the New York Observer, I always perused, as soon as issued, with deep interest and profit. But especially was I gratified with his 'Kirwan's Letters.' How admirably suited to the popular mind are these letters! They are powerful in argument, and yet not at all heavy in manner. The style is so racy, every page is illuminated with such flashes of the finest natural wit, and the whole work breathes such hearty good-humor, that the reader never tires. None but a man of genius, a scholar, a Christian, and a true Irish gentleman too, could have written 'Kirwan's Letters.' No wonder the archbishop fled so precipitately from the field. There was no standing before such volleys of logic, keen sarcasm, and indignant rebuke, though animated throughout with the spirit of Christian kindness, and clothed in the language of true Christian courtesy.

"Dr. Murray, as Moderator, opened the General Assembly in Cincinnati in the year 1850. His distinguished reputation as a preacher and an author had preceded him. His great honor, it was soon seen, sat well upon him; there was nothing arrogant, nothing assuming about him. He was the same frank, genial brother, only more matured in wisdom, love, and other Christian excellences.

"A few years after this, Dr. Murray came to our city by invitation to lecture. The congregation of the Seventh Presbyterian Church, which had then finished a very spacious and beautiful edifice for public worship, called him to their pastoral charge.

"During this visit he had much conversation with me upon the call then in his hands. He said, among other things, that he could not accept it; that he was frightened off; that he was expected to be not only pastor of the church, but also a professor in the Theological Seminary then existing in this city; that he felt himself incompetent to fill both positions at the same time; that some ten or fifteen years of close study might make him what he ought to be as a professor, but that such application was inconsistent with the duties of the pastoral office, and, consequently, if he at once undertook both, he would certainly fail, and therefore he must decline the position.

"I acquiesced, because I believed his views eminently judicious and safe. And yet I had suggested him to the people, and greatly regretted that he could not come, not only for his usefulness' sake in our city, but because I anticipated great pleasure and profit in our future intercourse as ministers laboring together in the same city. I will simply add that both as a preacher and a lecturer he was heard among us with deep interest by his crowded audiences.

"Shortly after his return home he wrote me a long letter, in which he spoke of the good hand of his God upon him in his whole journey, in so upholding him and ordering all his ways that he was enabled to fill every appointment in the different cities to which he had been invited to lecture. He expressed his great happiness in our intercourse, and his increasing attachment to me. He urged me, as soon as I could, to visit him at Elizabethtown; but even in so serious a letter his usual good-humor would gush out somewhere. He closed with the playful alliteration, 'Come, dear brother, when you may, you will always find with me a pulpit, a plate, and a pillow.' Your brother and servant in the Gospel, B. P. AYDELOTTE."

The Rev. Dr. Joshua N. Danforth, in writing of Dr. Murray, says:

"I first made his acquaintance in 1828. He was then a member of the Theological Seminary, and agent of the Tract Society, with his head-quarters in Philadelphia. He filled well that sphere. Having within him a certain inborn energy, it was ever developing itself in the duties of his office. Ingenious in constructing plans for the promotion of that good cause, he took care that they were promptly carried into execution. In doing such work, he had great tact in putting to good use the faculties and talents of others, which he was quick to discern. If he desired to raise a given amount of money for a specific object, he formed his plan in view of it, and steadily pushed it through in the face of all obstacles; in fact, they seemed to disappear, to melt away before his genius. No man would have made a more admirable secretary of a benevolent society; but he never would have been content with any employment beneath that of the ministry of reconciliation. Whatever engaged his attention, he held that incessantly in view, and he lived to magnify it.

"About this time he visited the celebrated watering-place Cape May. Wherever he was, he sought to keep his *mind* in action. He was fond of discussion, and skillful in argument. We were accustomed to have preaching every night at one of the public halls, in which Murray, though not yet licensed, took a great interest. Crowds attended those meetings; some, perhaps, as seasons of relaxation while away from home. A bold and daring nature may sometimes be inferred from a small circumstance; and I confess, when I looked at some of the marine exercises of my friend, when I saw the fearful distance oceanward to which he would allow himself to be carried on the back of a stalwart swimmer, I trembled for the safety of a valuable life. To him it was a joyous pastime; and when he returned from Europe I expected certainly to hear that he had been on the summit of Mont Blanc; but there are few, I believe, who attain to that elevation."

Having spent a year and a half in the service of the Tract Society, and by close economy having made these months yield him a sufficient sum of well-earned money to sustain him through the remainder of his theological course, he returned to Princeton, and resumed his studies with the class he left. During this period of travel, correspondence, lecturing, and teaching, he had been hard at work, in his leisure hours, keeping up with the class in the Seminary.

So successful had he been in the prosecution of the studies of his class, that his certificate of dismission from the Seminary, signed by all the professors, states that he entered the Seminary Nov. 9, 1826, and "that he has been ever since a regular student in the Seminary." This was given May 7, 1829.

Extracts from his private Letters.

"*Princeton, Dec.* 20, 1828. The year is coming to a close, and I imperceptibly recur to the days of my boyhood, when the holidays opened upon me many sources of enjoyment and pleasure. With the thought many others are connected. My early friends pass in review before me; and as I recognize their countenances, passing one after the other in the glass of memory, I feel sad—sad, as there is a probability that I shall never see them more this side of eternity. My father died while I was yet young. I recollect him lying in his coffin. I remember the feelings which possessed me while following his remains to the grave. It was near the New Year when he was buried. I then thought the grave in which he was buried should be mine, when, like him, I was cold in death. But the *New Year* came, and I was gay as ever. Shortly afterward I became a clerk in the store of a relative at some distance from home, where I spent three New Years with other companions than those of my boyhood. Since the close of those years, as respects me, all my relations are as if in the grave of my father. Away from country, home, friends, relatives, I have spent thirteen New Years, and now am about entering on another.

Although not yet twenty-six, I have seen a checkered life. I have seen more of the bustle of the world than I wish to see again. But I ought to be thankful. Far from home, I have found friends, and, as I hope, a Savior. In the midst of darkness light sprung up, which revealed to me the path in which I should walk.

"There are thoughts and feelings which present themselves to the mind, which, when unbosomed, give relief. Among these are thoughts of home and friends. The attachment of the Irish to their country is proverbial. And, although causes have operated very strongly to weaken this attachment in me, I yet feel it in some degree, and delight in chanting the bold anthem of '*Erin go Bragh.*'"

"*Jan.* 1, 1829. The hour I have taken for writing calls for serious thought and consideration. While the gay and thoughtless dance on the grave of their years as they join the caravan of those that preceded them, and hail with mirth the commencement of the new, it becomes the serious and thoughtful to note time by its loss, and to hail every New Year as a messenger who precedes and notifies the approach of Him who bears a warrant for our departure. Although the day is like others—the sun unchanged—the same clear blue sky enveloping the world, still, from the bustling throng, the joyous countenance, the sounding knell, we learn that unwonted thoughts occupy the mind. Some, who reckon their existence by their *years*, march slowly in the procession of the old, as of some dear friend; and when deposited in old Time's vault, reflect that with it they shall shortly rest. Those are sad because they are wise. The beginning of the new year is to me an occasion on which I look down, as from an eminence, upon the long vista of years. There are times when thoughts too ponderous for utterance come over my mind—when the *past* marches in review before me, and I feel my situation to be somewhat like that of a mariner on a plank: my mates (I mean my early ones) are gone down; from the fleet with which I commenced the voyage of life I am separated, and looking abroad, as I have been this day, on the wide ocean, I see not even their wreck in view. Oh! let me then be wise, and as my years, like sands, are running, forget not that with trumpet tongue they proclaim a shortening life."

"*Feb.* 20, 1829. Yesterday and to-day I have been striving to bring a ruffle on the dead sea of feeling, but in vain. This is to me a strange and unaccountable state of mind, as I am not given to melancholy. But the proverb is, 'It is the darkest hour just before daylight.' I hope, for one, there is a sun in the clouds which will shortly pour its cheering beams on me. I feel at times as if the enjoyment of such feelings was a luxury. There is something in a continuous flow of feeling which is buoyant and pleasant; it gives a sweetness to the sweets of life, and frequently gilds prospects that otherwise would be gloomy enough. But the uninterrupted enjoyment of such a state is not desirable. We are carried along by it unconsciously like a man asleep in a ship. We desire to look on the sunny side of every object, and to dwell more on fancied than real life. Our tone of feeling becomes monotonous, and we live like the insect that revels in the light, and sleeps when it has retired. Living so, life is no luxury. The man who eats from the same dish every day has his appetite satisfied, but no more: vary his dishes, and his taste will become interested. Thus it is very much with life. The hermit, after a long seclusion from social man, on his return (unless his feelings in the mean time are soured) enjoys friendly intercourse, and when tired again enjoys his retreat. I have often observed that those habituated to depression of spirits have usually a more intimate acquaintance with themselves than others. This has led me farther to remark that what we usually term *blues* may be the state of a man who has abstracted himself from the world around him, and retired into himself, for the purpose of studying that divine mechanism which has so wisely adjusted every chord in our system to its particular function, and placed them all, in their almost infinite and complicated variety, under the control of the will. This, to me, would be a pleasing theory if I found myself within myself, if I found my hidden nature developing itself in greater strength and resolution to use every talent God has given me for His glory, and to the elevating to the dignity of the sons of God our species. From the world we can expect nothing. Its breath is cold and chilling, and its ruling passion selfishness."

"My life has been a diversified one. I have passed through deep waters, but they have not overwhelmed me. I have been in the wilderness, and yet felt not its dreariness. I was early separated from the fleet with which I commenced the voyage of life, and thrown on the wide ocean, a toy for its billows to play with, and that, too, without pilot, rudder, anchor, or polar star to pierce the clouds that gathered around me, and yet I have been, by infinite mercy, preserved to mix with the friends of religion, and to lend my feeble talent to vindicate the ways of God to man."

"You have often heard that the course of the scientific man and student are more barren of interesting incidents than that of any other class of men. Shut out from the world as they are, and from the communion of men, their history is known only to themselves, and the novelty with which they are conversant is only that of diversified thought and variety of opinions. This is truly my case. Were it necessary or expedient, I could tell you something about the Socinian controversy, respecting the learned Fathers many a long story, but in reference to the moving, mixing men around me I am in prison. The walls of my little square room bound my horizon; my companions are the mental remains of the departed; my employment, cogitation. Through the same unvaried scenes I have daily to pass; along the same beaten path I have daily to walk; with the same companions I have daily to mix, and with the same stubborn heart daily and hourly to contend. When wearied with study I leave my books. When my mind regains its elasticity I return to them with renewed ardor. That 'all beside the *present hour* is a mere feather on the torrent's side' is more poetical than true.

That we have no lease of life is acknowledged, but not that we may expend it as a profligate does his money, and live to-day regardless of the good we may do to-morrow. If this were not fallacious, I should not be here poring over old Latin theology, collecting mental treasure from the mines of antiquity. If prospective usefulness is a mere feather on the torrent's side, it is a situation highly perilous; and, if true, I should break away from those halls erected for the education of the prophets, and launch into the world. What holds me here? A desire of *prospective* usefulness. And it is this desire that gives energy to study, invigorates my prayers, cheers my heart, and enables me to wade through the rubbish of antiquity for the purpose of collecting and digesting materials for future use. I will pray for future and extensive usefulness. Hope is an anchor to the soul both sure and steadfast; and if the comfort it administers is taken away, earth becomes a prison-house, into which not a ray of light enters to cheer its prisoners."

CHAPTER VI.

Sketches of the Professors Archibald Alexander, D.D., and Samuel Miller, D.D.—Their Influence on Mr. Murray's future Character. —His grateful Recollections of their Instruction and Example.

If the power of Dr. Griffin was felt and seen while Mr. Murray was in college, rapidly and wonderfully developing and cultivating his intellectual faculties, and preparing him for his useful career, not less was the influence on his mental and moral training by the venerable men at whose feet he sat in the seminary at Princeton. Having read his recollections of the president, we will here recall the account which he gave in after life of the venerable professors, whose intimate friendship he enjoyed from the time he was their pupil till they ceased to live on earth.

THE REV. ARCHIBALD ALEXANDER, D.D.

A LETTER TO A FRIEND.

"My dear Sir,—The true idea of Dr. Archibald Alexander must be ever confined to those who knew him, and who were capable of appreciating his character; and that idea, even with such, like the idea of the true or the beautiful, is more easily felt than expressed. You ask me to give you my idea of him. It is impossible for me to transfer it to paper just as it lies enshrined in my own mind; but, for the sake of those who never saw or knew him, and who may desire a portrait of the man, I will make the attempt to comply with your request.

"My first sight of the man and interview with him was in the month of November, 1826. My first feeling was that of disappointment. He was small of stature, rather slender in person, negligent in dress, rather reserved in company, and with a voice in conversation pitched on a higher key than ordinary, and rather inclining to a squeak. Having just passed from under the tuition of Dr. Griffin, the contrast between my past and future teacher was too great not to be felt at the moment. He placed me, however, by his kind and cordial manner, soon at ease; and as he was reading my introductions and papers, I sought, as well as I could, to read his person and countenance. I soon concluded that his broad and strongly-marked forehead, his dark and penetrating eye, his brief but comprehensive questions, and his rapid conceptions, meant something; and I left his room deeply interested and impressed by the interview. On the next Sabbath, in the afternoon, I heard him, for the first time, preach in the oratory of the Seminary. He spoke sitting in his chair. He read a passage of Scripture, and then, as was his manner, raising his spectacles from his eyes to his head, he commenced talking. His voice was peculiar, and his manner; his matter was simple. As he progressed, I became interested—absorbed. Although seated in the middle of the room, and in the midst of students, I thought he was preaching to me, and revealing the very secrets of my heart; and as his penetrating eye glanced from seat to seat, I instinctively shrunk behind the person that sat before me, in order to avoid his reading me through and through. That first sermon I have never forgotten. As a preacher to the conscience and to the experience of men, I have never known or read of his superior. While under his instructions, my esteem grew into respect, my respect into love, and my love into admiration of the man; and my intercourse with him in subsequent years, on more equal terms, and on a wider platform than that of a student, has left the impression on my heart, that in all the elements of true greatness the Church of Christ has had but few such ministers.

"'What makes you think Dr. Alexander a great man?' said rather a captious minister to me one day. 'That is a question I never thought of,' was my reply. And the question was a natural one for persons to ask who but occasionally saw him, and who heard him but occasionally preach. He was not eloquent, like Chalmers and Robert Hall; he was not learned, like Bentley and Porson; he was not polished to cold elegance, like Blair, nor into crimson gorgeousness, like Melville; nor was his a courtly polish of manner in public or in private, which often makes weak men quite impressive. In what, then, you will ask, consisted that emphatic character which so deeply impressed itself upon all who ever knew him, and, indeed, upon his age? In a rare combination of characteristics, so nicely blended as to conceal each other, and as yet to make an almost perfect whole.

"He was a man, if not of various, of solid learning. To this all his students and his works testify. He was a child of nature in all his habits; in his modes of thought, in his manner of expression, in his tones of voice, in his gestures, in his keen wit, in his occasional sarcasms, in his very laugh, he was perfectly natural. It would seem as if the idea of doing a thing genteelly, or according to rule, or for effect, was never before him. This was one of the highest charms of his character. He was a man of godly sincerity. He had no concealed ends—no hidden plans to produce future results. He manifested all that he felt. In an intercourse with him, of more or less frequency, for twenty-five years, some of which was confidential, I have never known him to advocate policy. His was the most simple-hearted piety; he read the Bible like a child, and he exercised a simple faith in all it taught and promised. There was no effort to explain away its doctrines, or to modify its principles by the teachings of philosophy, falsely so called. He was a metaphysician, and yet all the metaphysics and German mysticism upon earth weighed not a feather with him against one simple text of Scripture fairly interpreted. His mind and heart were imbued with divine truth, and his experience of its power was rich and ripe. He had a sympathizing heart; no person ever resorted to him in vain for counsel or aid. He entered into your circumstances and feelings, and soon felt as you felt. Indeed, I have known his sympathies produce in him a nervous excitement, so as greatly to interrupt his comfort. He knew when to speak and when to be silent. It was in the month of January, 1842, he came to my bereaved family to bury one of our children, the second taken from us within a few days. He sat by my side without saying a word for some time; at length, breaking the silence, he uttered this memorable expression: 'I have not come to comfort you, my friend; the Lord only can comfort you;' and again a long silence ensued. After the emotions excited by our first meeting subsided, the conversation became natural, and on his part instructive and greatly comforting. He was a preacher of the rarest excellence; natural, scriptural, pungent, experimental, and, at times, overwhelming in his application of truth to the saint and to the sinner. Nor had he lost any of his interest down to old age. The last address I ever heard from him was made to the Synod of New Jersey, at its meeting in Elizabethtown in 1850, and I never heard a better one, or one that more deeply interested his crowded audience. As a professor of theology, he was able, discriminating, sound in the faith, and most ardently attached to the great doctrines of grace; and as a teacher, he was as a father to his pupils. Their location, their joys and their sorrows, their failures and successes, seemed all known to him; their names seemed ever before him, and he never met them but with paternal emotions. His death was just like his life — calm, natural, collected, and pleasant. None would have it, indeed, otherwise. There was no pain of body — no anxiety of mind — no fears as to the Church. His family was all around him. The Synod of New Jersey was in session. His beloved seminary was flourishing. 'My work,' said he, 'is done, and it is best I should go home.' And he went home.

And the Synod of New Jersey, and many ministers from other synods, and from distant places, carried him to his burial."

REV. SAMUEL MILLER, D.D.

"Among the most polished, popular, and learned ministers that have adorned the American Church was the Rev. Dr. Samuel Miller. In stature of the medium size, formed with remarkable symmetry, with mild blue eye, bald head, high forehead, and a countenance remarkably bland and prepossessing, he immediately commanded the respect of all with whom he came in contact. His politeness was such as to gain for him the sobriquet of the American Chesterfield; his affability was such as to attract even the fondling attention of children; so ready was he in conversation, and so full of anecdote, as to make him the attractive centre of every circle which he graced with his presence; and so wise and prudent was he withal, that his advice and counsels were sought by his brethren and by the churches as if he were an oracle. In his youth he was greatly popular as a preacher, and down to the close of his long life was remarkably solemn and instructive. Thoroughly evangelical and devotedly pious, his ministrations were sought beyond those of almost any of his contemporaries. He was a man of varied learning—of retentive memory; was a graceful, easy, and polished writer, and, to as great an extent as almost any man of his day, enjoyed both an American and European reputation. He was a voluminous author, an able controvertist, a fine ecclesiastical historian, and an able and beloved professor in the Theological Seminary at Princeton, from its foundation to the close of his long and brilliant life. Dignified without haughtiness, condescending without descending, affable without garrulity, polite without the cold correctness which chills, firm in his opinions without bigotry, catholic without any approach to latitudinarianism, and remarkably generous in all his sympathies, he made even his enemies to be at peace with him, and embalmed his memory in the hearts of all good men; and the hundreds of students that enjoyed his instructions as a professor, while they reverenced him as a teacher, loved him as a father.

"The Historical Society of New Jersey met at Princeton, now a place of patriotic, and classic, and sacred associations. It was a noble gathering of men distinguished in their various professions as jurists, advocates, professors, and divines; and there was a most cordial greeting and commingling of these historic associates. All differences in sentiments, professions, and politics were laid aside while in the pursuit of the one common object of honoring New Jersey by collecting materials for its history, and to rescue from oblivion the names of her many heroic and distinguished sons.

"But one was absent who had rarely been absent before, and who was one of the founders and vice-presidents of the Society; one whose bland and polished manners always attracted regard, and whose venerable aspect always deeply impressed. His absence from the meeting, and in the town of his residence, excited inquiry; and when it was announced that Dr. Miller was very seriously sick, there was in the meeting a deep expression of sorrow and sympathy. It was solemnly felt by all that in those historic gatherings we should see his face no more.

"His son conveyed to me a message from his father that he would like to see me on the morning of the next day, if convenient. The hour of our interview was fixed; and, as other engagements required punctuality, I was there at the moment; but, as the barber had just entered the room, he was not quite ready to see me, and he sent requesting me to wait half an hour. This my other engagements absolutely forbade; and on sending him word to that effect, he invited me to his room. As I entered it, the picture which presented itself was truly impressive. The room was his library, where he had often counseled, cheered, and instructed me. There, bolstered in a chair, feeble, wan, and haggard, was my former teacher and friend, one half of his face shaven, with the soap on the other half, and the barber standing behind his chair. The old sweet smile of welcome played upon his face, and having received his kind hand and greetings, he requested me to take a seat by his side. His message was a brief one; he had written a history of the Theological Seminary for the Historical Society which was not yet printed, and he wished an unimportant error into which he thought he had fallen to be corrected; and, that there might be no mistake, he wished me to write it down, thus showing his ruling passion for even verbal accuracy. When his object in sending for me was gained, he then, in a most composed and intensely solemn manner, thus addressed me:

"'My dear brother, my sands are almost run, and this will be, probably, our last interview on earth. Our intercourse, as professor and pupil, and as ministers, has been one of undiminished affection and confidence. I am just finishing my course; and my only regrets are that I have not served my precious Master more fervently, sincerely, and constantly. Were I to live my life over again, I would seek more than I have done to know nothing but Christ. The burdens that some of us have borne in the Church will now devolve upon you and your brethren; see to it that you bear them better than we have done, and with far greater consecration; and as this will, no doubt, be our last interview here, it will be well to close it with prayer. As I am too feeble to kneel, you will excuse me if I keep my chair.'

"I drew my chair before him, and knelt at his feet. The colored barber laid aside his razor and brush, and knelt by his side. As he did not indicate which of us was to lead in prayer, I inferred, because of his feebleness, that it would be right for me to do so; and while seeking to compose my own mind and feelings to the effort, I was relieved by hearing his own sweet, feeble, melting accents. His prayer was brief, but unutterably touching and impressive. He commenced it by thanksgiving to God for His great mercy in calling us into the fellowship of the saints, and then calling us into the ministry of His Son. He then gave thanks that we ever sustained to one another the relation of pupil and teacher, and for our subsequent pleasant intercourse as ministers of the Gospel. He thanked God for the many years through which He permitted him to live, and for any good which He enabled him to do. 'And now, Lord,' said he, 'seeing that Thine aged, imperfect servant is about being gathered to his fathers, let his mantle fall upon Thy young servant, and far more of the Spirit of Christ than he has ever enjoyed. Let the years of Thy servant be as the years of his dying teacher; let his ministry be more devoted, more holy, more useful; and when he comes to die, may he have fewer regrets to make in reference to his closing ministrations. We are to meet no more on earth; but when Thy servant shall follow his aged father to the grave, may we meet in heaven, there to sit, and shine, and sing with those who have turned many to righteousness, who have washed their robes and made them white in the blood of the Lamb. Amen.'

"I arose from my knees, melted as is wax before the fire. My full heart sealed my lips. Through my flowing tears I took my last look of my beloved teacher, the counselor of my early ministry, the friend of my ripening years, and one of the most lovely and loved ministers with which God has ever blessed the Church. Every thing impressed me: the library, his position, the barber; his visage, once full and fresh, now sallow and sunken; his great feebleness, his faithfulness, his address, and, above all, that prayer, never, never to be forgotten! He extended his emaciated hand from under the white cloth that draped from his breast to his knees, and taking mine, gave me his parting, his last benediction. That address—that prayer—that blessing, have made enduring impressions. It was the most solemn and instructive last interview of my life.

"When I next saw him he was sleeping in his coffin in the front parlor of his house, where he often, with distinguished urbanity and hospitality, entertained, instructed, and delighted his friends. That parlor was crowded by distinguished strangers, and by many of his former pupils, who mourned for him as for a father—for a father he was to them all. And as they passed around to take a parting sight of his countenance, from which even death could not remove its accustomed placid, benevolent smile, their every bosom heaved with intense emotion, their eyes were suffused with tears; and could every tongue utter the emotions of their hearts, it would be in the language of Elisha when he gazed on Elijah ascending before him unto heaven, 'My father, my father, the chariot of Israel, and the horsemen thereof.'

"His death was as calm and triumphant as his life was pure, disinterested, and lovely; and as pious men carried him to his burial, and as we covered up his remains under the clods of the valley, the prayer arose at least from one heart, 'May I live the life of this righteous man, and let my last end be like his.'

"There are many scenes in the life of Dr. Miller that memory frequently recalls—scenes in the class-room, in the General Assembly, in the Synod of New Jersey, in the pulpit, in the social party—scenes which occurred during the conflict of parties, and in the frank and unrestrained intercourse of social life. In them all Dr. Miller was pre-eminently like himself. But the scene by which I most love to recall him, and which memory most frequently recalls, is that parting scene in his study. Oh, may that parting prayer be answered!"

F

CHAPTER VII.

Licensed to Preach the Gospel.—Labors as a Domestic Missionary.—Conflicting Calls.—Offers of Secretaryships.—Passages from his Diary.—Recollections of his Youth.—His first Sermon.—Sketch of Ashbel Green, D.D.—Goes to Wilkesbarre.—His Call.—Remarkable Reply.

"I CONTINUED my studies in Princeton until April of the present year (1829), when I was licensed to preach the Gospel by the Presbytery of Philadelphia. The period of my licensure was to me one of great interest. The ministry was brought home to my door which for years I had been viewing at a distance. I was licensed in Frankfort, Pa., in the church of Mr. Biggs. I think I felt an unwonted spirit of prayer on the occasion. My first sermon was on the Sabbath after licensure, in the church of Dr. Ely. Many of my special friends came out to hear me. I felt much agitated, but the Lord was truly with me. Dr. Green came into the pulpit to me, and made a prayer at the conclusion that warmed my heart. I returned to Princeton, where I remained until the middle of May, when Mrs. Janvier, with whom I boarded, died, and I returned to Philadelphia; and, having a Presbyterial appointment at Norristown for six weeks, I proceeded to fulfill it. After preaching three of my Sabbaths, I sent the Rev. Wells May to take my place, and on the 8th of June accepted an appointment of a mission from the Board of Missions of the General Assembly to the borough of Wilkesbarre, Pa., for two months. Having preached the amount of time specified, a call was put into my hands from the churches of Wilkesbarre and Kingston to become their pastor. [Kingston was just across the Susquehanna River, and connected by a bridge with Wilkesbarre.] As it was the first I had formally received, I knew not what to do. The Church of Wilkesbarre was congregational, and otherwise in peculiar circumstances. But I concluded to leave the result to Providence. I went to Philadelphia for the purpose of giving myself time to consider the matter. Between me and the committee several letters passed, which resulted in my acceptance of the call. On Thursday, the 24th September (1829), I returned to Wilkesbarre by the way of Easton, and commenced my labors as the pastor of the two churches."

This year was one of great anxiety. While he was looking forward with interest and hope to the pastoral work, he was perplexed by other and conflicting calls. Among his letters we find one assuring him that the people of Montrose, Pa., would give him an invitation to settle with them, if he would encourage them that he would favorably entertain the proposal. But this suggestion did not embarrass him. The American Tract Society, in whose service he had been so efficient, sought to secure him as a permanent agent; and had he yielded to the repeated and pressing invitations from this quarter, the whole course of his future life would have been changed. At the same time, the

Presbyterian Board of Education elected him, before he was licensed to preach, to be assistant corresponding secretary and general agent. The Executive Committee then consisted of the Rev. Ezra Stiles Ely, D.D., chairman, Rev. Dr. Engles, Messrs. Alexander Henry, Solomon Allen, John Stith, and John M'Mullin. The Rev. Dr. Green pressed this appointment upon him with great earnestness. The Rev. Dr. Janeway was to be the secretary without a salary, and the chief duties and responsibilities of the work, then in its incipient stages, were to be confided to Mr. Murray. In a letter to him, the Rev. Dr. Green says: "I think, with Dr. Alexander, that in no other way can you probably be so useful as in being instrumental in bringing into the ministry some hundreds of young men, who, but for your labors, would never have entered it."

Both of these applications he declined; and having fixed his eye and his heart on the pastoral office, he went forward steadily to the work to which he was called. But it is evident that he had already made a deep impression on the minds of leading men in the Church. His business talents, his energy, his strong good sense, his pleasing manners and address, had marked him, even at this early period in his life, as one fitted for great and efficient usefulness.

A few passages from his letters at this period of his life are deeply interesting:

"*Wilkesbarre, June* 17, 1829. What the result of my visit at this place will be, I know not. The Church is in a most distracted state. There are two parties in it, neither of whom exchange words with each other.

But they seem to be tired of fighting. I have heard the leaders of both parties express themselves as anxious for a different state of things. On the Sabbath I preached twice to large and attentive audiences, and was caressed by both sides. I hope the Lord will keep me in my proper place, and give me an eye single to His glory."

"*Wilkesbarre, June* 29, 1829. The state of things here is becoming increasingly interesting. Since the town was settled there have been but few meetings as large as mine was on the afternoon of yesterday. For the last five years they have been a divided people; and it will take some time to wake them up to a proper spirit. To that spirit I think they are coming up fast. I preach three times on the Sabbath, have a meeting for the young on Monday evening, which is overflowing, preach on Wednesday about a mile from town, on Thursday evening lecture in the Academy, and on Friday evening preach at Kingston. This is the amount of my weekly duties. I am up in the morning bright and early, study until tired, then I make a few visits, and return to study again. I feel encouraged to go on in this way for a few weeks to come. When I came here I resolved to hear no stories on either side. The consequence is, I visit indiscriminately. Their feuds have become so ramified that the only way is to be neutral. At my last meeting for the young I have heard that two young ladies were very seriously impressed. May the Lord carry on His own work in this barren wilderness.

"As respects a settlement here, I can have it if I

wish; but, unless the old wounds are healed, I will not locate myself among them. I am not so anxious for a settlement as to plant myself on the sides of a volcano."

The venerable Ashbel Green, D.D, LL.D., of whom he speaks as being present, and in the pulpit with him when he preached his first sermon, was another of the men whose counsels and example were among the forming influences of Mr. Murray's character. The following sketch of his distinguished friend is at once graphic and faithful:

THE REV. ASHBEL GREEN, D.D.

"Although I had heard much of him from my boyhood, and had read some of his writings, I never saw him until 1826; and the sight of him, at that time, would induce any young man to resolve to keep at a respectful distance. His form was full and commanding; his appearance was stern; his eye, gleaming through shaggy eyebrows, was penetrating; his step was firm, and from his cane to his wig there was something, which, to say the least, was more repulsive than attractive to a youth; and with this conclusion agreed many of the anecdotes which I had heard of him while President of Nassau Hall. My acquaintance with him commenced in 1827, and in this wise: Visiting Philadelphia as the agent of one of our national societies, I felt his approbation of my plans necessary to my success. I called to see him, and was introduced into his study. I soon found myself in converse with a courteous, kind, but dignified Christian minister. He not only approved my plans, but tendered his own subscription to the object. Finding, on inquiry, as I was about to retire, that I was a candidate for the ministry, he invited me to a seat by his side; and the impressions made upon my mind and heart by his kind inquiries, by his paternal advice, are vivid to this hour. He dismissed me with his blessings upon myself and my object. Never was a revolution more entire wrought in the feelings of a man, and from that day forward he was my counselor in cases of difficulty; and so pleasant and simple was he in private, that, on leaving my family after an occasional visit of a few days, my little children would cling to his feet and his garments, crying out, 'You must not go, Dr. Green.' I feel quite sure that those who only knew him in Presbyteries and Synods, and especially in the ardent conflicts of the General Assembly, of which he was almost a standing member, have the most erroneous views of his true character.

"His was a truthful character. Truth was to him truth; and what he believed he felt and acted out. His was not the policy to believe one way and act another. Such policy he scorned, and withheld his confidence from those who practiced it. A man cast in such a mould is likely to be unpopular with that large class of persons who regard truth with less reverence; who stretch it or contract it to suit circumstances; who, in the bad sense of the phrase, are ready to become 'all things to all men.' They are prejudiced, obstinate, bigoted, sectarian. But there is a better and truer explanation of all this. There is a deep and heartfelt reverence for the truth as such, which, on all occasions, and every where, forbids its compromise on the ground of mere worldly expediency. There is an inner reverence for it, in kind and degree, like unto that which is felt for God himself. This was conspicuous through the whole long life of Dr. Green; and often have I heard him censuring, with far greater severity, what he considered the crooked policy of his friends, who always acted with him, than that of his opponents, who always pursued a different policy from his. His firmness was at an equal remove from fickleness and obstinacy, which are alike alien to a truly noble character. The one is barren of good as the yielding wave, the other as the unyielding rock. Although holding his opinions strongly, he was ever willing to yield them for good reasons. A fool never changes his opinions, but a wise man always will for sufficient cause.

"He was a most fervent and instructive preacher. Although I never heard him preach until he had passed the meridian of life—until, fearful of attacks of vertigo, to which he was subject, he generally declined the pulpit; yet the few sermons I have heard him deliver very deeply impressed his hearers, and very obviously indicated that, in the prime of his years, he was a man of no ordinary power. His utterance was distinct, his manner was calm and dignified; if he never rose to the higher style of action, he always attained its end, attention and impression; he made you feel that he entirely believed every word he uttered, and that it was of infinite moment that you should believe them also. The minister that uniformly makes this impression must be one of great power.

"Nor was the impression which he made simply that of manner; his matter was always weighty, well arranged, and instructive. If his topics were common-place, they were always important; if his discussions were sometimes dry, they were clear as a sunbeam; if you could not always adopt his opinions, there was no mistake as to what he meant. In all my intercourse with him, I had never cause to ask, 'What do you mean, sir?' nor do I remember a sentence in all his writings which is not entirely transparent.

"His most valuable lectures on the Shorter Catechism, and his published sermons, give a fair specimen of his ordinary style of preaching. If they have not the amplitude of Chalmers, nor the polished eloquence of Hall, nor the warmth of Davies, they have the purity of Blair, in union with a natural simplicity, which strongly fix their truly evangelical sentiments in the mind and heart. Hence the devoted attachment, both to him and his sentiments, of all who ever enjoyed his ministrations.

"He greatly excelled as an expounder of the Word of God. Of his talent in this way I had an abundance of opportunity of forming a judgment. The Sabbath-school teachers of Philadelphia adopted a rule to have the same Bible lesson taught on the same Sabbath in all schools of the city, and to have the lesson expounded to them by some clergyman. The lecture-room in Cherry Street was the place, and Dr. Green was the man selected. On each evening the large room was

F 2

crowded by one of the most interesting and interested audiences I ever beheld; and although Dr. Green was then approaching his threescore years and ten, never did I hear more clear, and full, and fresh, and pleasing expositions of divine truth. At the close of the lecture, opportunity was given for the asking of any questions upon any points that were left unexplained, which were always answered with a promptness which showed the remarkable fullness of his mind upon all topics connected with the exposition or elucidation of the Scriptures. I know not that I ever attended a more instructive religious service. I have learned that it was greatly blessed of God to the conversion and edification of Sabbath-school teachers. He served his generation in more dignified stations, but probably in none more usefully than when expounding the word of life to nearly a thousand young men and women, who, on each successive Sabbath, sought to impress those views received from him on the minds of ten thousand children. Might not this plan be successfully revived in all our cities?

"He was a truly devotional man. His public devotional services were always peculiarly impressive. They were solemn, pathetic, reverential, appropriate, and never unduly protracted. In the family he always commenced morning and evening prayer with imploring a blessing upon the service; and while engaged in them, all felt that he was conversing with God as a man converses with a friend. I have often heard him express his regrets at the little preparation ministers often make for conducting the devotional exercises of a congregation, and I have heard him state that in the early part of his ministry he was in the habit of writing prayers with equal regularity as sermons; and, while he never read them, nor committed them to memory, the writing of them furnished him with topics for prayer, and gave to those topics arrangement, and to the expression of them variety and appropriateness. For this thought he may have been indebted to his venerated tutor, Dr. Witherspoon, who always recommended devotional composition to his theological students, of whom Dr. Green was one.

"My first sermon was preached in the Third Presbyterian Church, Philadelphia, then under the pastoral care of the Rev. Dr. Ely, and from the text 'Compel them to come in.' Dr. Ely was absent, and to my confusion, Dr. Green entered the church just at the opening of the service. Feeling it better to have him behind me than before me, I sent for him to the pulpit. In my ardor to stimulate ministers and Christians to do their duty, I omitted almost any allusion to the necessary agency of the Spirit to secure their success. He made the concluding prayer, in which, with his accustomed felicity, he converted the topics discussed into supplications, and then brought out most prominently and emphatically the essential truth by me omitted. I felt that the whole congregation saw and felt the defect of my sermon. His kindness was marked at the close of the service. I went to my study, re-wrote my sermon, put into it the prayer of Dr. Green, and it is unnecessary to say that it was greatly improved by the addition.

"My very last interview with him impressed me with the depth of that spirit of devotion which characterized his life. He was feeble, and forgetful, and in a mood to talk but very little to any body. Hearing that I was in the city, he sent for me, that I might attend to a matter of business for him connected with the New Jersey Historical Society. I entered his study on a May morning about nine o'clock. His Greek Testament was open before him. He requested me to be seated. The business ended, he waved his hand, saying, 'My devotional reading is not yet concluded; I shall be happy to see you at another time;' and as I closed the door of his study, the prayer, 'God bless you,' fell upon my ear; the last words I ever heard him utter. All testify that the closing years of his life were marked by a spirit remarkably devotional.

"He possessed a truly catholic spirit. This assertion, perhaps, will startle some who only knew his public character, and who have only heard of him as an impersonation of Old-school Presbyterianism. Yet it is true to the letter. His own views he held strongly, but in perfect charity to those who differed from him. Although his contributions and exertions were mainly confined to the organization of his own Church, it was out of consistency with himself, and not out of illiberality to others. More than once have I heard him detail an account of a visit made by the venerable Dr. Woods, for so many years the ornament of the Andover Theological Seminary. They compared views on theological and other subjects, and while they differed a little in the explanations of some positions, they radically agreed. 'Would to God,' I have heard him say, 'that all our ministers and churches held the sentiments of my brother Woods.' And after the disruption of our Church, he never permitted a day to pass without the most fervent prayers to God on the behalf of the brethren to whom he was regarded as being so violently opposed. He had none of the narrow sectarianism that would confine the Church visible to those only who walked with him; and often have I heard him rejoice in the good that was doing by Methodists, Baptists, Episcopalians, to all of whom, as Christians and as ministers, he could extend the right hand of fellowship, although on all suitable occasions he could strongly maintain the positions on which he differed from them. There is not probably a national society for the spread of the Gospel in this land to which he was not a contributor, and of which he was not a member or a manager; while he may be considered the father of nearly all the Boards and Societies of his own deeply-venerated Church. 'Nobody will question the Presbyterianism of Dr. Green,' said an eloquent divine, during a debate in the General Assembly, 'as he was dyed in the wool.' 'The brother mistakes,' said Dr. Green, with that promptness of repartee which he possessed; 'the Lord, by his grace, made me a Presbyterian.' And although the principles of his Church were interwoven with his spiritual life, and formed a part of it, yet he had the most cordial love for the children of God, by whatever name called. Never have I heard him speak with more affection of any man than of his friend, the amiable and venerated Bishop White.

"He was remarkably gifted as a son of consolation to desponding souls. This, perhaps, was mainly owing to his own simple views of divine truth, and his rich experience of its power. He had the power of simplifying every subject on which he spoke or wrote, and of doing it in a few words. This is very apparent in his lectures on the Shorter Catechism, prepared for the youth of his own congregation. When anxious or desponding souls applied to him for direction, he first sought out the cause of trouble, and then, like a well-instructed scribe, he so simply presented and applied the remedial truth as to give, if not immediate, yet speedy relief. He acted upon the principle that, 'if the truth makes us free, we are free indeed.' Hence aged, desponding Christians, and individuals asking what they should do to be saved, and from different congregations in the city, were often found in his study seeking his counsels. On such occasions there was a kindness and blandness in his manner which formed the greatest possible contrast with his stern and unflinching position when contending for principles on the floor of the General Assembly.

"A case in illustration of this I will state. Twenty-five years ago, the name of Miss Linnard, whose memoir has since been published, was familiar to the pious female circles of Philadelphia. She shone conspicuously among them for her fine sense, great activity, and deep piety. A minister, still living, preached a preparatory lecture in the church in Spruce Street, of which she was a member, on the text, 'Lovest thou me?' which cast her into the deepest gloom. Such were the strong and vivid representations which he made as to the necessary preparations for the right partaking of the Lord's Supper, that, conscious of not possessing them, she resolved not to commune. Her sense of duty and her deep depression of feeling came into conflict, and greatly excited her soul. In this state she had recourse to Dr. Green, who had heard the lecture. 'My dear child,' said he, 'our excellent brother seemed to forget that the Lord's table is spread, not for angels, but for sinners. He has come, not to call the righteous, but sinners to repentance. It is the weary and heavy laden He invites to Himself, and to the privileges of His house.' It was enough. She left his study rejoicing in the Lord; and a more joyful communion season she had never spent on earth. I heard the lecture, and the incident here narrated I have had from both parties. And this, I feel persuaded, is a fair illustration of his skill and success as a comforter of the Lord's people, and as a director of the inquiring to the cross of Jesus Christ.

"It remains for me only to speak of him as a literary man. As his life and writings will do his memory full justice upon this subject, I need say but little upon it. His academic habits he carried with him into his pastoral life, and always took rank in the very first class of the educated men of his own age—with such men as Dwight, and Smith, and Wilson, and Mason. If he was excelled in brilliancy by these, and others with whom he ranked, he was fully their equal in all solid attainments. It was no ordinary tribute to his literary character that he should be selected to succeed Dr. Smith as the President of Princeton College, in which position he discharged his duties as instructor with distinguished ability, and, in a religious point of view, with distinguished usefulness. It was during his presidency that the revival occurred which, under God, brought into the Church and into the ministry such men as Dr. John Breckinridge, Dr. Hodge, Bishops M'Ilvaine of Ohio, and Johns of Virginia. On retiring from the presidency, he commenced the Christian Advocate, which he edited for twelve years, and whose twelve volumes give the most ample testimony to his rich scholarship, his keen discrimination, his metaphysical acumen, his sharpness as a critic, and to the extent and variety of his reading. Some of the ablest productions of his pen were written after he had passed his fourscore years; and to the very close of his life his Greek Testament was his daily study, and he could repeat passages from the Greek and Roman classics with the interest and vigor of a school-boy. His habits of study he never surrendered to the last; and I have in my possession a note written to me on business in his eighty fifth year—written with as clear, bold, and steady a hand as if written in his fortieth year. In this respect he is an example worthy of imitation by all literary men in advanced years, to study, write, and work to the last. Still waters soon stagnate; running waters never. The mind, unemployed, like the blade of Hudibras,

"'Which ate into itself, for lack
Of somebody to hew and hack,'

preys upon itself, and soon passes away.

"Such is my estimate of the character of Dr. Green. On the whole, I esteem him as among the ripest scholars, the most able divines, the most useful men which our country has produced."

From his Diary.

"*Wilkesbarre, Aug.* 19, 1829. For the last few days my mind has been much distracted on the subject of my call to the pastoral care of these churches. It was put into my hands a week since, and as yet I am undecided what to do. It is unanimous, with a salary of six hundred dollars. There are many things inviting, and some serious obstacles. I pray the Lord to direct me. On the Sabbath previous I preached at Montrose. They would have given me an immediate call had I given them the least encouragement. But I have determined to be no coquette.

"Much labor and study have impaired my health considerably. I feel not so strong as I have done, and need a little relaxation again to invigorate me. I have reason to believe my labors here have been blessed; and if I shall conclude to stay, a prospect of usefulness spreads itself before me."

He went to Philadelphia to consult his friends and give the subject more deliberate attention; and while there he addressed the following letter to the united congregations from which the call had come. As an answer to the first call he received, it is certainly a remarkable paper:

"Wilkesbarre, August 21, 1829.

"GENTLEMEN,—As the signers of a document purporting to be '*a call*' from the united congregations of Wilkesbarre and Kingston, I take the liberty of addressing to you the following communication, as the organs of these churches respectively.

"Since that paper was put into my hands it has caused me many hours of anxious solicitude. As far as I can see duty, the beam of Providence seems to hold no steady position, sometimes inclining to the one side, and sometimes to the other. This is my great difficulty. Professing some independence in thought and action, let me assure you that if I saw the way of Providence clear, and my duty manifest, nothing could make me hesitate for a moment.

"In each of your churches there are many things well calculated to deter *a young man* from becoming their pastor, and any man from connecting himself with them. Many of these things are of long continuance, and to eradicate them will require years of laborious faithfulness. Dissension and misrule have rent the one into opposing and contending parties; coldness and decay are the characteristics of the other. The one is without any regular organization; the other possesses little but the name. And both are very much destitute of that freshness and activity which show that the heart performs its appropriate functions. Besides this, the support offered is utterly incompetent to place a man beyond the reach of care and anxiety as it respects his subsistence. And even if raised to the amount contemplated in the few lines annexed to the call, which is altogether hypothetical, still it would be incompetent. This will appear evident to any mind who sits down and counts the cost. And the very fact that two churches of so much comparative wealth can not raise a competent support for a minister, is itself a strong presumptive argument against them. If a minister is bound to make sacrifices for the good of any particular Church, it is equally the duty of that Church to make sacrifices for his support. It is a wrong explication of the law that places all sacrifices to the account of the ministry. But, in reply to all this, it may be said there are many reasons which should induce me to stay. It is true there are; and it is on this ground that I hesitate. The union of feeling and sentiment in myself, from a people so distracted, is one of the most clear indications of Providence that I see; all other reasons that should induce me to stay, arising from the surrounding destitution, and the prospect of doing good, are common to this, with nearly every vacancy in our country.

"Without farther preliminaries, I will merely state that I think duty requires me to give the following answer. I feel inclined to think favorably of connecting myself with your churches in the relation of their pastor on the following conditions:

"1. That the Church of Wilkesbarre become, previous to my ordination, Presbyterian.

"2. That my salary, as stated in the call, be paid punctually, to the day, without any interference whatever on my part.

"3. That the committee accept of the assistance offered by the Missionary Society until such time as they can do without it.

"4. That no more than four weekly services be required at my hands; all over that shall be at my own pleasure. This I insert, because many are to be found in every congregation who think they know the minister's duty better than he does himself.

"5. That, if possible, the Church of Kingston shall make arrangements to have meetings permanently at one place on Sabbath morning.

"6. That, as soon as possible, the meeting-house shall be repaired and rendered more commodious for public worship; and that some place shall be prepared for evening and occasional services.

"Farther than this I can not say at present, as the call has not been put into my hands in due form. I wish it also to be understood that if, previous to my receiving the call from the hands of the Presbytery, any reason of sufficient weight shall appear to me why I should decline settlement, I hold in my hands the power of making such declination, without subjecting myself to any censure whatsoever for so doing.

"Yours, gentlemen, in much Christian love and affection, NICHOLAS MURRAY.

"To Messrs. Haff, Anhauser, Collins, Hollenback, Brower, Parker, Hice, and Hoyt, Committee of the Churches of Wilkesbarre and Kingston."

The conditions having been substantially accepted, he gave his formal acceptance of the call, and in September went again to Wilkesbarre. In a letter to a friend, written after his arrival, he says:

"September 28, 1829.

"I found every body on the eager look-out for me, and, as the stage passed along, I saw a head from almost every door and window looking out. My reception by my friends was most warm and gratifying. On Thursday and Friday I was principally employed in attending to the examinations in the schools, and in making and receiving visits. Saturday I spent in Kingston, where I preached yesterday morning. In the afternoon I preached here, to a very full house, from the text, 'Fear not, little flock, it is your Father's good pleasure to give you the kingdom.' It was more still than I had ever seen it previously. Many came out, no doubt, to hear what I would say for the first time; but, with the exception of what I said in prayer, there was nothing peculiar in the exercises. This evening I held my meeting for the young; on Thursday evening my weekly lecture. I found three individuals rejoicing in hope on my return; one of them as interesting a convert as I have ever known. I hope the Lord may multiply the number like the drops of the morning dew. Last evening a young man called on me for the purpose of religious instruction. There is a great work to be done here. May the Lord grant me courage and strength to perform it."

CHAPTER VIII.

Ordained, and Installed over the Churches of Wilkesbarre and Kingston.—His Description of Wyoming Valley, in which he resides.—Incidents of Pastoral Life.—The Hay-mow.—Mr. Murray's Marriage.—Sketch of Rev. Mr. Rhees, the Father of Mrs. Murray.—Too late for the Wedding.

"*Wilkesbarre, Nov.* 4, 1829. This has been to me, beyond all odds, the most solemn and important day of my life. The Presbytery of Susquehanna met here this day for the purpose of ordaining me to the work of the Gospel ministry, and to constitute me the pastor of these churches. On the last evening they took me under their care, and passed me through a full examination. The examination of my fellow-men I stood very well. Would that I could say the same as it respects God! I think that, in the whole course of my life, I have been mercifully directed by the Lord, and that, by His good hand upon me, I have been brought into the ministry. At times, many stumbling-blocks were thrown in my way by myself and others, but, in great goodness, they were all removed. The business of this day was entered on by me not without prayer. I think the Lord was with me through the service; and in the Lord's strength I hope to be enabled to perform the high duties and obligations devolving on me."

In a letter written a few days afterward, he says:

" *Wilkesbarre, Nov.* 9, 1829. The exercises of my ordination were solemn and interesting. Dr. Janeway preached a good didactic sermon, which he will publish. The charge of Rev. Mr. Gray to the pastor and people, also to be published, was certainly very fine. The house was full, and we hope an impression was made favorable to the cause of Christ in the Valley. Before the hands of the Presbytery were fifteen minutes off my head, I was called upon to marry a couple, and had to ride nine miles to do it. This, they say, augurs favorably. Dr. Janeway paid me a distinguished compliment in leaving the ordination of his son to come to me. He was delighted with the Valley of Wyoming, and said that to see it was a sufficient compensation for coming up. Yesterday I preached my introductory to a full house; it is the longest sermon I have ever preached; I was upward of an hour in delivering it, and the house was perfectly still. My remarks were strong, decided, and pointed; suited, as I thought, to the people; but what impression it has made is yet to be learned. I am now entered on the full duties of the ministerial office. Never have I had such feelings as have pressed my bosom since Wednesday. Hitherto I have been viewing the ministry at a distance, now it stares me fully in the face. My fervent prayer is, that the Lord may give me strength to fulfill my ordination vows, and to live only to his glory and for the good of my fellow-men. This is my constant, fervent, and, I hope, sincere prayer. Both my congregations are united in me, and I hope the Lord may give me some souls to be stars in the crown of my rejoicing. Next Sabbath is my first communion: three persons stand propounded for admission; one of them one of my own spiritual children, the first fruits of my ministry here, and others would come forward if encouraged, but we have deferred them for another time. On the following week I have to assist in organizing a new church eight or ten miles from this place. Next month I have to attend to the installation of a minister fifty miles from here, in Susquehanna County."

The Valley of Wyoming, in which Wilkesbarre and Kingston lie, is celebrated in song and story. Dr. Murray describes it in the introduction to some incidents of his early ministry:

"The valley is beautiful beyond description. A broad and winding river enters it at the north, between two high, rocky peaks, which bear the evidence of being torn from each other's embrace by some dread concussion of nature; and, after a course of fifteen miles, takes its exit at the south, and through a gap probably made in the same way. On either side of this river the bottom-lands are exceedingly rich. As you leave the river, these lands gradually undulate, until, at the distance of about two miles, they rise into mountains on the east and west, which seem built of heaven to guard the quiet vale from all disturbing intrusions. As the traveler reaches the brow of the eastern mountain, a scene of surpassing loveliness spreads itself beneath him; and he feels that if peace has not utterly forsaken our world, its residence must be there. The valley seems as if expressly made for the home of the Indian; and for moons beyond the power of his arithmetic to calculate, the red man fished in that river, and planted his corn in that rich bottom, and sought his game upon the mountains. And before he could be compelled to yield it, he made the white man feel the power of his anger in many a dreadful surprise.

"But sin, and in its very worst forms, found an entrance into this beautiful spot. Early in the history of the settlement, a Church was collected there, which continued a feeble existence until 1829, when I became its pastor. Young, ardent, and without experience, I here commenced my ministry, in a community proverbial both for its intelligence and its disregard of religion; amid external opposition, and with a Church small, and rent by internal discords. A more unpromising field none could desire.

"I entered on my duties with zeal, and was diligent in their performance. I prepared my sermons with care, and thought them conclusive; but few heard them, and none seemed convinced by them. I felt deeply myself, but my hearers seemed unmoved. Months thus passed away without, to my knowledge, a religious impression being made on any mind; and, feeling that I labored in vain, and spent my strength for naught, I was about giving up in despair. My preaching seemed more to excite the opposition of the wicked than the prayers of the pious.

"There was among my people a man in mid-life, a German by birth, and a remarkably simple-hearted, pure-minded Christian. Whoever was absent, he was always present at the place of prayer. One evening, early in December, as I was about retiring to rest, I heard a knock at my door, and my German friend was introduced, his countenance full of emotion. On taking his seat, his first words were these: 'My dear pastor, I have come to tell you that the Lord is about to revive his work here.' Surprised at his appearance and language, and at the lateness of his visit, I asked him, 'Why do you think so?' He replied as follows: 'About eight o'clock this evening, I went up to my hay-mow, to give hay to my cattle, and while there the Spirit of God came upon me, and has kept me there praying until now. I feel that God is about to revive his work, and I could not go in to my family until I told you.' The entire simplicity and earnestness of the good man convinced me that God had vouchsafed to visit his servant. After some conversation we parted, mutually agreeing to pray and labor for a revival of religion, and to engage as many as we could to do the same.

"Every meeting for religious services was now to me one of intense interest. A few days convinced me that the spirit of prayer was on the increase. Meetings for prayer were numerously attended. The church on the Sabbath became more full and solemn; and a few weeks after that evening of wrestling with God on the hay-mow, found me in the midst of the first revival of my ministry, and one of the most precious I ever witnessed.

"Among the first that expressed seriousness was a

fashionable and well-educated young lady, belonging to one of our richest families. She was the pride of a mother whose ambition it was to have her shine in elegant society. Miss E—— expressed a hope in Christ. In a few days she was sent to spend the winter in one of our principal cities with some gay friends, who were directed to take her to all the fashionable amusements. She yielded to the temptation; and when she returned in the spring, seemed farther from the kingdom of heaven than ever. Another refreshing was soon enjoyed, when the former feelings of this young lady returned. She became hopefully pious, and in a few months the wife of a godly minister. And her large family, perhaps influenced by her example, followed her into the fold of Christ.

"There was in the place a young man, a profane, but yet an industrious mechanic. Like Nicodemus, he came to me by night to know what he should do to be saved. His feelings seemed of the most pungent character, and his visits were often repeated. He thought he understood, and could joyfully embrace, the plan of salvation through Jesus Christ. Yielding to the influence of one wicked companion, in a few weeks he forsook the house of prayer and the people of God. As long as I knew him afterward, he was among the most obdurate men I ever knew. He ripened for ruin; and not long ago, with one stroke, as the woodman removes the saplings out of his way, God cut him down. It is a fearful thing to quench the Spirit!

"Mr. C—— was a pleasant, moral, and interesting

man. Under the prayers and conversations of a pious mother, he grew up a friend to the institutions of religion. His mind became deeply interested. But a more convenient season was always an excuse for the putting aside of present duty. In the midst of the revival, when some of the sturdy cedars of Lebanon were bowing, his aged mother, and with tears, besought him to make God his portion. 'Mother,' said he, 'you are dependent upon me for a subsistence, and so are my motherless children. To provide for you all is my pleasure and my duty. I am now engaged in a very profitable work among the mountains, and when I have made enough to support you all comfortably, in connection with my own industry, I promise you I will attend to religion; but you must excuse me now.' And with a solemn warning against the folly of such reasoning from the lips of his aged mother, he hastened to his business among the mountains. On the evening of the third day from his departure, he was brought back to that mother, and was laid at her feet a mutilated corpse. Before he could escape its track, a log of timber, rolling down a steep precipice, caught him, and, rolling over him, almost ground him to powder. And as we laid him down in the grave, I heard that mother exclaim, in the bitterness of her sorrow, 'Would to God I had died for thee, my son, my son!' Oh, the folly of boasting of to-morrow, as we know not what a day may bring forth!

"Some of our pious people undertook the circulation of religious tracts. The tract 'The Way to be Saved' was selected for the purpose of placing in the hands of our people a plain and simple guide to the Savior of sinners. One of these was placed in the shop of a mechanic who was noted for his profanity and vulgarity. Blotting out the word 'saved' in the title of the tract, he wrote in its place 'damned,' so that the title, thus amended, read 'The Way to be Damned.' Now tearing it nearly in two, he flung it into the street. It was soon picked up by a young woman, deeply serious, and who, although shocked by its title, carried it home. She read it with care. She pasted the torn leaves together, and read it again and again. She went as directed, and found peace and joy in believing. And in a conversation with her about her hope, she drew from her bosom this mutilated tract, saying, 'This is the little book that told me the way to the cross.' If yet alive, I have no doubt she preserves it among her choicest treasures. Thus it is that God often makes the wrath of man to praise him.

"Many instances like these occurred during that revival, which the time would fail me to enumerate. But even these emphatically teach us,

"1. That when faithfully and prayerfully discharging duty, ministers must not be unduly discouraged by unpropitious external circumstances. If they go forth weeping, bearing precious seed, they will return again with rejoicing, bringing their sheaves with them.

"2. They teach us the power of prayer. It moves the hand that moves the world. That revival, with its consequent blessings, I have ever traced, under God, to that prayer on the hay-mow. The prayer that God inspires He will answer.

"3. They teach us the awful guilt of parents who sacrifice the souls of their children at the shrines of worldly ambition. And, alas! how many such parents there are!

4. "They utter warning notes in the ears of those who quench the strivings of the Spirit, or who postpone the duty of submission to God *now* to an uncertain future.

5. "They teach us that even pearls cast before swine may not be in vain. Through the wickedness of the wicked, God is ever accomplishing his purposes of love. How invincible the combined agencies of mercy, when even one mutilated tract becomes the instrument of life from the dead to a human soul!

"Years have passed away since this revival occurred. Some of its subjects have already entered on its reward. That simple-hearted, pious German has gone up to his Savior. But the influences of that prayer on the hay-mow will live forever. Good men never die; they rest from their labors, but their works do follow them. May our churches never want members like him who wrestled and prevailed with God on the hay-mow."

While Mr. Murray was in Philadelphia, connected with the American Tract Society's operations, he had interested the ladies of that city in the distribution of tracts, and had also identified himself with other departments of Christian benevolence. In his visits to the various churches he became interested in the Sabbath-school of the First Presbyterian Church, and he took charge of a class of boys who had up to that time been under the care of Miss Eliza J. Rhees. These boys became the objects of his deepest solicitude. He increased the class by adding to it several from the Sixth Presbyterian Church, and he had the joy and reward of knowing that they were converted to God; and some of them are now well known in Philadelphia as useful citizens and elders in the churches there.

The young lady whose class of boys he took upon his hands was to be the partner of his future labors, and to relieve him of a thousand cares. The acquaintance formed in these fields of Christian labor grew into a holy affection, which continued through life. She was the daughter of a distinguished and eloquent Welsh clergyman, whose remarkable history was written by Dr. Murray for the American Pulpit of Dr. Sprague, and is worthy of being recorded in this connection:

"Morgan John Rhees was born in Glamorganshire, Wales, on the 8th of December, 1760, the son of highly respectable and pious parents. As he early evinced superior talents, and a great love for study, they gave him a finished education. He first devoted himself to teaching, and soon acquired a high reputation for brilliant writing and eloquence. He became hopefully pious, and connected himself with the Baptist Church, which was the Church of his fathers. After a full consideration of his duty, he consecrated himself to the work of the ministry, and, to prepare for his high calling, he entered the Baptist College at

Bristol. On leaving the college he was ordained over the Church of Peny-Garn, in Monmouth, where he labored with great ability and success, and where traditions illustrating his power and eloquence are yet abroad among the people. While here he wrote many sacred lyrics and other poetical pieces, which are yet in high repute among his countrymen.

"With a soul all alive to the wrongs of the oppressed, and to the universal extension of liberty, he became an enthusiastic advocate, at its commencement, of the French Revolution. Indeed, he resigned his charge, and went over to France in order to witness the glorious triumphs of liberty. He was, however, soon convinced of the unprincipled selfishness of the chief actors in that memorable drama, and returned to Wales determined to defend his own principles the more zealously, and for this purpose he established a quarterly magazine, called the 'Welsh Treasury.' In this, with high eloquence and terrible sarcasm, he exposed the policy of the English ministry. But he was compelled to relinquish it; and knowing that he was suspected of being friendly to the French interests, and that the Tory ministry only needed a fair pretext to subject him to prosecution, he called many of his friends around him, and, as the protector of a Welsh colony, came to America, where he landed in February, 1794.

"He was most kindly received by the Rev. Dr. Rodgers, then pastor of the First Baptist Church in Philadelphia, and provost of the University of Pennsylvania. Between these two there existed ever after a cordial friendship. Finding the civil institutions of the country in harmony with all his political views, and nothing in the way of religious intolerance to fan his excitable feelings, the religious sentiment soon rose to the supremacy in his heart, and, as if he had never turned aside from the ministry, he again preached the Gospel with great power and success. He was followed by admiring crowds wherever he spoke, and preached Christ with an earnestness and an unction but rarely witnessed since the days of Whitfield. He traveled extensively through the Southern and Western States, preaching the Gospel of the Kingdom, and in search of a suitable location for his colony. On his return to Philadelphia he married the daughter of Col. Benjamin Loxley, of that city, who was an officer of the army of the Revolution, and a man of high character and standing. After two years' residence in Philadelphia, he, in connection with Dr. Benjamin Rush, purchased a large tract of land in Pennsylvania, which, in honor of his native country, he called Cambria. He also located and planned the capital of the county, to which he gave the name of Beulah. To this place he removed his own family, with a company of Welsh emigrants, in 1798, which was increased from year to year by others from the principality.

"Here he was intensely occupied, for several years, with the duties which devolved upon him as a large landed proprietor, and as pastor of the Church of Beulah. For the benefit of his increasing family, he was induced to remove to Somerset, in Somerset County, where he died of a sudden attack of pleurisy, and in the triumphs of faith, on the 7th of December, 1804, in the forty-fourth year of his age. Indeed, his departure seemed rather a translation than a death. He left a widow and five children to mourn his loss.

"The following letter was addressed by Dr. Rush to Mrs. Rhees, in reference to the death of her husband, and it shows the writer's exquisite sensibility and sympathy, as well as his high appreciation of Mr. Rhees' character:

"'My dear Madam,—Accept of my sympathy in your affliction. While you deplore the loss of an excellent husband, I lament the loss of a sincere and worthy friend. His memory will always be dear to me. Be assured of my regard for you and your little family. May a kind and gracious Providence support you! And may you yet have reason to praise the orphan's Father and the widow's God in the land of the living!

"'From, my dear madam, your sincere friend,

"'Benjamin Rush.

"'Philadelphia, January 26th, 1805.'

"A glowing but chastened enthusiasm was a leading characteristic of Mr. Rhees, and gave form and hue to his entire life. He had a highly poetic temperament. This was apparent from his earliest life—not merely from the lyrics of which he was the author, but from the ardor with which he devoted himself to every subject which interested him. He was, while orthodox himself, a liberal in religion and a democrat in politics. Hence he was a lover of all good men, and threw the mantle of charity even over persons whose opinions he considered honest though unsound. Hence he was the intimate friend of Dr. Priestley, and of Jefferson, while utterly eschewing their religious opinions, because they agreed with him on the agitating political topics of the day. He was a most fervent preacher and orator, and gave to his sentiments a point and intensity which made them deeply felt. And down to the present day, his name is as ointment poured forth among the old settlers of Cambria and Beulah. And if any excuse is necessary for the degree to which he united the religious and the political in his life, it may be found in the circumstances of his times, which induced many of the ablest divines of his native and adopted country to pursue the same course.

"Mrs. Rhees was a woman of high character. On her great bereavement she returned to her native home, where, upon her patrimonial inheritance, she educated her children, and lived to see them all not only members of the Church of Christ, but filling posts of high honor and usefulness. Endowed with a mind of the strongest original texture, polished by education, stored by reading and reflection, and by grace subdued to the most humble obedience to the truth, she was efficient in action, wise in counsel, strong in faith, and untiring in doing good. A spirit of self-sacrifice, connected with the deepest humility, was her leading characteristic. But few have lived a life more consistent and lovely, or died a death more cheerful, calm, and confiding. She rested from her labors on the 11th of April, 1849, in the seventy-fourth year of her age.

"The earlier productions of Mr. Rhees were published in the Welsh language, but few of them have been translated. The few orations and discourses, written and published by him in this country, exhibit great vivacity and eloquence."

The daughter of Mr. Rhees had been for nearly three years engaged to be married to Mr. Murray. In the month of January, 1830, he went to Philadelphia to bring back his bride. It was then more of a journey than it is now, to cross the rough country, in the midst of winter, in the old stage-coach. The day was appointed for the marriage, and he left Wilkesbarre in time, but the course of true love did not run even so smoothly as usual in this case. The day arrived, but the bridegroom came not. The evening came, and the hour, but no bridegroom. There was no telegraph to announce the cause of detention, but it was soon ascertained that the stage had not arrived. The next day brought him on, bruised and sore, but still alive and well. The coach had been upset near Bethlehem, and several of the passengers injured. Mr. Murray escaped with a cut on one of his fingers, which required a surgical dressing, and the circular scar which he always carried he called his wedding ring. The marriage was deferred a week, and then he carried his wife away to his new home. It was a cold and fearful journey, and the delicate bride would have suffered by the way but for the buoyant spirits and unfailing humor of the young husband, which kept the company in a state of pleasurable and healthful excitement all the way. They spent a Sabbath at Easton, where Mr. Murray preached for Rev. Dr. Gray. The journey over the mountain on Monday and Tuesday was made in an open sleigh, in bitter cold, but on the second day they reached Wilkesbarre, and were cordially greeted by a circle of refined, cultivated, and devoted friends, who at once made the minister's young wife at home among them.

CHAPTER IX.

The Valley of Wyoming.—The Freshets.—The Drift-wood.—A Type of Society.—A Classmate and two more.—Other Characters drawn.

The beauties of the Valley of Wyoming, as they never weary the eye of the dweller or the visitor, were often the theme of Dr. Murray, when he would draw striking and strong illustrations. One of his most characteristic sketches was suggested by the habits of a class of people among whom he was first settled. He writes:

"It has been my lot to wander upon foreign shores. I have gazed upon Italian skies and scenes; I have wandered over the mountains and vales of Switzerland; I have traversed the Rhine, the Rhone, the Clyde; I have gazed upon most of the beautiful scenery of Britain, and yet I turn to Wyoming as unsurpassed in quiet beauty by any vale that I have ever seen.

"'A valley from the river shore withdrawn;
* * * * *
So sweet a spot of earth, you might, I ween,
Have guessed some congregation of the elves,
To sport by summer moon, had shaped it for themselves.'

"The river by which it is divided, enriched and greatly beautified, is subject to freshets. This is caused, in the spring, by the sudden melting of the snow in the mountain ranges in which it has its rise, and at other seasons of the year by heavy rains. When swollen, as I have often seen it, it rushes on with fearful rapidity and violence, sweeping to destruction every thing that lies in its way; and, when thus swollen, often have I stood on its banks and gazed with trembling on the terrific current, sweeping away houses, mills, trees torn from its banks, and rotten wood of all kinds and sizes, and whirling them in every direction as if they were but corks.

"These freshets were occasions of some importance to that class of people, too large in every community, who live by their wits. These, taking their position on the bank of the river, with fit implements, were laborious in their efforts to fish from the turbulent current the floating timbers. They were often successful, and in a few days would pile on the shore drift-wood enough to supply them with fuel for a few months. It was quite amusing to witness the scenes which often occurred. When a large timber was seen in the distance, each was anxious to be its captor. One would harpoon it, and when shouting out 'I have it,' the force of the current would sweep it away; and thus many would successively harpoon it, but yet it would escape from them all. The size of the log and the force of the current gave it a momentum that no arm could resist. Great exertion was often made to bring a drift to the shore; but, when caught, it was found worthless, and was cast back again into the foaming waters. At a sharp turn in the river much lumber was driven on shore, and to that spot many would rush, hoping there to catch a fine log, but it would shoot round the corner and disappoint them all. Some lumber would float into an eddy, or would get entangled among the trees on the low bottoms, or would be caught by a pier, where it was considered secure; but, on a sudden, the power of the current would drive it into the middle of the river, and down it would go, disappointing all hopes. When the freshet rapidly subsided, much lumber was left upon the dry land, there to remain until another should come and carry it farther down toward the ocean. It was not even picked up as fuel for the fire. One thing was very observable, that the drift-wood was but rarely fitted to be wrought into a building, or to be used for any ornamental purpose. It was usually gathered into heaps, and when sufficiently dry, to be burned.

"And all this is but the type of what is constantly occurring in society around us. Are there not freshets in society as upon our great rivers; excitements, political, moral, and religious, which work great changes, which reveal men of principle, which tear up and send adrift those not rooted and grounded in the truth? In what community or in what calling are not persons to be found whose only fit emblem is drift-wood?

"I had a college-mate of many good qualities. He was fluent, rapid in his conceptions, a professor of religion, but vain and ambitious. He was a candidate for the ministry. But there were indications that his vanity was stronger than his principles, and that to feed the one he would sacrifice the other. The freshet came in our Junior year, when, on the giving out of the appointments which indicated the standing of the students as scholars, he failed to obtain any. He expected one of the highest; he got none. His pride was mortified beyond endurance—he left college—he gave up the ministry—he made shipwreck of faith—he went out upon the sweeping tide of politics, where, no doubt, unless radically changed, his principles are yet the weaker, and his vanity the stronger power. Such persons can never be any thing but drift-wood.

"I had a theological classmate of very good qualities. He was good-looking—he dressed well—he wrote poetry—he flattered, and was flattered by, the ladies. He knew more about Tom Moore than Turretin; he read Greek less than Goethe; he preferred Walter to Thomas Scott, and could quote Byron at least as well as the Bible. Vanity was his besetting sin. He got license to preach, but could get no settlement. Thinking that the people of the Church of his fathers were too dull to appreciate his shining qualities, he passed over to another. To be in keeping with his high flights, he became High-Church, and whither the freshet has carried him I know not. He has written a book, as I learn, on 'The Succession,' of which he knows as much as about the precession of the equinoxes, and which has only served to prove that he was, or is, drift-wood.

"I had yet another fellow-student. He was young, ruddy, and prepossessing. Although yet in his teens, he was deeply imbued with the spirit of New Measures, then on the high tide of successful experiment. He denounced his teachers as pharisees and fogies.

While yet a student, he practiced his new notions in a small way. Finding but little encouragement for his novelties, he changed his latitude for more congenial climes. He entered the ministry a New-measure man, greatly exciting the hopes of their friends. He went abroad, and became enamored of the old, petrified measures of the Old World, and on his return deserted his former friends. Now, excitements were only injurious, and Church power and set forms were every thing. This was a change from the equator to the poles. For a while he linked himself with the straitest sects of the Church of his fathers, but that did not long suffice. He was on the bosom of the swollen river, and could not stop. At a bound he became a Puseyite, and, whether for funds or to make friends, wrote one of the most disgraceful and truthless books known to theological controversy in modern days. The book by 'One of Three Hundred' proves, at least, that its author was of the drift-wood species. He had no root in himself; he was the prey of every current; and if he had remained a little longer, another swell of the freshet would have swept him from his Oxford eddy, and would have left him deep in the mud of the Tiber, praying to the Virgin to take him out and clean him off.

"Another specimen of the same genus. He was bold, bluff, and self-confident. When a student he went to three colleges, and claimed credit for it! He went, at least, to three seminaries, to get the good of each. He was educated a Presbyterian, ordained a Congregationalist, became, I believe, a Methodist, then a Baptist; but what he now is I know not, nor does he know himself. Each thought they had him, but he escaped from them all. The harpoon entered the log in a soft place, where it could not hold. What has become of him I know not; but when next drawn to the shore, he may be cast back again into the current as too worthless to repay the trouble of fishing him out.

"There are exceptions to all general rules. In the course of his studics, a young man may see reasons sufficient to leave the Church of his early education for some other. No man is bound to the faith of his fathers, because, if so, the Jew must remain a Jew, the pagan a pagan, the papist a papist, forever. No young man is to be censured for departing from the faith of his fathers, if he does so for reasons, and wisely. But when men have formed their opinions, and preached them for years, and then change them, it is an evidence of a restless, disordered state of mind. One or two attacks of any disease render the system liable to its return; and one or two changes in opinions are liable to convert the individual into a changeling, and to send him out upon the stream of life as drift-wood.

"And how many there are connected, as private members, with the churches whose only fit emblem is drift-wood. They go here and there as prejudice, or passion, or fashion, or some disappointment may sway them. I knew an elder twice censured in a Presbytery, who, in revenge, became a most violent High-Churchman, and had all his children rebaptized for conscience' sake! Mr. —— and family were from

England; according to their own showing, they left the husks of the Establishment for the simple truth of the Independents. They then attached themselves to the ministry of some supralapsarian shoemaker. They came to this country, but for a long time could find no suitable successor to the shoemaker. As I was considered as coming nearest to him, they placed themselves under my ministry. For a time they would have plucked out their eyes and given them to me; but the Millerite fever became epidemic, and they caught it badly. The fanatics of that threadbare nonsense became their favorites. I no longer preached the Gospel, because I did not preach up the destruction of the world about Easter, and advise the faithful to commence cutting their ascension robes. They were swept out as drift-wood upon the bosom of the freshet, but where it has carried them is hardly worth the inquiry.

"And persons of whom drift-wood is the true emblem are to be found in every community, and attached to all congregations. They are as numerous as those who are ungoverned by fixed principles. There are those in the ministry who can pass from this body to that, from this school to that, with all ease. These regard themselves, and would be regarded by others, as moderate and catholic. But there is another explanation for all this; their own lines of opinion are drawn with invisible ink, and can be shifted to suit circumstances; they have no root in themselves. There are those in the churches upon whom you can make no calculation. The next freshet may carry them into some new connection, or work a change in their entire views and feelings. I look around me, and see persons who have been connected with three churches in less than three years. I see others who have passed from one denomination to another because their minister did not like secret societies, or preach up, to the point of scalding heat, the efficacy of some plans of social reform. And there are but few churches in the land where the freshets to which human opinions and society are ever liable have not deposited some of this drift-wood, where it will remain until the rise of another freshet, when it will be again swept out and whirled we know not whither. When the tree is torn up by the roots and swept into the current, there is no telling where it will stop; and if brought to shore, it will be difficult to replant it. It will not pay for the labor. Dr. Priestley was once a high Calvinist, then a low one; then an Arminian; then a high Arian, then a low one; then a Unitarian; then a Humanitarian; and he was once heard to say, 'If God spares me a few years more, I know not what I shall be before I die.' When a stone is started on the brow of the mountain, it is hard to stop it until it reaches the bottom.

"Many make a great noise when a minister, or persons in high position, pass over to them. But they have caught only drift-wood. How long they can keep them is uncertain; and to what use they can put them is often a question.

"There are those who are steadfast, immovable, always abounding in the works of the Lord, and those who are ever learning and never coming to the knowledge of the truth. The first are as the cedars in Lebanon, that bear fruit even to old age, and that are fit to be converted to the most useful purposes in the house of the Lord; the second are but drift-wood, scarcely fit to feed the fires that warm it."

CHAPTER X.

Zeal and Self-denial.—The People.—Their want of Punctuality.—Free-thinkers and Infidels. — Characteristic Letter from one of them.—A Protracted Meeting.—A Lawyer enraged.—Beasts at Ephesus.—Is invited to go West.—Declines.—Builds a new Church.

Two congregations, on opposite sides of the river, were now upon his hands. A small church was at Kingston, with no house of worship except an old building at Forty Fort, where he preached every Sabbath morning. This is a famous spot in early American history, and is associated with the bloody story of the Massacre of Wyoming. Here he lectured every week, spending the afternoon of the same day of the lecture in visiting his people from house to house. Up among the mountains, in the most retired and difficult passes, he sought his sheep, gathered them into the fold, and under the influence of his ministry. The same indefatigable energy, the same zeal and perseverance that had marked his pursuit of knowledge in preparation for his work, were now displayed with intenser ardor and self-denial. On foot or on horseback, in the midst of storms and cold, he pursued these labors with a diligence and spirit that could not fail of success. Even beyond the mountains, in Northmoreland, he pressed his way to carry the Gospel as a volunteer missionary beyond the bounds of his own parish, and there are now five or six churches to be found in the region where this young and ardent minister used often to administer the sacrament of the Lord's Supper to a few scattered and pious followers of Christ. His absence on these expeditions was often protracted to the anxiety of his friends in Wilkesbarre, where was his home; and once, when attempting to raise his umbrella while riding on horseback in a storm, his horse threw him and ran away, leaving him to find his way home in the night, bruised and battered, but not disheartened.

In Wilkesbarre he found a large, intelligent community, among whom were men of high professional standing, and a circle of cultivated society. It was necessary for him, at the very outset of his ministry, to meet the demands that would be made upon him by a refined and intellectual people; while all around him, on both sides of the river, there were multitudes of the poor and the ignorant, to whose spiritual wants it was at once his duty and his joy without cessation to minister.

A more systematic man in all his habits, public, social, and private, scarcely ever lived. He had a time for every thing, and every thing was done in its time. He made it a rule in early life, and through life, to do every thing as well as he could; and, certainly, the best of men can do no better.

The people here had never been accustomed to habits of punctuality in their attendance upon church, expecting their indulgent minister to wait until they had come before he commenced the Sabbath service. Mr. Murray told them that ten o'clock in the morning meant sixty minutes after nine, and that, when the hour for public worship had arrived, he should always begin, if there was one person present besides himself. At first they came dropping in, one after another, until the close of the sermon; and many amusing stories he could tell of fat old ladies coming running, out of breath, to get seated before the service began; but, soon finding that they had lost more than they could well afford, and that the young minister was not disposed to defer to their laziness and neglect, they reformed their habits, and became a punctual as well as an attentive congregation.

In this beautiful valley, and in the old town of Wilkesbarre, there were not a few who gloried in being known as Free-thinkers, though they would be more justly called infidels. Scarcely had Mr. Murray begun his labors before they were disturbed by his preaching and success. Perhaps his keen observation had already discovered the various characters around him, and his natural shrewdness was shown in directing his efforts where they were most required. Threats of personal violence were made if he did not moderate his tone. The following letter, received by the young pastor, would open his eyes to the peculiar wants of the people among whom he had been settled. It was filed away among his papers, with this indorsement on the back of it:

"*An Infidel's Letter. I do like to hear the devil beat his drum; it is a good sign that his ranks are thinning.*"

The letter is in these words:

H

"Wilkesbarre, August 21.

"SIR,—As a spirit of free inquiry has gone abroad among the people of this land, which will tend greatly to decrease the demand for 'spiritual doctors,' I would advise you, as a friend, to abandon your present occupation, and seek some more honorable calling by which to obtain a livelihood. I repeat it, priestcraft is on the wane in this country. As the people become more enlightened, and the march of mind progresses (and they become more capable to discriminate truth from falsehood—reason from error), the less need will we have for the *services* of men of your profession. The minds of the people 'are being' opened to your real designs. The cord with which you have so long held their minds in bondage is becoming enervated, and will soon be entirely broken and separated. They see that your object is, not *their own* welfare and happiness, but your own aggrandizement—the gratification of your own sordid minds. They have good reason to believe that you would suck their very life-blood (as leeches) to gratify your unhallowed purposes. Your 'four days' meeting' may probably have a tendency to prolong their thralldom and your influence, but it will eventually fail before the light of truth and reason. VERITAS.

"N.B.—I would advise you, as a friend, to adopt the spirit of the sentence in the Book of Moses, which is said to have come directly from the mouth of God: 'Six days shalt thou labor,' and instead of laboring one day, labor six."

For such men, whether they wrote him anonymous

letters, like this from Veritas, or attacked him openly, he was always ready. His mode of dealing with them is well illustrated in an account he gives of a protracted meeting in a neighboring church, where he was one of the preachers:

"When I commenced my ministry, 'protracted meetings' were popular, and the evangelists, by whom they were conducted on the highest key of excitement, were regarded as 'the angels of the churches.' And although connected with a class of ministers who never favored 'the revival evangelists,' and who opposed the 'new measures' of which 'anxious seats' were the representative, yet we yielded so far to the popular feeling of the Church as to hold protracted meetings, which were conducted by ourselves, without foreign aid and without new measures. For the purpose of illustrating the power of the Gospel, and the kind of opposition which it has not unfrequently to meet, I will give a brief narrative of one of those meetings:

"T—— was a town of some importance in Northern Pennsylvania. Its first settlers were chiefly from New England—men of enterprise and shrewdness, but without religion. It became the county town, and had its court-house, and jail, and taverns, but no church of any kind. Universalism and infidelity were there, and united their forces to oppose every effort to introduce the Gospel into the community. The only preaching-place was the Court-house, and, as every body had a right to go there, many thought they had a right to treat the minister when preaching as they were accustomed to treat the politician when making a political harangue, and especially to treat with rudeness what did not agree with their prejudices; and this right was often queerly exercised by interrupting a preacher, by putting questions to him in the midst of his sermon, by persons getting up and leaving the room, and, as they retired, pronouncing some truth declared to be a lie. Nor were these things done simply by the rabble; they were practiced and countenanced by men of intelligence and position. These things, and the morals which they cherished, obtained for the town, at a distance, the name of 'Satan's Seat,' and caused many a good minister to fear to preach the Gospel there, lest he should be attacked and insulted by these emissaries of Satan, these beasts at Ephesus.

"It was in this town that a neighboring pastor of excellent and prudent character resolved to hold a protracted meeting, and to invite some of his brethren to his assistance. I was of the number invited. Our only preaching-place was the Court-house, which was duly secured for our purposes, and the meeting was generally advertised for weeks previous; and expectation was on tiptoe as to our meeting, its disturbance, and its results. Threats were made beforehand, and by men who lacked neither the energy nor the impudence to carry out their most wicked purposes. To be forewarned is to be forearmed, and we went to the Court-house prepared for an attack, but in what way it was to come we knew not.

"It was in the evening. The room was crowded. It was with difficulty that the ministers could make their way to the seat occupied by the judges when the court was in session. As the preliminary services were being performed, I strove to read, as I could, the crowd around me. Just beneath me was the green table around which the lawyers sat when at court, and around the niche in that table sat a few individuals, whose object in coming to the meeting could not be mistaken. Their whisperings, winkings, and noddings satisfied me as to the quarter from which difficulty might be expected; and I plainly saw that they had their sympathizers and opposers in the crowd. Conspicuous among them was a Campbellite Baptist preacher, of low character, and a lawyer of the place, who was said to be like his father, and a little more so; the character of that father was a hybrid, such as we might expect to be produced by now pettifogging, and now acting as Universalist exhorter. These two men were the leaders.

"As I arose to preach, I paused a moment to take a close survey of these men. They were just beneath me. As their gaze met mine, they dropped their heads. I saw in a moment they were only braggarts that could be soon driven to the wall. Save the rustling of their paper, on which they were making notes, every thing was quiet to the close of the service. The moment the benediction was pronounced, the Campbellite Baptist sprang to his feet and screamed out, 'I wish to know whether I may ask the preacher a few questions?' The crowd, which had commenced moving, was brought to a dead pause, and waited in breathless silence for a reply. Some felt that the fight was now fairly opened. After a brief pause, I replied as follows: 'We have come here to preach the Gospel for a few days to those who may choose to come and hear us. One of our principles is to disturb nobody in their religious worship; and another is, to allow nobody to disturb us. There is a law to protect us from disturbance, and we shall see that that law is enforced.' Then turning to the man who asked the question, I said to him, 'You are either an honest or dishonest inquirer: if an honest one, you may come to my lodgings, and I will answer, as far as I am able, any of your questions; if a dishonest one, as I fear you are, I wish to have nothing to do with you, here or there.' He could make no reply, and the crowd dispersed applauding the positions taken, but yet feeling that the end of the chapter was not yet.

"As the meetings progressed, a deep solemnity was soon observable. As the gainsayers were regularly at their post, there was a constant crowd in attendance, in expectation, daily, of some conflict. In the evening they came in great numbers from the surrounding country, and long before the hour of service the Court-house was crowded to its utmost capacity. At the conclusion of a deeply solemn service one evening, we invited the serious to retire to a room in the building for religious conversation. As we entered the room, to our astonishment, we found there a large number of persons deeply anxious, among whom were some prominent citizens; and conspicuous among them was the Campbellite preacher and his friend the lawyer. I saw, at a glance, that accounts must first be settled with these before we could proceed; and, approaching the preacher, I asked him sternly, 'What, sir, is your object in coming here?' 'I want you,' he replied, 'to give right instruction to these anxious sinners; and for this purpose I wish you to read this chapter.' And, suiting the action to the word, he put a small Bible, opened, into my hands. Amazed at his cool impertinence, I returned the Bible, saying, 'When, sir, we need your counsel and aid, we will send for you; and as we did not invite you here, you will leave the room.' And as it was now my turn to suit the action to the word, I gently laid my hand upon his shoulder and pointed to the door, and, to my surprise, he went quietly away. Wickedness is always cowardly.

"Having gotten rid of one customer, I then approached the lawyer, who had obviously more daring about him than the ignorant, unmannerly preacher. 'And what, sir,' said I, 'is your object in coming here?' Stretching himself to his highest altitude, and in a semi-comic way, designed to produce merriment in that anxious-room, he replied, 'You have said something in your sermon to-night about the devil, and I thought I would come and ask you who the devil is.' Feeling that it was one of those occasions which would justify the answering of a fool according to his folly, I replied, 'You are the first man I have met, for some time, that did not know who his father was.' The question and answer were heard by all in the room. I then said to him, as to his companion in wickedness, 'As we did not invite you here, sir, you will leave the room.' Soon the comic was changed to the tragic aspect, and he declared, 'I will not leave the room; this house is a county house, and is free and open to us all; I have as good a right to be here as you have.' It so happened that among the inquirers was an aged, athletic man, a prominent citizen, and an associate judge of the county; and I said to him, 'Judge, will you see that Mr. —— leaves the room?' He rose at once, and said to him, 'Mr. ——, you will leave the room, sir.' There was no alternative but to leave, and he went out enraged; and he went down the stairs swearing that he would shoot me, as sure as he was a living man. The door was then closed; we proceeded with our service, and a more deeply-impressed company of anxious inquirers, asking what they should do to be saved, I never saw.

"The services of the evening ended. There was a deep excitement upon many minds as to what the enraged lawyer would do. Six or eight men accompanied me, or kept near me, on my way to my lodgings. They feared his violence; but when I knew their object, I told them there was nothing to fear, as I soon saw the man was only a braggart. The question he asked up stairs, and the reply to it, soon got into circulation. The interview was all over town the next day, and every where the old man was hailed as 'the old devil,' and the enraged lawyer as 'the young devil.' There were some who affirmed that rarely could the epithets be more appropriately applied.

"That was the end of the lawyer as far as our services were concerned; but the preacher regularly attended them. He lodged at the public house, and it was whispered that he did not always drink cold water. After a solemn meeting, in which the preacher strongly presented the idea that morality, however spotless in the view of man, could not save a sinner, in making his way through the crowd, he said, 'Let me go where morality is more respected than here!' I saw the hit would have its effect upon some minds, and in a low, but yet audible tone, said, 'The gentleman wants to get to the tavern.' He got out, and that was the end of him.

"The services subsequently proceeded without any disturbance of any kind. The solemnity increased from day to day. The Gospel was joyfully received by many in that town and in the surrounding country. A Church was organized, of which those hopefully converted at that protracted meeting were the main elements. A church was soon erected. That ungodly clique was broken up, and its chief members converted into laughing-stocks. Twenty-five years have nearly passed away since that meeting, through which its influence for good has been felt on all the interests of society. That once wicked town is now the seat of several churches, and of, at least, one moral and educational institution, which is destined to shed its light on the surrounding country, and for ages to come.

"What has become of that Campbellite preacher I know not. He was, beyond doubt, a bad man. If yet living, may the Lord convert him. The lawyer, to get rid of the sobriquet, 'the young devil,' went to parts unknown, and thus happily relieved the community from his evil example. One of the beloved men who preached on that occasion has gone up to his reward, while three yet survive who were engaged in this conflict with beasts at Ephesus.

"The malignity of these men was overruled for good. They overshot the line of even allowed opposition there, and disgusted many. They made show of fight, and attracted multitudes to witness the affray. Thus they multiplied the hearers of the Gospel and the trophies of the Cross. The Lord often makes the use of wicked men that sportsmen do of their dogs—the dogs start the birds, and then the sportsmen shoot them; so that beasts at Ephesus have their place in the economy of redemption. What they mean for evil the Lord overrules for good."

In the fall of 1831, the American Tract Society made a new and strenuous effort to induce Mr. Murray to embark in its work, and now presented him the wide and inviting field of the Valley of the Mississippi, a far more extended valley than that of the Susquehanna. The Rev. Dr. Hallock writes to him:

"New York, November 2, 1831.

"MY DEAR BROTHER MURRAY,—It is now about eighteen months since Brother Eastman ceased his labors as general agent for this Society at the West, during which time, except a little done in Kentucky, we have had no agent south of the Ohio River. That whole country lies comparatively desolate in respect to this cause; for, though Depositories have been formed in most of the larger towns, and many small auxiliaries around them, the whole are becoming inactive, and will doubtless continue so till some one is raised up, in Providence, to go and rouse them to effort. North of the Ohio we have four agents: one a young preacher in Missouri and Illinois, one a layman in Indiana, and two laymen in Ohio; they are men of a good spirit, but there exceedingly needs some one to go in and aid them in all the large towns. In New Orleans a special effort is imperiously demanded this winter. We have looked earnestly, and with much prayer to God, for the man for this important service, and at length our executive committee have unanimously fixed on you. The place of your location for your family will be at your own election—probably Cincinnati. The committee have proposed what they suppose will provide comfortably for your family; but if experiment should show it is insufficient, your safety will lie in the principle by which the committee are governed, that those who labor for the Society must be clothed and fed, and comfortably sustained. We now lay our claim before you; we rejoice that *you* can see it somewhat in its extensive bearings, and we feel that the stock of Tract information, and Tract fire and zeal which, in Divine Providence, you have, is an important argument why *you* should enter on this service. We beg you and Mrs. Murray to ponder the subject, and weigh it in all its import, and carry it to the Throne of Grace, and may God, in great mercy and kindness to His own cause, direct you. If you decline, we know not what to do for securing another in your stead. If there are any obstacles in your mind, we should be glad to have you communicate them, and to answer any inquiries you may propose; or to see you here, if you would visit us with reference to the agency. We believe you will be acceptable to all the friends of this cause, and that you can do *very much* for it, by God's blessing, at the West.

"Your brother in Christ,

"WILLIAM A. HALLOCK, Cor. Sec. A. T. S."

At a meeting of the Executive Committee of the American Tract Society, New York, November 1st, 1831, it was unanimously

"*Resolved*, That Rev. Nicholas Murray, of Wilkesbarre, Pa., be commissioned to act as General Agent of the Society for the Valley of the Mississippi, with especial reference to raising funds and promoting the general interests of the Society in that interesting portion of our country, and that he receive as compensation eight hundred dollars and his traveling expenses.

"A true copy, from the Minutes.

"WILLIAM A. HALLOCK, Cor. Sec. A. T. S.

"New York, November 2, 1831."

He had now no hesitation in declining this great work, and quietly went on with his duties at home.

The Church in Wilkesbarre greatly needed a new house of worship, and, with his characteristic energy and enterprise, Mr. Murray undertook to see the work done. Having exhausted the ability and disposition of the congregation, he went abroad from place to place, wherever he could get permission to present the object, and in the course of a few months he collected means sufficient to enable the people to complete the edifice. An incident in the course of his visits in this service he has recorded, as producing an important influence upon him through his future ministry.

In the autumn of 1832 he went to Morristown, N. J., to preach, by previous appointment, a sermon before the Synod of New Jersey, there in session, on the subject of Domestic Missions. The Rev. Dr. M'Dowell, then pastor of the Church in Elizabethtown, was present, and Mr. Murray asked him if his people would listen to an application from the congregation in Wilkesbarre for assistance. Dr. M'Dowell replied that if he would come to Elizabethtown and preach the same sermon there that he had just preached before the Synod, something might be done. Accordingly, Mr. Murray went to Elizabethtown and preached on the following Sabbath. He writes:

"The Sabbath was a chilly one in October; and in the middle of the sermon I saw an old man rise at the end of the church, with a large handkerchief thrown over his head, and, placing his stick on the seat of the pew before him, leaned on its top to the close of it. The attention of the old man was obviously fixed. His movement and appearance were so peculiar that I was induced to make inquiry in reference to him, when I learned that he was a pensioner of the Church, of marked character, of subtle mind, of remarkable Christian experience, and of the most fervent piety. When he felt in the least drowsy under the preaching of the Word, his habit was to stand up, so as to hear the Gospel with his powers all awake to the importance of the message.

"In going my rounds the next day among the people to receive their donations to aid me in the erection of my church, I met this old man. He was in an old dilapidated gig, drawn by a horse just like it, with his aged wife sitting by his side. They seemed all well stricken in years. He stopped, and Dr. M., who was going round with me, introduced me to Father Miller, when the following colloquy took place: 'You are the minister that wants aid to build a church, eh?' 'Yes, sir; but I do not wish you to give any thing.' 'Then you don't take any thing from poor people like me, eh? The Savior did not prevent the widow from giving her mite—all that she had; and are you kinder to the poor than your Master?' I knew not what to reply. 'Take what he gives you,' said Dr. M. So, after searching his pockets, and whispering to his wife, he handed me two shillings and sixpence, saying, 'I wish it was a hundred dollars, but it is all we have; God never permits us to want; we have always a little for His cause. We give you this with our prayers. The whole thing was said and done with a tone, simplicity, and earnestness that very deeply affected me.

"Having emptied his pockets, he then commenced to speak to me from the fullness of his heart. 'You,' said he, 'are the young man that preached to us yesterday.' 'I am.' 'Well, that was a kind of a missionary sermon, and I liked it very well. It is necessary to preach such sermons occasionally; but they are not the Gospel. You are young, and I am old; you know a great deal more than I do; but, dear young minister, preach Christ. If you wish to be useful, preach Christ. If you wish to be a blessing to the Church, preach Christ. You may never see this poor old man again; if not, let my last words be to you, *preach Christ.*'

"I was moved beyond the power to reply. After slapping the old horse three or four times with the reins, he slowly walked away. Upward of a quarter of a century has passed since that interview. Father Miller and his wife have long since gone to heaven, but the impressions it made abide. The spot where it occurred—the appearance of the aged couple—are indelibly impressed on my mind. Had I the pencil of an Angelo, I could paint them to the life. I subsequently became his pastor. His entire life, to its close, was in perfect keeping with that first interview. For him to live was Christ. Every thing to him was dross and dung that he might win Christ. And although for years a pensioner of the Church, we all felt, when he fell, that one of the strongest pillars of our Church was removed.

"'If you wish to be a blessing to the Church, preach Christ!' How often have these admonitory words rung in my ears and burned on my heart! To preach Christ as Paul preached Him—the world over—to saint and to sinner—as the great remedy for all the moral woes of our race—this is the grand duty of the ministry. To this one duty every thing must be made subordinate and subservient by the ministry. The ministers who have preached Christ—as did Payson, Nettleton, Richards, Alexander, Rice, Baker—are those who were a blessing to the Church. And such are the men who are a blessing to it now; the men who permit not themselves to be drawn away from the Cross to a crusade against particular sins, or in favor of certain schemes of social or political reform. And the men who turn away from the preaching of Christ *to preaching for the times*—who are seeking to rise to prominence by connecting themselves with the excitements of the day, are the men who are dividing their own churches, and who are casting around them firebrands, arrows, and death, to the extent of their power. Their progress is marked, like that of the conflagration or freshet, by the ruins they leave behind them. Without benefiting any human interest, they destroy their own usefulness, and bring a reproach upon the entire Gospel ministry.

"Among ourselves there are sectional jealousies and political excitements for which the preaching of Christ is the best remedy. Abroad, every thing is tending in one direction. The great drift is toward right civil and religious institutions. India, China, Japan, Turkey, Sardinia, and even Mexico, by recent treaty, are open to the Gospel; and the gates of those nations yet closed must be soon unlocked. And if *every* minister of the Gospel would, from this time forth, preach Christ and nothing else, in the spirit and power of their commission—if they would abandon sectarian strife, and doubtful schemes of reform, and devote their united energies to the simple preaching of Christ, within a very brief period the Gospel might be carried in triumph from pole to pole—on the Eastern Continent from Senegambia to Japan, and from Hudson's Bay to Cape Horn on the Western.

"In the language, then, of the old patriarch to the young minister, I would say to every minister of the New Testament, '*If you wish to be a blessing to the Church, preach Christ.*'"

On returning home, he resumed and continued his pastoral labors with great enjoyment and success.

CHAPTER XI.

Called to Elizabethtown, N. J.—Advice of Friends.—Letter from Rev. John M'Dowell, D.D.—Letter from a venerable Elder.—He accepts the Call.—His Installation.—A new Era.—Habits of Study.—History of Elizabethtown.—Pastors of the First Church. —Reminiscences.

In the month of April, 1833, the Rev. Dr. John M'Dowell was dismissed from the pastoral charge of the First Presbyterian Church in Elizabethtown, New Jersey, having been called to the Central Presbyterian Church of Philadelphia.

Before leaving Elizabethtown, Dr. M'Dowell called the elders and trustees of the Church together to learn whether they would take any action in reference to a successor. Their attention was at once directed to the man who had visited them a few months before for the purpose of getting assistance to build a church. A letter was written to Mr. Murray at Wilkesbarre, but he was at that time in Philadelphia, attending the General Assembly. A committee of the elders then proceeded to Philadelphia, and requested him to visit Elizabethtown, and preach as a candidate in their vacant church. This he steadfastly refused to do, but was finally prevailed on to supply the pulpit for two Sabbaths, while the General Assembly was in session. Dr. M'Dowell left Elizabethtown May 13th, 1833, and on the two following Sabbaths Mr. Murray preached in Elizabethtown. The congregation met June 3d, the Rev. Dr. Magie, pastor of the Second Church, presiding, and with entire unanimity made a call for Mr. Murray, offering him a salary of one thousand dollars per annum, and the use of the parsonage house and lands.

This call opened a new field and a perplexing question to the mind of the pastor in the Valley. He sought the heavenly guidance and the counsel of his friends. The advice he obtained was almost as unanimous as the call of the people; but he had formed new, strong, and endearing ties, which it was hard to sunder, and it may be truly said they never were sundered, for he and the people of the Valley cherished the warmest reciprocal attachment so long as he lived. Some of them insisted that he was under obligations to them to stay. With that independence of spirit that always marked his language and conduct, he replied, "I am under obligations to no man."

Dr. M'Dowell, feeling naturally deep concern for the people he had left, wrote to Mr. Murray:

"Philadelphia, June 15th, 1833.

"My dear Brother,—I rejoice to hear that my former people at Elizabethtown, still dearly beloved, have, at a full meeting, unanimously made out a call for you to become their pastor. By a letter which I have recently received from Elizabethtown, I find that there is a deep interest felt in the result of this call, and much anxiety, and doubtless much prayer (for I know that they are a praying people), that, if it is consistent with the Divine will, you may be induced to accept; and I unite with them in the hope that this may be the result. I view the hand of God as remarkable in this call—that, so soon after the departure of their late pastor, and when they were foreboding disunion, and that it would probably be a long time before they would be able to call a minister, they should so soon, and so cordially and harmoniously unite. The Lord, I sometimes think, has a great work for you to do there, and that he suffered the events to take place which issued in my removal, to open the door for your introduction to reap the harvest. Nothing but something like what did take place would probably have removed me from that people. I pray that the Lord may be with you, and direct you in this solemn business; and if it is for His glory, and the interests of Christ's kingdom, and consistent with His will, I pray that you may decide to go; and if not, however anxious I feel on this subject, I desire with submission to bow. I can tell you what my wishes are, but I dare not say what is duty. I am not sufficiently acquainted with your present situation, and I feel too much interested on one side to place great confidence in my own decision. I can only place before your mind the state of things at Elizabethtown, and leave you to contrast them with your present situation. The congregation, in itself, is a very important one, containing about 400 families and near 600 communicants; it has had, and is calculated to have, a commanding influence on the surrounding country throughout the Presbytery; it has been, and is calculated still to be, an efficient congregation in the benevolent enterprises of the day; and it has been, and I hope ever may be, an example of sound principles in doctrine, of moral habits, and of Church order; and much will be lost to the cause of correct doctrine, and order, and of benevolence if this congregation should languish and decline, or fall into some hands; and I fear this will be the result if you decline. They are an affectionate and kind people, as much so as any minister ought to desire. The little leaven of new measures which gave me trouble is purged out, and I think is in such bad savor that my successor will not be likely to have any trouble from this source. The salary they offer is competent. The situation is a pleasant one in itself, and is rendered more so by its contiguity to our great cities. The house is a very convenient one; the garden excellent. The immediate neighborhood quiet and good; a small, but good ministerial library for its size. The congregation has a share in the Widows' Fund, which will yield something annually to a widow or children, in case the pastor dies. I mention these things that you may have before your mind desired light in seeking for the path of duty.

"Yours, with sincere respect and affection,

"JOHN M'DOWELL."

Other brethren in the ministry wrote to him, urging him to go. Private individuals and elders in the Church in Elizabethtown sent importunate appeals. A venerable elder wrote him a letter which could hardly fail to make a favorable impression. It was written after reading a letter from Mr. Murray, in which he gave no encouragement that he would yield to the call. The good old man thus pours out his heart:

"Elizabethtown, June 15th, 1833.

"REV. AND DEAR SIR,—I have just returned from Mr. Meeker's, after perusing your letter. While I duly appreciate the spirit in which it is written, I must confess it has cast a gloom over my heart. It is a feeling that I very seldom indulge. I have had so many instances of God's goodness to me, that I more frequently raise my Ebenezer to God than indulge despondency. And in no case through life did the providence of God more clearly point out the path of duty than in this. When I think of your first introduction to us during last winter, the difficulties that took place in Philadelphia, the call of the doctor to Philadelphia, all of which were necessary to open the door for you here; and that so large a congregation as ours, without any management or effort by the leading members of the congregation, should, of their own free will and accord, give you a unanimous vote, without a single dissenting voice (for that was the case on the day of your election, when the call was made out for you), and add to this that you preached for us the very next Sabbath after the doctor left us, I must conclude the hand of the Lord is in these events.

"My prospects brighten while I write. The gloom disappears. Surely the Lord that has led us so far prosperously will not now disappoint us. But let me, dear sir, reason with you a few words. You remind me of a valuable friend I had who is now no more. He was frequently in spiritual darkness, when all his friends thought him a man eminent for piety. He would always look on the dark side, and instead of rejoicing in the glorious liberty of the children of God, he was often bound fast in the chains of despair. Permit me, dear sir, to tell you I can see no just cause, in the providence of God, to cast a cloud over you; every thing seems to me to be suited to your wants. Do you wish to support your family decently, and give your children a good education (which is the duty of every Christian; for 'he that provideth not for his own, and especially for those of his own household, hath denied the faith, and is worse than an infidel')? Here, then, the Lord has provided the means for you; for the salary you will receive in Elizabethtown will, with prudence and economy, supply your every want. Do you wish to be useful in converting souls to the Redeemer, and in building up believers in faith and holiness? Here the Lord has provided this also for you. You will not here have to cultivate a barren soil; the ground is, in some measure, prepared; in every part of our congregation we have our prayer-meetings—our Aarons and Hurs—to sustain you, and hold up your hands; so it may be said, 'The fields are already white unto harvest.' Why, then, hesitate about taking the good the Lord provides for you?

"I would farther remark, sir, that our people fully participate with you in seeking Divine direction; for in all our prayer-meetings petitions are put up for you and for ourselves, that we may be *divinely* directed, and that, if the Lord should send you unto us, 'you might come in all the fullness of the Gospel of Christ.'

"I would farther respectfully suggest, if you conclude not to accept our call, that you would let us know in your next letter, as I am appointed one of the commissioners. An old man, laboring under some of the infirmities of age, would feel much disappointed if, after going to Wilkesbarre, he could not accomplish his object. And I know every thing depends on you. If you throw the responsibility on the Presbytery, they will not dismiss you. But I must come to a close. My rheumatic shoulder dislikes writing. Give my respects to your lady; tell her the people of Elizabethtown long to see her, and become acquainted with her, from the interesting character Professor M'Clain, of Princeton, gave me of her.

"I shall, every morning and evening, meet you at the throne of grace, to seek for the Lord's direction.

"Respectfully yours, JAMES ROSS.

"Rev. Nicholas Murray."

He had made the decision with his accustomed promptness, and in less than two months from the time of receiving the call he was settled in Elizabethtown.

Before leaving the people of his first love, as he was accustomed to call the churches of Wilkesbarre and Kingston, he preached a farewell sermon, from which, as a fitting close to his brief but useful ministry in the Valley of Wyoming, we make a few extracts:

Extract from a Sermon preached in Wilkesbarre, Pa.

"Permit me to say a few words in reference to the choice of a future pastor. You are now united; let no step be taken that will tend to disunite. A Church distracted is a Church declining. A Church torn by dissensions is a Church merely in name—the vital principle of godliness has departed.

"During my ministry among you, this has been a frequent topic of remark; and now, on the eve of my departure, I would pray you to love one another. Let no root of bitterness spring up; let no subject of dissension find admission; let no hard feelings be indulged; let no jealousies be manifested. There are those around who are looking for your halting. Disappoint their expectations, we pray you. United you stand and will be useful; divided you may maintain a weak and sickly existence, but you will be useless. By your own comfort and happiness, by your individual growth in grace, by your increase and prosperity as a Church, by all that is dear to the salvation of souls, I charge you to keep the unity of the Spirit in the bonds of peace. And let your increasing cry to God be that He may preserve you from every thing that tends to slacken or untie the cord of Christian love. And in your choice of a pastor, look at the *substance*, not the *show* of a man. Show without substance, however it may please for the moment, soon becomes disgusting. The most pleasing manner, without the aid of strong sense and sterling piety, soon becomes commonplace. Substance, on the other hand, is the more valued the more it is known. Like the precious metal, it becomes bright by use. Show soon cloys the mental appetite, substance renders it increasingly craving. And as you need a holy light constantly in your candlestick, choose that which burns longest in preference to that which burns brightest. The flaming comet in its eccentric course soon burns out, but the mild light of the fixed star is never extinguished.

"And in the choice of a pastor, be unanimous, if *possible*. Let every individual act on broad Christian principles. And even *this* is possible. When the majority express their decided preference, the minority should cordially unite with them where there is no positive, reasonable, or conscientious ground of objection. It is the glory of our Church that we have no hierarchy. We are governed by majorities. And unless we are willing to submit to our brethren in the Lord, there is an end to all order in the community of the saints. Thus uniting, your pastor will be the pastor of the whole Church, and not of a party. He will come among you without hostile feeling on the part of any, and you will be all prepared to receive benefit from his ministrations. And when God sends you a pastor, oh sustain him by your prayers, assist him in his labors, co-operate with him in every good word and work! Leave him not to labor alone. Like Aaron and Hur on the mount with Moses, sustain his hands, and then God will distill the dews of His grace upon you. As a Church and as a people, you will be happy and blessed. Your great Shepherd will lead you into green pastures and beside still waters.

"Thus acting, and thus living together as the heirs of the grace of God, you will put into operation an influence which eternity alone can measure. I leave you in peace, and may the God of peace abide with you. To the elders I bid an affectionate *farewell*, praying you to take good heed unto yourselves, and to all the flock over which the Holy Ghost has made you overseers. To the members of this Church I bid an affectionate farewell, praying and exhorting you to grow in grace, and in the knowledge of our Lord and Savior Jesus Christ. Unto those collected into the Church under my ministry, I bid a special farewell; upon you I look as the seals of my ministry—as my dear children in Christ. So live and so act as to be to me a crown of rejoicing in the day of our Lord Jesus Christ. To the unconverted members of this congregation I bid an affectionate farewell, praying that the labors of some future pastor may be more blessed to you than mine; praying that you may never be permitted to exchange worlds until you are washed and made white in the blood of the Lamb. And now, brethren, I commend you to God, and to the word of His grace, which is able to build you up, and to give you an inheritance among all them which are sanctified. May you be peaceful and happy, your church crowded with devout worshipers; and may this whole congregation, under the culture of a faithful minister, become fair and blooming in the garden of the Lord.

"Very soon we shall all take up our abode in the home which admits of no removal until the morning of the resurrection; and when that time arrives, may we together see the Lamb in His glory, and enter with Him into an eternal rest."

The installation services were held July 23, 1833, at eleven o'clock A.M. The Rev. Joseph M. Ogden, D.D, of Chatham, preached the sermon, from 2 Corinthians, iii., 15, 16. The Rev. Dr. John M'Dowell gave the charge to the pastor, and the Rev. Mr. Thompson, of Connecticut Farms, gave the charge to the people.

From this hour we may date a new era in the life and progress of Nicholas Murray. He was now thirty-one years of age. In excellent health, with a robust manly form, ardent zeal, and exuberant spirits, his highest ambition already attained in the pastoral charge of a large and flourishing congregation, he now consecrated himself to the work of the ministry with singleness of devotion and steadiness of purpose. His habits of study and pastoral labor were formed; he had only to adapt them to the circumstances of the new field upon which he was entering, and to make the previous results of his study and experience available for increased usefulness.

A few days or weeks after his settlement, he was met by one of the members of the congregation, who said to him,

"You may have heard, Mr. Murray, that I did not vote for you when the call was made?"

"No," said Mr. Murray, "I have never heard of it; I understood the call was unanimous."

"So it was," replied the gentleman; "I did not vote against it, but I did not vote for it. I had no objections personally to you, but the truth is, I do not like your preaching."

"Well," said the pastor, "there you and I agree exactly; I don't think much of it myself."

The same conversation has been repeated of other ministers and parishioners, and Mr. Murray alludes to it in his work on "Preachers and Preaching;" but we have his own authority for saying that it actually occurred in his own experience, and that the parishioner was so well satisfied with the answer of his pastor, that he remained till death a warm and valued friend.

The church and town to which he has now been introduced have a rich and honorable history, and Mr. Murray himself became the historian. After he had been settled here about ten years, he prepared a series of historical discourses, which, at the request of his people, were published in one volume, giving a minute account of the settlement and progress of the town. He begins the history with the taking of Constantinople by the Turks in 1453! mentions the art of printing in 1455, the discovery of America in 1492, and the Reformation in 1517. It is not important for us to consider the relation of these great events to the settlement of Elizabethtown, but we may go back to "the month of August, 1665, when the ship Philip dropped its anchor at Elizabethtown Point. It conveyed from England to the shores of New Jersey Philip Carteret, the first governor of the province, and about thirty emigrants. These debarked, and, together with the dwellers in some log huts, which had been previously erected, formed the first settlers of Elizabethtown. The persons residing in the log huts were from the east end of Long Island, induced to remove here by John Ogden and his associates. The persons who settled Long Island were generally Puritans from England and New England; and as John Ogden was a pious Puritan, we may infer that the first white inhabitants of Elizabethtown were pious persons, and of the old Puritan stamp.

"As in those days the emigrants from England to the Northern States were generally persons whose religious principles subjected them to persecution, we may infer that the settlers brought here by Carteret were mainly of Puritan faith. And this inference is greatly strengthened by the fact that we find them heartily agreeing with the people of Newark, who were decided Puritans, 'to be of one heart and consent, with God's blessing, in endeavoring to carry on their religious concernment;' and that until 1704, when the Episcopal Church was organized, the First Presbyterian Church was the only one in the town.

"As the Church Records were lost during the war of the Revolution, and the Records subsequent to that, to the year 1800, during the partial insanity of the Rev. David Austin, we have no Session minutes previous to the settlement of the Rev. Dr. Kollock. We know not when the Church was first organized. Because of the character of the first settlers and of the leading associates, we conclude that the Church was formed immediately after the settlement of the town. Hence this claims to be the oldest congregation in the state worshiping God in the English language. Nor has it any competitor for this honor save its venerable sister Church of Newark, which dates its existence from October, 1667.

"Nor is it known whether the people first organized as a Presbyterian or as an Independent Church. The churches of Newark and Woodbridge were Presbyterian. There was very early a large emigration here from Scotland. There is neither record nor tradition that it ever changed its polity, or that it was ever any thing else than Presbyterian. It is very likely that for some years its government assumed no particular form, but that when it did, it took a Presbyterian form, which it has ever since maintained. The influence of the Church on the community was very early apparent, as Rudyard, in 1683, describes the people as 'generally a sober, professing people, wise in their generation, and courteous in their behavior.'

"Nor is it known when the first church edifice was erected. It stood where its more imposing successor now stands. It was a building of wood, with galleries; and when first erected was small. It had a high steeple, with a town clock in it; and it was probably in it that the Legislatures under the Proprietors, and the Supreme Court held their sessions. It was enlarged and beautified on several occasions. Fired by the torch of a refugee, it was burned to ashes on the 25th of January, 1780.

"The foundations of the present church were laid in 1784. While yet incomplete, it was dedicated to the public worship of God by the Rev. Dr. M'Whorter, of Newark, in January, 1786. Its fine steeple was erected during the ministry of Mr. Austin. It was reseated and greatly repaired in 1842; and in the year 1851 it was enlarged and placed in its present state of beauty and taste, at an expense of about ten thousand dollars.

"The first minister of the Church of which we have any record was the Rev. Seth Fletcher. He died in 1682. It is very probable that from the founding of the Church to the settlement of Mr. Harriman, there was no settled pastor, the people depending, as do many new congregations now, upon occasional supplies.

"The Rev. John Harriman became pastor in 1682, and died in 1704."

The Rev. Mr. Melyne was settled here in 1704. Whence he came we are not able to say, but there is a tradition in respect to his departure to this effect: Being strongly suspected of intemperance, he took offense at a piece of music sung as a voluntary by the choir on a Sabbath morning. Descending from the pulpit in the midst of the singing, and taking his wife, he walked out of the church, and never entered it again. In his time the whole town contained only about three hundred families.

"The next pastor was the Rev. Jonathan Dickinson, the impress of whose character is yet visible on the town, and, indeed, on the whole of the eastern section of New Jersey. This great and good man was born in Hatfield, Mass., April 22d, 1688, and was graduated in Yale College in 1706. He was settled here two or three years afterward, and when he was about twenty-one years of age. Of this congregation and town he was for nearly forty years the joy and the glory. 'He had a mind formed for inquiry; and to a keen penetration he united a disinterested attachment to truth. With a natural turn for controversy, he had a happy government of his passions, and abhorred the perverse disputings so common to men of corrupt minds. The eagerness of contention did not extinguish in him the fervors of devotion and brotherly love.' He advocated with great zeal the doctrines of grace, and adorned them by a holy life devoted to doing good. He was valiant for the truth. Unlike many at the present day, he never consulted his own ease or popularity at the expense of God's truth, nor stood neutral to see which side would prevail, and then throw himself on the popular current. Armed with the weapons of truth and love, he boldly resisted every attack on the truth and order of God's house, and manfully defended from the assaults of error all the great fundamental doctrines of our most holy religion. And his published works praise him in all the gates of Zion, and will transmit his name to all future generations. The most complete list of his published writings that we have seen is contained in Dr. Green's very valuable history of the College of New Jersey.

"During his ministry this congregation prospered greatly. It shared largely in the glorious revival with which God favored the country during the ministry of Whitefield, Edwards, Brainerd, and the Tennents, who were all his contemporaries; and in 1740 there was a large addition made to the communicants of the Church. It is a pleasant fact in our history that here the beloved Brainerd delighted to visit, and to commune with his brother Jonathan. During the second visit of Whitefield to this country in 1740 he visited this place; and at the very short notice of about two or three hours, preached at twelve o'clock to an audience of seven hundred people. At the close of the service he took up a collection, probably for the Orphan Asylum, the largest in the list of collections for the year. From this fact we infer the great popularity of the preacher, that the town must have been considerably populous, and that it must have been a time of more than ordinary attention to the subject of religion.

"This parish is now a large and laborious one; but in the days of Mr. Dickinson its boundaries were much more extensive than now. It then included all of Rahway, Westfield, Connecticut Farms, and Springfield, and even a part of Chatham. Then the people of Westfield would walk here to worship God; but those from Chatham were oftentimes in the habit of riding. Nor in those primeval days were the people much deterred by bad roads or bad weather. The Gospel was precious to them, and they could encounter difficulties to hear it.

"Between the Elizabethtown Associates and the New Jersey Proprietors, the different parishes were not forgotten. The former set apart a town lot of the largest size for the minister, and the latter appropriated two hundred acres for each parish. It is more than probable that the lot given by the Associates lay in that part of the town through which Race Street now runs, as Mr. Dickinson resided in a house which stood a few yards north of the present residence of Capt. Charles L. Williamson. But what became of the grant of the Proprietors, or whether it ever came into the possession of this congregation, there is no means of ascertaining. There is a tradition that Mr. Dickinson, on his decease, gave to the Church several acres of land, to be added to the original town lot. The great cheapness of all the necessaries of life, together with the use of that lot and the parsonage, and their devoting a part of their time to other pursuits than those directly ministerial, account for the small salaries given to the different pastors. Mr. Kettletas was paid but two pounds ten shillings per Sabbath. Mr. Caldwell was paid three pounds one shilling and sixpence per Sabbath. In 1776 his salary was raised to one hundred and eighty pounds, and he was paid by the week, and punctually every Monday morning. Mr. Linn was settled on a salary of three hundred pounds York currency, with the parsonage house and lands. But then all other things were in proportion. The governor's salary in East Jersey was one hundred and fifty pounds, in West Jersey two hundred pounds; and at one time they were paid that in peas, and corn, and tobacco, at fixed prices. Beef and venison were a penny a pound, corn was two shillings and sixpence per bushel, barley two shillings, and all other things in proportion. Making due allowance for the changes that have taken place, there is no doubt that pastors were much better paid then than now.

"A controversy which had existed for some time in the Synod of Philadelphia, then representing the whole Presbyterian Church in the Provinces, resulted in dividing that Synod into two parts in 1741—the Synods of New York and Philadelphia. From the time of their separation each made strong exertions to educate youth for the ministry, with the mingled purpose of elevating the standard of ministerial education and of strengthening their party. New Jersey went nearly unanimously with the Synod of New York; and as the Presbyterian Church was much stronger here than in New York, it was determined, if possible, to establish a college, and to locate it in New Jersey. Dickinson was the leader of his party in the old Synod of Philadelphia, and after the separation was by far the most able man in the Synod of New York. He it was, no doubt, that gave being and shape to the deliberations that resulted in the creation of the College of New Jersey. He had been for several years a very popular teacher of young men; and when the institution was resolved upon, every eye rested upon him as best qualified to lay its foundations and to superintend its concerns. A charter for a college was sought, and granted by John Hamilton, who acted as governor (being the oldest member of the Council) between the death of Governor Morris, in May, 1746, and the induction of Governor Belcher into the chair of state in 1747. The college thus founded was commenced in this town, and Mr. Dickinson was chosen its first president. It is now in a flourishing state, with an able and extended faculty, numerous buildings and students; but then, with the exception of an usher, the president was the only teacher. The number of students was about twenty, who boarded with the president and other families in the town. The Academy, which stood where the Lecture-room now stands, and which was burned down during the war of the Revolution, contained the first recitation-room of the first classes ever attached to New Jersey College. Although brought into existence by the influence of Dickinson, he was spared to act as its president but one year, as he died October 7th, 1747. The students were then removed to Newark, and placed under the government of the Rev. Aaron Burr, who was the second president of the college. In 1757, when about seventy in number, they were removed to Princeton, where the first college edifice was erected, and which, in honor of William III. of England, Prince of Orange and Nassau, the assertor of Protestant liberty, was called Nassau Hall.

"The great and good Dickinson died in the sixtieth year of his age, although not full of years, yet full of honors. His must have been a life of great activity and industry when it is remembered that in addition to his duties as a pastor, and teacher, and farmer, and the studies imposed by his numerous and ardent controversies, he was a practicing physician, and obtained a considerable medical reputation. So devoted was he as a minister, so untiring were his efforts to do good, so discriminating and powerful was he as a preacher, so dignified and bland were his manners, so ardent was his attachment to the truth, and so firm and cogent was he in its advocacy, that his memory is yet inestimably precious. It must have been a sad day in Elizabethtown when Mr. Dickinson, and Mr. Vaughan, the rector of the Episcopal Church, who are said to have come to this place on the same day, and after laboring here forty years together, were both corpses on the same day, the former having died but a few hours before the latter.

"Mr. Dickinson left behind him three daughters: one of them married a Mr. Sargeant, of Princeton, of whom the Hon. John Sargeant, of Philadelphia, is a descendant. Another married the Rev. Caleb Smith, pastor of the Church in Newark Mountains, now called Orange, of whom the family of Greens of Lawrenceville are descendants, one of whom, H. W. Green, of Trenton, is one of the ornaments of the New Jersey bar. And the other became the wife of a Mr. John Cooper. The remains of this venerated man sleep in our grave-yard, and hallowed be the spot of their repose until they awake to newness of life."

The successor of Mr. Dickinson was the Rev. Elihu Spencer, D.D., who was installed Feb. 7, 1750. He continued a faithful and useful pastor until 1756, when he removed to Trenton, N. J., and became pastor there. He died in Trenton Dec. 27th, 1784, in the 64th year of his age. On his tomb it is written, "Possessed of fine genius, of great vivacity, of eminent and active piety, his merits as a minister and a man stand above the reach of flattery. Having long edified the Church by his talents and example, and finished his course with joy, he fell asleep, full of faith, and waiting for the hope of all saints."

Dr. Spencer was succeeded by the Rev. Abraham Kettletas, installed Sept. 14, 1757. He was here but two or three years. He went to Long Island and settled at Jamaica, where he died September 30, 1798, aged 65 years. He was an able man and a warm patriot, and his writings were influential in the war of the Revolution.

"The Rev. James Caldwell, of Revolutionary and patriotic memory, whose tragical end gives to his history all the interest of romance, was the successor of Mr. Kettletas. Between the removal of the one and the settlement of the other, the pulpit was supplied by many individuals, no doubt, as candidates for settlement. As they were in the habit of paying the preacher every Monday morning, the Treasurer's account is the only testimony we have as to who they were. Mr. Kilpatrick, Mr. Treet, Mr. Carmichael, Mr. Horton, who afterward settled at Bottle Hill, Mr. Elmore, Mr. Woodruff, Mr. Parkhurst, Mr. Green, afterward or at that time settled in Hanover, and the father of the venerable Dr. Green, Mr. More, Mr. Pierson, Mr. M'Whorter, Mr. Halsey, and a Mr. Jones, are among the number. But Mr. Caldwell was selected from them all, and was installed in December, 1761, although he preached here several Sabbaths between August, 1760, and the date of his settlement.

"We learn from some of the descendants of this

distinguished man, of whom there are many, that his family was of French origin. Driven from their country by the fierce persecution against the Huguenots, they went over to Scotland. In the reign of James I., a branch of the family went over to Ireland and settled in the county of Antrim. From this branch John Caldwell was descended, who emigrated to this country, bringing with him, besides his wife and children, four single sisters. He first settled in Lancaster County, Pa., but soon removed to a settlement called Cub Creek, in what is now called Charlotte County, Virginia. There James was born, April, 1734, the youngest of seven children. He was sent to Princeton College, where he graduated in 1759. In about a year afterward he was licensed to preach the Gospel; and while the dew of his youth was yet upon him, he entered upon the charge of this then large congregation. Soon after his settlement he was married, March 14, 1763, to Miss Hannah Ogden, of Newark, who was in every respect a help meet for him, and whose cheerful piety and unshaken fortitude sustained and comforted him amid the dark and trying scenes through which he was called to pass.

"Shortly after the settlement of Mr. Caldwell here, those differences between the colonies and Great Britain commenced which resulted in the war of the Revolution, and subsequently in the independence of the United States. Descended from the Huguenots, he early learned the story of their wrongs, and may be said to have inherited a feeling of opposition to tyranny and tyrants. Possessing warm feelings, and fine genius, and great muscular energy, he entered with all his heart into the controversy. He acted as the chaplain of those portions of the American army that successively occupied New Jersey, accompanied the Jersey Brigade to the northern lines, and is said to have held the station of commissary for some time. He was high in the confidence of Washington, with whom he was on the most intimate terms of friendship; and in times of gloom and despondency, by his eloquent and patriotic appeals, contributed much to excite and sustain the drooping spirits of officers and soldiers. And perhaps no one man in this part of the State of New Jersey contributed so much to give direction and energy to the movements of our citizens. His popularity with the soldiers and people was unbounded, and his practical wisdom was held in the highest estimation.

"But the very things that made him popular with the friends of his country, made him equally unpopular with its enemies. To avoid the danger to which he was constantly exposed from the Tories, and the enemy then in the possession of Staten Island and New York, he was compelled to remove his residence from this place to Connecticut Farms, where he resided until the day of his murder.

"He was sustained in his political action by his congregation with scarcely a single exception. The church in which he preached was cheerfully yielded as a hospital for sick, and disabled, and wounded soldiers, as some of the aged ones yet among us testify. It was its bell that sounded through the town the notes of alarm on the approach of the foe; its floor was not unfrequently the bed of the weary soldier, and the seats of its pews the table from which he ate his scanty meal. Its worshipers on the Sabbath were not unfrequently compelled to stand through the service because of the greasiness of their seats, and the fragments of bread and meat by which they were covered. In vengeance on the pastor and the people, this church was fired on the 25th of January, 1780, by a refugee called Cornelius Hetfield. On the 25th of the following June, while General Knyphausen was on his way to Springfield, Mrs. Caldwell was shot at Connecticut Farms by a refugee, through the window of a room to which she had retired with her children for safety and prayer; two balls passing through her body. Her lifeless corpse was drawn from the building and laid in the open street, when it was fired; and soon all the surrounding buildings were in ashes. And on the 24th of November, 1781, Mr. Caldwell himself was shot at Elizabethtown Point, whither he had gone for a young lady who had come under the protection of a flag of truce from New York. The ball pierced his heart, and he expired in a moment. His corpse was laid in the body of a wagon covered with straw, and was carried to the house of Mrs. Noel, his unwavering friend, whence it was buried. Dr. M'Whorter, of Newark, preached his funeral sermon from Ecclesiastes, eighth chapter and eighth verse. The remains of himself and wife lie together in our grave-yard. He died in the 49th year of his age, leaving a name as dear to the state as it is to the

Church of Jesus Christ. Thus, in less than two years, this congregation was bereft of its church, and next of the inestimable wife of their pastor, and next of that pastor himself. And as a proof of the estimate in which he was held, his name was given to one of the townships of this county.

"The funeral of Mr. Caldwell was one of the most solemn scenes that this town has ever witnessed. He was shot on Saturday afternoon, and many of the people were ignorant of the tragical deed until they came to church on the Sabbath; and instead of sitting with delight under his instructions, there was a loud cry of wailing over his melancholy end. There was a vast concourse assembled to convey him to his tomb on the following Tuesday. After the religious services were ended, the corpse was placed on the large stone before the door of the house of Mrs. Noel, now the residence of Miss Spalding, where all could take a last view of the remains of their murdered pastor. After all had taken their last look, and before the coffin was closed, Dr. Boudinot came forward, leading nine orphan children, and placing them around the bier of their parent, made an address of surpassing pathos to the multitude in their behalf. It was an hour of deep and powerful emotion; and the procession slowly moved to the grave, weeping as they went. And as they lifted their streaming eyes to heaven, they besought the blessing of God upon the orphan group; and His kind interposition to crown their efforts against their oppressors with success.

"So vivid are the recollections of many yet among

us of this devoted patriot and pastor, that we can describe him almost to the life. He was of middling size, and strongly framed. His countenance had a pensive, placid cast; but when excited, was exceedingly expressive of resolution and energy. His voice was sweet and pleasant, but, at the same time, so strong that he could make himself heard above the notes of the drum and fife. As a preacher he was uncommonly eloquent and pathetic, rarely preaching without weeping himself, and at times would melt his whole audience into tears. He was one of the most active of men, and seemed never wearied by any amount of bodily or mental labor. Feelings of the most fervent piety and of the most glowing patriotism possessed his bosom at the same time, without the one interfering with the other. He was one day preaching to the battalion, the next marching with them to battle, and if defeated, assisting to conduct their retreat, and the next administering the consolations of the Gospel to some dying parishioner. His people were most ardently attached to him, and the army adored him. His shed blood is mingled with our soil, and his ashes repose in our cemetery. Let his name be had in everlasting remembrance.

"He was shot by a man called Morgan, who was tried and found guilty of murder. It is said that it was proved on his trial that he was bribed by British gold to commit the murderous deed. He was hung, giving signs of the most obdurate villainy. The day of his execution was intensely cold, and his last words were, addressing with an oath the executioner, 'Do your duty, and don't keep me here suffering in the cold.' The place of his execution is about half a mile north of the Westfield church, and is called Morgan's Hill to this day.

"Mr. Caldwell left behind him nine orphan children, with but very little provision to sustain or educate them. The Lord raised up friends to protect them, and they all lived not only to become members of the Church of Jesus Christ, but to occupy places of distinguished usefulness."

Mr. Caldwell was succeeded in the ministry by the Rev. William Linn, D.D, June 14, 1786. He remained but a few months, and was dismissed to become a pastor of the Reformed Dutch Church, in the city of New York.

"The successor of Dr. Linn was the Rev. David Austin, whose name and fame will be long remembered in this part of the country. He was born in New Haven in the year 1760. His father was one of the earliest settlers of that place, and was a man of great respectability, of piety, and wealth. He was for many years collector of the customs, and afterward a successful merchant. David was the eldest of a numerous family, all the members of which who lived to maturity became truly pious. He was early fitted for college, and graduated at Yale in 1779. After graduating, he pursued his theological studies with Dr. Bellamy, of Bethlehem, in his native state, and, according to the custom of that day, was soon licensed to preach the Gospel. He preached with great acceptance, and in several places was strongly solicited to settle as a pastor. Having determined to visit Europe before taking a pastoral charge, he declined all these proposals, some of which were highly flattering and advantageous. He spent some time in foreign travel, and returned with an ardent desire for the work of the ministry. He married Miss Lydia Lathrop, of Norwich, whose father was a wealthy and highly respected citizen of that town, and shortly afterward, September 9th, 1788, he was here ordained and installed pastor.

"From the time of his settlement he continued his labors here, greatly beloved and extensively useful, until the close of 1795. The effect of a natural eccentricity, connected with the most enlarged benevolence, which his private fortune enabled him to exercise, was only to increase the number of his ardent friends. In that year he had a violent attack of scarlet fever, from which he but slowly recovered, and which very seriously affected his mind. During his recovery he commenced the study of the prophecies, and the effect was soon obvious in a mental derangement from which he never wholly recovered. When he resumed his labors, he commenced preaching on the 60th chapter of Isaiah, from which he taught the doctrine of the personal reign of Christ, and that His second coming was to take place on the fourth Sabbath of May, 1796. The attention of the people now became wonderfully excited, and such was the rush from neighboring towns, that multitudes on the Sabbath could not get room to stand in the church.

"At length the appointed day drew near. On the

previous evening a meeting was held for prayer and preparation in the Methodist Church, and the house was crowded. He dwelt on the history of the Ninevites who repented at the preaching of Jonah, and exhorted to imitate their example. Weeping and mourning were heard in all parts of the assembly. The next day the sun rose with more than its usual splendor, and a vast multitude of people crowded the house and surrounded it. But the day passed away without any unusual occurrence; and many of his followers were only now convinced that he was under a delusion, and that he deluded them. His friends hoped that disappointment would dissipate his delusion, and the Session remonstrated with him; but his ingenuity soon found excuses for his Lord's delay, and his enthusiasm was only inflamed. He charged his Session, and the members of the Church that opposed him, with the sin and guilt of Uzzah, and stated that it was because of the mere mercy of God that they did not suffer his punishment. At this time he took the vow of a Nazarite, and preached incessantly, sometimes three sermons a day, through this part of the country. Wherever he went crowds followed him, and God overruled the excitement he produced to the conversion of many souls. His great theme was the near approach of the personal reign of Christ upon earth; and that as Joshua led the Jews into the promised land, as John Baptist was the forerunner of the Savior, so he was appointed of God to bring in the glorious millennial reign of righteousness.

"Finding the congregation seriously agitated by his

proceedings, and having declared that he was about to establish a new Church upon earth, a public meeting was called and a committee of eleven appointed to wait upon him. They stated their grievances, asked some questions as to his future proceedings, and requested in reply a written answer. The following is his answer:

"'To Jonathan Dayton, of the committee of eleven, appointed by the Congregation of Elizabethtown to wait on Mr. Austin, their pastor, in respect to the present course and object of his ministry, and of the concerns of the Congregation in general:

"'In conformity to the request of the committee, that the answer to their application might be given in writing, it may be said:

"'In respect to that part of the paper read, which hinted at and complained of an avowed design of the pastor to institute a new Church, and to set up a new order of things in ecclesiastical concerns, "independent of Presbytery, of the Synod, or of the General Assembly," it may be openly answered that such is my fixed and unalterable determination! For a warrant thus to proceed, reference may be had to the third and sixth chapters of the prophecy of Zechariah, and to many other passages of Scripture, which foretell of these things and of these days.

"'On the testimony of the Scriptures, and on the inward teachings of the Holy Spirit of God, and on the present aspect of Providence, and on uncommon and extraordinary revelations of the mind and will of God to this point, dependence is had in proof of a special and designating call to proceed in this solemn and interesting work.

"'Be it known, then, to the committee and to the congregation, and to the Presbyterian Church, and to the world at large, that such extraordinary call I do profess to have received, and that it is my glory openly to avow, and solemnly to profess my determination to maintain and to discharge the duties of it, through the faith of that power and constant grace which hath called and accompanied me in this concern thus far!

"'Under such impressions, standing collected and firm, I again announce to the committee, to the congregation, and to all concerned, that implicit obedience to the voice of Heaven is my fixed determination!

"'Let this declaration be productive of what consequences it may, be it remembered, that the anticipations of Divine support are so ready and abundant, that the instrument of the Divine designs feels himself ready, and professes himself willing, to meet all obstacles and to brave all dangers in the prosecution of the noble object which Infinite Wisdom hath placed before him.

"'The baptism of the cloud and of the sea opened the journey of God's ancient Israel toward the goodly land, and answeringly to the former example, the present course of spiritual journeying is now to be taken up; and if the scenes of the ancient warfare are again to be repeated, faith in God pronounces His eternal arm to be mightily sufficient to secure the victory in every conflict in which His own shall be engaged! and it may be well for opposition to the predestinated purposes of God to remember that the disasters of those whose carcasses fell through unbelief, and the utter extirpation of those who stood in the way of the advancing forward of the host of Israel in search of the goodly land, are but a lively figure of what those are to expect who are found imitating their faithless and wicked example in these later days.

"'Submitting the whole concern to the unqualified sovereignty of God, and to the decisions of those to whom these presents may come, subscribe to the congregation, an affectionate pastor, and to the people of God in every place, an unfeigned friend, and servant of God in Christ Jesus. DAVID AUSTIN.

"'Elizabethtown, Friday, April 7th, A.D. 1797.'

"Twelve days after the receipt of the above answer, the following petition was sent to the Presbytery of New York, with which the Church was then connected:

"'At a meeting of the Elders, Deacons, Trustees, and Members of the First Presbyterian Congregation in Elizabethtown, at their Meeting-house, on Wednesday, the 19th day of April, 1797, at two o'clock in the afternoon of that day, agreeable to adjournment, Mr. Elias Dayton was chosen Moderator, Mr. Aaron Ogden, Clerk. *Resolved unanimously*, That the following petition be presented to the Presbytery of New York at their next session:

"'The Elders, Deacons, Trustees, and Members of the First Presbyterian Congregation in Elizabethtown respectfully petition the reverend Presbytery of New York to dissolve the pastoral relation now subsisting between the Rev. David Austin and said congregation, provided they are of opinion that the following reason is a sufficient foundation for the application, namely, the declaration of the Rev. Mr. Austin's intention to set up a new Church, independent of Presbytery, Synod, or General Assembly; as will fully appear by an acknowledgment under his own hand, and herewith sent.

"'*Resolved unanimously*, That Messrs. Jeremiah Ballard, Benjamin Corey, and Shepard Kollock be a committee for the purpose of presenting the foregoing petition. ELIAS DAYTON.

"'Attest, AARON OGDEN, Clerk.'

"The following is the decision of the Presbytery in the case, which, while it dissolves his pastoral relation to the congregation, and protests against his errors, and warns the churches against him, yet bears ample testimony to his moral character:

"'Thursday, May 4, 1797.

"'The consideration of the petition from Elizabethtown was resumed. The commissioners from the congregation of Elizabethtown being asked whether they had any thing farther to offer respecting the business, answered, "Not at present." Mr. Austin being then called upon to know whether he had any thing to offer respecting the petition and application before Presbytery from the congregation of Elizabethtown, replied, That he had no objection to the Presbytery's deciding upon that petition as they should think proper; and that he took this opportunity to signify his intention to withdraw, and declared that he actually did then withdraw from his connection with this Presbytery, and from all Presbyterial connection and government.

"'The parties being removed, the Presbytery proceeded to deliberate and to form a judgment upon the case; and, after due deliberation, unanimously judged that the way was clear for granting the prayer of the petition from the congregation of Elizabethtown, to have the pastoral relation between Mr. Austin and said congregation dissolved, and did accordingly dissolve it, and hereby declare the congregation vacant.

"'With respect to Mr. Austin's declaration of his having withdrawn from his connection with this Presbytery, and from all Presbyterial connection and government, they also unanimously declare that they are sensibly and tenderly affected upon the occasion, and sincerely lament the unhappy circumstances which have led to these measures. And while it is their wish to treat Mr. Austin's person and character with all possible delicacy and tenderness, and while they declare that they have nothing to allege against his moral character, yet, as they are clearly of opinion that Mr. Austin is, and has for more than a year past been under the powerful influence of enthusiasm and delusion, evidently manifested by his giving credit to, and being guided by, supposed revelations and communications of an extraordinary kind; his alleged designation and call to particular important offices and services; his undertaking to fix the precise time of the commencement of the Millennium to the fifteenth day of May last, and to designate the circumstances of its commencement; and his present declaration of his intentions to institute a new Church, and to set up a new order of things in ecclesiastical concerns; and his having persisted and still persisting in similar views and conduct, notwithstanding his having been faithfully and tenderly dealt with on this head by the Presbytery in an extra-judicial capacity, as well as by individual members: the Presbytery having taken these things into consideration, feel themselves bound, in justice to the Church of Christ in general, and particularly to the congregations under their care, to declare that they can not recommend Mr. Austin as one who, while under the influence of this enthusiasm and delusion, promises usefulness in the service of the Gospel ministry; but, on the contrary, feel it to be their duty solemnly to caution all against giving heed to any irrational and unscriptural suggestions and impressions, as delusions of Satan, the effects of a disordered imagination, tending to mislead, deceive, and destroy the souls of men, and to affect the union, the peace, and the harmony of the Church of Christ.'

"After his removal by the Presbytery from his congregation, Mr. Austin preached in the surrounding country for a short while, when he returned to New Haven. Believing in the literal return of the Jews to the Holy Land, and that New Haven was to be the place of their embarkation from this country, he erected houses and a wharf for their use. Unable to pay the debts he incurred, he was imprisoned for some time. During his confinement his mind seemed in some measure to recover itself; but yet on the subject of prophecy was distracted. He returned to this town in 1804, when, being refused admission to his old pulpit, subscriptions were circulated for putting the Methodist church into a state of repair for his use. The object was obtained, and he preached there for a short while, but the state of his mind now became obvious to all; his friends could no longer encourage him, and he again returned to New England. His mind gradually emerged from the cloud that obscured it, and he again entered upon a career of usefulness. His excellent wife, possessed of an ample patrimony, exerted a most happy influence upon him, and greatly aided in restoring his mind to its former balance. For a number of years he preached in vacant churches in the eastern part of Connecticut. In 1815 he received a call from the Church in Bozrah, where he was installed on the 9th of May of that year. Here he preached regularly, and with great acceptance and success, until his death, which took place at Norwich, February 5, 1831, in the 72d year of his age.

"Mr. Austin was decidedly one of the most popular preachers of his day. Up to the time of his great affliction, no man could be more universally beloved and admired. Dignified in personal appearance, polished in manners, eloquent in his public performances, giving all his goods to feed the poor, he exerted a commanding influence, not only over his own congregation, but also over many of the leading minds of his day. His memory was retentive, and his conversational powers extraordinary. His devotional exercises were peculiarly happy and impressive; and all who remember him testify that few have ever surpassed him in public prayer. Besides performing a great amount of pastoral labors, he did good service for the theological literature of the country. He edited and published a Commentary upon the Bible, some of President Edwards' most valuable works; and he commenced a monthly publication of original sermons by living ministers, which reached its fourth volume, under the title of 'The American Preacher.' When at the high noon of his fame and usefulness, that thick cloud fell upon his intellect which was never wholly removed during his life. We have seen but one production of his in print, 'The Downfall of the Mystical Babylon,' save his 'Proclamation for the Millennial Empire,' published in folio sheet, in New York, in 1805.

"The successor of Mr. Austin was the Rev. John Giles. He was born in England, and came to this town in June, 1799, and buried his wife here on the 5th of August following. He was installed on the 4th of June, 1800; but such was the effect of the death of his wife on his health and spirits as to unfit him for pastoral duties, and he sought and obtained a dismission in the following October.

"The successor of Mr. Giles was the Rev. Henry Kollock. He was ordained and installed in this place December 10th, 1800. After a brilliant ministry of three years, of whose usefulness there are yet living witnesses, he removed to Princeton in December, 1803, because of his election to the office of Professor of Divinity in the College of New Jersey. He afterward settled in Savannah, where he died, universally lamented, December 29th, 1819. He was principally distinguished for his remarkable eloquence, which was unsurpassed in his day in the American pulpit.

"On the 26th of December, 1804, the Rev. John M'Dowell, D.D., was ordained and installed the successor of Dr. Kollock, and continued the minister of the Church for twenty-nine years, when he was dismissed, April 30, 1833, to become the pastor of the Central Presbyterian Church in Philadelphia. With the exception of Dickinson's, his was the longest ministry that the First Church ever enjoyed, and, probably, was the most useful of any. But as he is yet living, and active and useful, what might justly be said of him here must be left to his biographer to say after the good fight he has been so long waging is terminated, and he has gone up to wear his crown, and with those who have turned many to righteousness to shine as a star forever and ever."

During the ministry of the Rev. Dr. M'Dowell, the growth of the Church was so great that the house of worship was not adequate to accommodate them, and the number of families was too large for one pastor. He led the way to found a new Church, and certain individuals were selected and designated to embark in the enterprise. They went out with the prayers and benedictions of the pastor and people they left. They called the Rev. David Magie, one of their own number, a native of the town, to be their pastor. He accepted their call; and being settled over them, and married to one of their number, also a native of the town, has been their faithful, successful, and honored shepherd to this day. It is now more than forty years since Dr. Magie was settled over this, the Second Presbyterian Church. In numbers, strength, and efficient piety, the congregation is among the first in our country.

These historical reminiscences were essential to a proper appreciation of the field and the work upon which Mr. Murray entered. As the successor of a long line of distinguished ministers, and the pastor of a large and intelligent people that had been well instructed in the Word of Life from year to year, it was no small undertaking to sustain himself in such a position, and successfully build upon the foundation which these great men had laid.

CHAPTER XII.

The Field before him.—His private Devotion.—His Wit and Piety.—Systematic Study of the Bible.—Preparation for the Pulpit.—Pastoral Labors.—Knows every one.—A friend to all.—His Record.—His first Sermon as Pastor.—The Half-witted Hearer.—A Sorrowful Sermon.—The first Revival.—Incident in a Farm-house.

HIS life's work was now before him. Whether he had formed already the purpose of spending the rest of his days in this field, it is unnecessary to inquire; but we have evidence enough that he determined to enter upon his labors, and pursue them with the same diligence and devotion that he would summon to the work if here only he was to win the reward of a good and faithful servant.

When he entered the Seminary at Princeton, he records in his journal that hitherto he had been actuated by unholy ambition in the pursuit of knowledge. On the threshold of his ministerial studies, he resolved to sacrifice that passion, and to be hereafter governed by the single desire to honor God and do good to his fellow-men. And now, at the outset of his ministerial life in Elizabethtown, he makes a holy resolution to devote his whole energies to the simple service of his Master, in the advancement of the best interests of the Church and the world.

Every thing in his present situation was favorable to the development of his plans of usefulness; and, with a method and precision scarcely if ever equaled, he commenced his labors, and pursued them steadily and successfully to the close of his earthly career.

Before all else, he was systematic and constant in his habits of private devotion, seeking, in intimate and regular communion with God, the inspiration and strength that were essential to the successful prosecution of his duties in the study, the pulpit, and the congregation. In the social circle, and especially in the society of his ministerial brethren, he was always so full of pleasantry; the humorous story, the lively repartee, the sudden flash of wit, and the hearty laugh were so frequent with him, that persons who associate spiritual piety with habitual solemnity may have been under the impression that Dr. Murray was not a man of devotional habits. But those who knew him more intimately were well aware that all his springs were in God. He drew from the Fountain of living waters daily and hourly supplies. This was the secret of his success in the execution of all his plans of life. He began, continued, and ended them with prayer.

He devoted part of every day to the systematic study of the Holy Scriptures in the original tongues. As it was comparatively late in life that he entered upon a course of preparation for the ministry, it was always his fear that this early deficiency would make him liable to mistakes; and the diligence with which he pursued his studies in later years made up for the want of opportunities in youth. Without pretending to be a critical scholar, by his progressive and patient pursuit of learning through every succeeding year of his life, he became mighty in the Scriptures, and distinguished as a defender of the truth.

Justly regarding the preaching of the Gospel as the primary business of the Christian minister, he adopted the most systematic and careful habits of preparation for the pulpit. Early in the week selecting his themes of discourse, and diligently investigating them with the aid of a well-selected library, he wrote out his sermons with the same fullness, completeness, and finish that he would attempt if each discourse were to be given to the printer on Monday morning. A thousand and sixty-five manuscript sermons are the proofs that he rigidly pursued this practice through life, and that he began as he designed to continue. Of his success in this work we shall see the fruit hereafter.

The same thorough and methodical habits were carried out in the pastoral care of his widely-scattered flock. With a faculty of adapting himself to all the people, equally conversable with the learned and unlettered, the young and the old, a welcome visitor at all hours and on all occasions, he excelled in his power to interest and instruct the families of his charge when he went from house to house as their pastor. Always ready to answer every call upon him to visit the sick and afflicted, he set apart certain seasons of the year for family visitation, when he called at every house in its order, instructing the children in the Catechisms of the Church, conversing with each member on personal religion, and praying with the family. These rounds of duty he pursued year after year, with no lack of energy or fidelity, as he became more involved in the public business of the Church at large. Whatever distinction he afterward attained as an author, and however widely his influence was extended, his own vineyard at home was never suffered to lie waste, nor did he neglect, on any pretense, the minutest duty required of the pastor of a rural parish.

To perpetuate the record of interesting and important events in the history of his congregation, and doubtless also to confirm his own habit of systematic attention to the duties of his office, he procured a large folio blank volume, like a merchant's ledger, in which he and his successors in the ministry of this Church might inscribe such facts as should be had in remembrance in after time. He opens the book with this brief preface:

"As this book is simply designed to be a register of facts, circumstances, and incidents just as they occur, for the purpose of keeping up a continuous history of this ancient congregation, it is hoped that all succeeding *pastors* will continue this registry from the point where their predecessors leave off.

"This registry is to be kept by the pastors in a plain hand, and this book is to be carefully preserved in the ministerial library.

"The facts here to be inserted are not to be exclusively confined to the history of the congregation. Those of general interest may not be excluded whose insertion would be either useful or interesting to future generations."

This register might with great propriety be transferred entire into this volume, as a brief, comprehensive, and statistical record of the pastoral life of Dr. Murray in Elizabethtown. But it necessarily omits many facts respecting himself, which we are able to supply from contemporaneous testimony, and we shall use it as a guide in the pursuit of his history from this time onward. He was also in the habit of keeping "note-books," in which he entered with great minuteness striking incidents in pastoral experience, with reflections which they suggested. These sources furnish ample stores to illustrate his public and private life, and with them all at our hands, we begin to trace the progress of his labors among this people, and we will commence with the first service on the first Sabbath after his settlement. He writes:

"On Sabbath morning, as I was retiring from the church, after preaching my first sermon, I was arrested by a man in the belfry in a way peculiar and striking. His garb was plain—his form of the middle size—his countenance had a vague, but yet a pleased expression. Without waiting for an introduction, he came forward and earnestly extended his hand to grasp mine. The pressure was painfully cordial; and while one hand pressed mine, and the other his own bosom, he said, 'I thank you for that sermon; it has done my soul good.' His voice was indistinct and husky, and his appearance not prepossessing; but there was a heartfelt cordiality in his greeting which impressed me with his thorough sincerity. On the next Sabbath, and on the next, he met and greeted me in the same way. As he had reached midlife, I marked him as a peculiar character.

"I soon visited the Sabbath-school; and the very

first person that arrested my attention was this man, sitting in one of the classes surrounded by young boys, and reciting with them his lesson. My curiosity being excited, I went and stood by his class, and found him spelling his way through a verse of one of the Gospels, and obviously without understanding the sentiment which it taught. On inquiry, I learned that he was the son of Christian parents; that his mother, who was a woman of marked piety, had been deceased for years; and that, because of the great feebleness of his intellect, he could never be taught to read. As the name of the Savior was constantly on his lips, as his piety seemed to be of the most ardent character, my curiosity was greatly quickened to learn the details of his religious history, which is briefly as follows:

"As his mental debility early developed itself, his pious mother became the more solicitous that he should be taught of the Spirit of God. Daily did she pray with him; and, selecting the simplest truths of the Gospel, daily did she seek to impress them on his mind. But if his mind was feeble in sense, his heart was strong in depravity, and these means were ineffectual. After he reached mature years, there occurred a gentle refreshing of the Spirit. A meeting for conference with the serious and inquiring was appointed, and he was among those who attended. From week to week his seat was never vacant. When candidates for the communion of the Church were invited to meet with the Session, he was among those that attended. When asked if he hoped he was a Christian, his emphatic reply was, 'I hope I am.' About the doctrines of the

Church he knew absolutely nothing, and when questioned in reference to them he made no reply. He could give no reason for the hope which was in him. When asked why he hoped he was a Christian, laying his hands on his heart, he answered, 'I feel that I am, here.' With some fears, he was admitted to the Lord's Supper, and the whole of his subsequent life demonstrated that he was born from above.

"In the year that he made a profession of religion his mother died. Feeble as was his mind, the impressions which she made upon it were never erased. His very highest conception of heaven was that it was the place where his mother went to see Jesus, and his highest ecstasy was induced by the thought that when he died he would go to heaven to see Jesus and his own dear mother.

"There was but one thought which seemed to enter his soul, and that entirely occupied it. This was constantly obvious. Preach on what subject I might, nothing was understood, nothing felt, unless it was the love of Christ. For years, rarely a Sabbath passed away without his greeting me in the belfry; but nothing was said about the sermons unless they dwelt upon the love of Christ. Then his usual expression was, 'That sermon is good to my soul; it told me about the love of Christ.'

"He frequented prayer-meetings sustained by the young people and for their mutual benefit. One of his weaknesses was to make exhortations in these meetings, and until they became an annoyance. But he never succeeded in getting beyond one idea; and upon that—'the love of Christ, the love of Christ'—he would ring changes for fifteen minutes together. That one idea occupied and filled his whole soul. It was the one constant theme of his conversation every where. The only hymn that ever seemed to have impressed him, or whose singing he ever seemed to enjoy, was that called 'Loving Kindness.' However dull and uninterested he seemed to be in a prayer-meeting, the moment the first notes of the hymn

> "'Awake, my soul, to joyful lays,
> And sing thy great Redeemer's praise,'

fell upon his ear, his countenance brightened up, and his whole soul was in sympathy with the song of praise. And when in a social meeting which did not greatly interest him, his peculiar voice was often heard saying, 'Sing Loving Kindness.'

"His zeal, though not always according to knowledge, was of the purest character, and knew no relaxation. Was any person sick in his neighborhood? He was among the first to find it out and to visit the sick-bed. And feeble as was his comprehension of truth, and broken and repetitious as were his prayers, I have often heard the sick speak of the comforts which they received from his visits. He often preceded the minister and the elder—often conveyed to them the information of sickness and affliction, and solicited their attention; and often prayed and exhorted where their services might not be kindly received. The perfect confidence entertained by all in his sincerity induced them to forget his extreme feebleness, to overlook what would be regarded as intrusion in others, and to put the best possible construction on all that he did. I heard a profane scoffer say, after recovering from a sick-bed on which he had been often visited by this man, 'Well, if there is a Christian upon earth, it is Uncle Nehemiah.' More than once, when his minister was sick and in affliction, did he come and ask the privilege of praying with him and his family. Such was his life for years together.

"And in full keeping with his life was his death. During the protracted sickness which brought his days to their close, I frequently visited him. There was an unshaken confidence in Christ—a cloudless enjoyment of the light of his countenance; the love of Christ was his constant theme. The very last words that he ever uttered in my hearing were about going to heaven to see Jesus Christ and his dear mother.

"There are a few truths which this narrative of the life and death of 'Uncle Nehemiah,' as he was familiarly called, forcibly teach and illustrate.

"1. It teaches us how deep and durable aro the impressions which may be made on the minds of her children by a pious mother. Here was a mind, because of its feebleness, difficult of impression; yet a pious mother so impressed it, so engraved her own image upon it, as that nothing could erase her impressions or image. How deeply must it have been impressed with a sense of her piety, when its highest idea of heaven was that it was the home of Jesus and his mother! What might the sons of the Church be, if all their mothers were like the mother of Nehemiah!

"2. It illustrates the truth of the great doctrine of

regeneration. This consists, not in submission to the ordinances and forms of religion, but in being created anew in Christ Jesus. In his youth, Nehemiah was wayward, and, like persons of mental feebleness generally, greatly under the influence of passion. Submission to ordinances and forms could not correct this; the formal Jew, the Papist, the Mohammedan, can go out from their most solemn ritual observances as wicked and as turbulent as ever. Nothing but a change at the great spring of life can permanently change the life. There was no intellectual power here to moralize—no judgment to strengthen—no reason to wake up to its duty—no capacity to instruct. And yet there is a great, obvious, and permanent change. How account for it? In no way save on the ground of a change of heart by the power of the Holy Ghost.

"3. It also illustrates what is the great saving truth of the Gospel. It is a simple view of Christ as the Savior of sinners, and a simple resting upon Him as our Savior. Other truths are important—they are important to a well-balanced faith and life, but the great, essential truth is faith in Christ. 'He that believeth in the Lord Jesus Christ shall be saved.' This is so plain, that a wayfaring man, though a fool, need not err respecting it. When this faith is wrought in us by the Holy Ghost, then, whether we possess the expansive intellect of Paul, or the feeble one of Nehemiah, Christ is the polar star of the soul.

"Oh, if all the intellectual endowments of the professors of the religion of Christ were consecrated to His service, as was the one talent of this feeble child of heaven, how soon would the wilderness and solitary portions of earth rejoice, and the desert blossom as the rose! How hath God chosen the foolish things of the world to confound the mighty!"

"A few months afterward I spent one morning in my study in preparation for the Sabbath, with no excitement of thought or feeling on my mind or heart. The most important truths had lost all their connection, vitality, and freshness, and seemed to lie before me like a bundle of dry sticks; and to produce a thought seemed as impossible as to draw water from an empty well with a bucket without a bottom; and the morning was spent in the vain effort to arrange some ideas on a selected text worthy of being placed on paper. Mind and heart seemed as barren as the sands of the desert.

"The afternoon was given to preparation for the evening lecture, but there was no lifting up of that 'blackness of darkness.' It became denser with the approach of evening. The Bible was turned over from cover to cover, but not a text could be found from which a sentiment or meaning could be drawn adapted to the occasion or to the audience which usually met in the lecture-room. The very avenues to the throne of grace seemed barred up against all access to God, so that I could truly say, in the language of Job, 'Behold, I go forward, but He is not there; and backward, but I can not perceive Him; on the left hand, where He doth work, but I can not behold Him; He hideth himself on the right hand, that I can not see Him.' Of all the days of my life, that was the day in which I could say most emphatically, as to spiritual things, that 'a horror of great darkness' had fallen upon me. The sun, moon, and stars had all gone out in my spiritual sky.

"The bell rang for the evening service, and its first notes fell upon my ear as a death-knell. Slowly and sorrowfully I went to that meeting with my people, my mind a perfect blank, and without a text or subject on which to discourse to them. It was a charming night in October, when the moon was shining brightly, and, to my regret, I found the lecture-room unusually full. I resolved to change the service into a meeting for prayer, and commenced it with the hymn,

"'How long wilt Thou conceal Thy face?
My God, how long delay?
When shall I feel those heavenly rays
That chase my fears away?'

I called upon an aged elder to pray, who prayed with remarkable devotion of thought and with great unction. Because in consonance with my feelings, I read the 42d Psalm, and my heart could truly respond to the sentiment of the Psalmist: 'O my God, my soul is cast down within me . . . all Thy waves and Thy billows are gone over me.' But I was yet without a text or subject on which to address the people. I called upon another elder to pray, who in his supplications entered fully into the spirit of the psalm; and while he confessed and bewailed our spiritual desertion, most fervently implored that the Lord would again 'give us a little reviving in our bondage.' It was during this prayer, and, indeed, by the prayer itself, that the topic of 'declension in religion' was suggested as a theme for remark. Drawing largely on the existing feelings of my own mind and heart, without a text, and without knowing what I was going to say when I commenced, I entered upon the topic, and said something on the causes, marks, and remedy of spiritual declension. The following language of Cecil was brought seasonably to my remembrance, and was quoted for substance: 'A Christian may decline far in religion without being suspected; he may maintain appearances. Every thing to others seems to go on well. He suspects himself; for it requires great labor to maintain appearances, especially in a minister. Discerning hearers will, however, often detect such declensions. He talks over his old matters. He says his things, but in a cold and unfeeling manner. He is sound, indeed, in doctrine; perhaps more sound than before, for there is a great tendency to soundness of doctrine when appearances are to be kept up in a declining state of the heart. Where a man has real grace, it may be a part of a dispensation toward him to permit him to decline. He walked carelessly; he was left to decline, that he might be brought to feel his need of vigilance. If he is indulging a besetting sin, it may please God to expose him, that he may hang down his head as long as he lives. But this is pulling down in order to build up.'

"As I proceeded, the subject seemed to open up before me, but I felt that I condemned myself at every sentence; and at the conclusion of a disconnected, fragmentary address, I called upon another person to conclude the meeting with prayer. On the conclusion of the services, I returned to my study dejected, and oppressed with a sense of my being forsaken of God, and grieved that I had ever assumed the responsibilities of the ministry.

"On the afternoon of the next day, an intelligent and pious female called to see me. She alluded to the service of the previous evening as being one of the most solemn she had recently attended. I heard her with silence, and made no response. One of the men who prayed soon afterward called; he made the same remark. The solemnity of that evening's lecture was a topic of conversation for some days with those who were present. The prayer-meetings were soon more fully attended. There were searchings of heart among the people. Our public and social services increased in attendance and solemnity. The praying and the anxious ones, as they invariably do, multiplied simultaneously; and thus opened the first revival, in Elizabethtown, under my ministry, and which continued for upward of a year, gently distilling its blessed influences, multiplying the followers of Christ and their graces. Some of its subjects are now faithful and useful ministers of the Gospel. Never did I more fully realize the truth of the proverb, that 'the darkest hour is just before the light,' or of the saying of the Psalmist, 'He that goeth forth and weepeth, bearing precious seed, shall doubtless come again with rejoicing, bearing his sheaves with him.'

"This dark and yet joyful incident is here noted, not because of its peculiarity, as there are but few ministers who have not a similar experience, but for the purpose of bringing out a few of the principles of which it is an illustration.

"The hiding of God's countenance is not always desertion. We are backward in duty, we are negligent in its performance, we are self-confident, we are worldly. We keep not the Lord always before us. For these, or for some other sins, and for their reproof, God may withdraw the light of His countenance; and then we walk in darkness, as does the traveler at midnight, when the sun, moon, and stars have withdrawn their shining; and on all such occasions the people of the Lord should inquire, 'Why art thou cast down, O my soul, and why art thou disquieted within me? Hope thou in God; for I shall yet praise Him who is the health of my countenance and my God.' On due inquiry, we will find that no new thing has happened to us—that a part of God's dispensations to His people is to show them their weakness by leaving them to themselves, and to demonstrate their constant need of Him by leaving them occasionally to tread the weary ways of life by the light of the sparks of their own kindling. And we should be careful how we violate the principles thus taught and sung,

" 'Judge not the Lord by feeble sense,
But trust Him for His grace;
Behind a frowning providence
He hides a smiling face.'

"May it not be that ministers preach too little from their own varying experience? If truly good men, their experience, in its main outlines, is that of all the

Lord's people. Preaching on doctrines strengthens and enlightens—on duties, stimulates to action: exhortatory preaching may quicken the footsteps of the indolent; but when they preach from their own deep, heartfelt experience, and whether the string they touch gives forth notes of joy or sorrow, they find notes responsive in the hearts of many hearers. The seat of religion is the heart; and when they preach from an experience of the power of the grace of God in their own hearts, they are more likely to reach the hearts of their hearers.

"May it not be that the unvarying sameness which has obtained in our stated public and social services, detracts from their power and usefulness? How often do ministers hear least about the preparations on which they have bestowed most labor; and most about the warm, heartfelt addresses made to meet an emergency, and without any previous preparation! I have often observed that a warm, blundering man does far more for the world than a stately, correct, and frigid one. When we get into the habit of inquiring on all occasions, great and small, as to proprieties and expediencies, life is too often spent to little purpose. Nature craves for variety; and ecclesiology would reduce every thing to an unvarying form in public and social worship. Such forms of worship are as unnatural as they are injurious. Sermons occasionally without texts—sermons sometimes without music or prayers—and prayers and singing sometimes without sermons, would break in upon the monotony which has almost universally obtained, and would, at least, so far lead to awaken attention to the truth of God. We would not imitate the example of the eccentric preacher, who, on seeing his hearers sleeping around him, cried out 'Fire! Fire!' and when the aroused people asked 'where? where?' replied, 'for sleeping souls in hell;' but we would recommend a studied effort to introduce variety into all the services of God, for the sake of our common humanity, and because of the good which may result."

This revival was in the winter and spring of 1834, and resulted in the addition of more than sixty persons to the communion of the Church; and the sweet influence of the work, the pastor records, was felt through the whole year.

An incident in the month of November, 1833, the year of his settlement, while pursuing his first regular pastoral visitation, he enters afterward in these words:

"On a damp and chilly day, I went forth on a pastoral visitation among my people. As the day was drawing toward its close, I entered a farm-house wearing externally and internally an air of comfort. Every thing was in pleasant preparation for my reception. On either side of a glowing fire sat the father and mother of the household, now well advanced in years; and ranged between them were the other members of the family, the youngest child, then a lad of about fifteen years, holding his catechism in his hand. He could repeat it from beginning to end, showing that, as to the theory of religion, his education was not neglected. I went round the family group conversing with each as to their personal interest in the work of

Christ for the salvation of men. Every thing was free, social, and pleasant; but while with an intelligent understanding of the plan of salvation, and while freely admitting that there was no way for them to heaven but through faith in Jesus Christ, I found, to my great grief, that parents and children were aliens from the commonwealth of Israel. After giving to each a word of instruction adapted to their circumstances, and to the views expressed by them in conversation, we bowed together before the high and lofty One; and having implored for them all temporal and spiritual good, I bade them farewell.

"The father, whose natural strength many years had not impaired, and whose kind and gentle manners made him a favorite among his neighbors, followed me to the door, and, closing it after him, stopped me on the porch. His countenance gave strong indications that there was something pressing upon his soul which he wished to communicate. Hoping that the Holy Spirit had blessed my visit to his conviction, I waited with anxiety to hear what he had to say. After a considerable pause, taking me by the hand, he thus addressed me:

"'I thank you for this visit; although the first you have made us, I hope it will not be the last. I thank you for all the advice you have given us; and as you have but just commenced your labors among us as a minister, I wish to give you a word of advice, based on my own experience. Let us old people alone, for we are hopeless subjects, and devote your labors to the youth of your flock. Forty years ago, when Mr. Austin was our pastor, I was greatly anxious about my soul. Many were then converted, but I was not one of them. During the ministry of Mr. M'Dowell I was often greatly anxious about my soul—I went to the conference-meeting—many were converted in the successive revivals enjoyed, but I was not one of them. And now, for years that are passed, I have not had a single feeling on the subject. I know that I am a lost sinner—I know that I can be saved only through Jesus Christ—I feel persuaded that when I die I shall go to hell forever—I believe all you preach—I believe all you have said to me and my family, but I feel it no more than if I were a block of marble; and I expect to live and die just as I am; so that my advice to you is to leave us old people to ourselves and our sins, for you can not do us much good, and devote yourself to the work of seeking the conversion of the young.'

"And all this, and more, was said with a kind and pleasant bearing, which forbade every thing like suspicion of his motives; and yet with a cool deliberateness which made me feel that the man was a mystery. After placing before him the fullness of the redemption which is in Christ Jesus, we parted.

"I remembered the incident, and watched the progress of this man. His seat was rarely vacant in the sanctuary. To hear the Word preached, he breasted many a storm which kept the professor of religion at home. I made him other visits; and while he admitted all I said, and freely confessed his lost state, I never witnessed in him the slightest ruffle of religious emotion. He was a true prophet of his own fate. He lived as he predicted, and so he died. And we laid him down in a hopeless grave, after having spent his threescore years and ten without repentance toward God, or faith in our Lord Jesus Christ, in the midst of a congregation over which God has often made windows in heaven."

CHAPTER XIII.

The Faithful Pastor.—Testimony by the Rev. David Magie, D.D., Pastor of the Second Church.—The Number and Nature of Dr. Murray's Labors.—Visits to the Sick and Afflicted.—Public Usefulness.—Untiring Industry and Energy.

It occurred to me, while reviewing the pastoral life of Dr. Murray, that no one could give a more accurate and reliable view of his habits and success than the venerable and beloved man who had been pastor in the same town and by his side during the whole of his residence in Elizabeth. For more than a quarter of a century, Dr. Magie had been associated with Dr. Murray in kindred and common labors. Dr. Magie was pastor of the Second Church when Dr. Murray was called to the First. Their flocks were side by side, and mingled during the week, and often fed in the same pastures and by the same waters. It was a delicate matter to ask the testimony of one so related to Dr. Murray so long, but the record will be read with admiration of the character it portrays, and of him who delights to bear such testimony to the fidelity and success of his neighbor in the ministry. Dr. Magie writes:

"You ask me for some memorial of Dr. Murray as a pastor, and I cheerfully comply with your request.

"More than twenty-seven years of labor side by side in the same field, with our congregations intermingled, not in the city merely, but in every surrounding neighborhood, gave me the fullest opportunity of learning all his plans, and marking his going out and coming in from the beginning to the end of his ministry here. No one could know him better as a shepherd among his flock, and I am ready to testify that he discharged his duty well and faithfully.

"The people committed to his care were numerous, and they had been accustomed to see their minister frequently, as well at the fireside as in the pulpit. Long had it been their habit to look upon the man who taught them out of God's law on the Sabbath as a friend to whom they might have ready access, and who would be a guide and counselor in the various scenes of daily religious life. His predecessor, the Rev. Dr. John M'Dowell, still living happily and usefully at the age of upward of fourscore, was always regarded as a model pastor, familiar with the families of his charge, catechising the children, and conversing with individuals of all classes of society on the subject of their personal relations to God and preparation for eternity; and Dr. Murray nobly carried on the same blessed work. The period of their labor here was of about the same length, and very much the same indomitable energy and perseverance characterized them both. If the two men differed in many respects, and differ they unquestionably did, no one could say that the service, taken as a whole, fell off in the hands of the latter. The Church, and congregation too, expected a great deal from their pastor, and seldom had they reason to feel disappointed.

"Besides a regular weekly lecture, for which he prepared as punctually as for the claims of the Sabbath, he delighted to be present in the more retired praying circle, and often was he found mingling his sympathies and tears with the afflicted. So naturally did he care for the state of his people as to rejoice with those that rejoiced, and weep with those that wept. Most readily did he enter the humblest abode, to carry the consolations of the Gospel to the bedside of the sick, and direct the thoughts of the dying to Him who is the resurrection and the life. It was not difficult for him to accommodate himself to such scenes of sadness and sorrow as frequently meet the eye of the faithful pastor; and I have no doubt that some of the sweetest moments he ever spent on earth were those in which he was occupied in speaking to departing saints of another country, which is a heavenly. No one can estimate the amount of work which he thus performed in season and out of season, while watching for more than a quarter of a century over a Church of between five and six hundred members, and a congregation of upward of three hundred families. Few men could have done so much, or done it so well. Had he not been blessed with a remarkable love for his work and a naturally robust constitution, he never could have borne the burdens so long and with such unabated exhilaration of spirits. Discouragement is a feeling to which he never seemed to give place—no, not for an hour.

"It is difficult to say whether he excelled more at home or abroad; in the routine of weekly and daily duty among his own people, or serving the cause of truth in a sphere of greater publicity and observation. Multitudes knew him as an earnest, impressive speaker, bringing out the great truths of the Gospel in his own nervous and pointed style, and invited him here and there to deliver addresses and preach ordination and installation sermons. Often was he listened to with delight as he stood on the platform, and, with a happy admixture of Irish wit and pleasant seriousness, advocated the claims of piety and benevolence. And the letters which he sent out by scores and hundreds through the periodical press were read with eagerness far and wide. His fellow-citizens, too, always found him prompt to take part in plans for advancing the moral, educational, and industrial interests of the place where his lot was cast. These things seemed enough to fill the heart and hands of an ordinary man, had he never published a book, made a visit of condolence to the house of mourning, or superintended the concerns of a parish.

"If it be asked how he accomplished so much, and did it so thoroughly, the answer is found in his untiring industry and energy. To a resoluteness of will, never baffled or turned aside by ordinary obstacles, an admirably adjusted physical frame, a large flow of the most genial feeling, deep and earnest conviction of whatever was true and good, and the constant presence under his own roof of one ready to cheer him on in his noble work, he added a perseverance which never gave way to discouragement. His motto seemed to be, Labor here, Rest hereafter. He made full proof of the Christian ministry, giving himself to it year in and year out, as if he could never sufficiently magnify his office. I have seen many active, diligent men, but I have never seen one in any walk of life who excelled Dr. Murray. Scarcely was he through one undertaking before he entered upon another. The text for the next Sabbath morning was often chosen after the close of a third service on the same Sabbath evening. Instead of letting his work drive him, producing confusion, hurry, and disorder, he always drove his work, and thus was able to see his way, and have his mind clear and tranquil. His example in this respect is a legacy of untold value. Were all who deem themselves called to serve God in the Gospel of His Son to make equally full proof of their ministry, the happy effect would appear in the strength and permanence of the ties which bind pastor and flock together.

"To those who knew him at all, it is superfluous to remark that there was nothing of the recluse in his nature; nor was he insensible to the claims of social life. Seldom did he find himself so pressed with business that he could not spare half an hour for a friend, or give an evening to a pleasant gathering of neighbors, or take a few days for recreation at a spring side or on a mountain top. In his hands, the bow carried the arrow to its mark all the better for being occasionally unbent. No ability which he possessed of making an impression by unstudied efforts ever led him to dispense, whenever it was practicable, with careful previous preparation. If ever his reproofs took on them the form of cutting, biting sarcasm, as withering as an autumnal frost, it was when compelled to listen to the empty, jejune deliverances of preachers who think themselves smart enough to bring something out when nothing has been put in.

"Much of his power to gain the affections of his people so fully, and hold them so long, consisted no doubt in the cheerful smile he wore, and the friendly greeting he gave, meet them when and where he might. His genial spirit was delightfully contagious. It was difficult to be gloomy or downcast in his presence. Few men are able, in an equal degree, to make themselves agreeable to all classes, old and young, rich and poor, educated and uneducated. There was a certain something about him, in the twinkle of his eye, the shake of his head, and the tones of his voice, which could scarcely be resisted. If severity seemed necessary, nobody could be more severe; or if blandness and condescension would do better, they were always at hand. When he undertook to carry a point, few had tact or boldness enough to interpose any effectual resistance. Head of the congregation he felt that he ought to be, and would be, and, as such, he expected to be treated with all proper tokens of deference and respect, every where and at all times. There are prerogatives of office and position which he would never relinquish. Nobody knew better than he how to pour contempt upon religious nostrums of every sort, or send the pseudo-reformer from the door in disgrace. Yet it is but justice to add, he had the wisdom to reach and maintain this eminence in a way which generally left well-meaning people entirely satisfied with themselves. They felt that their pastor was a man of talent and great force of character, and it was easy for them to yield to his sway.

"No wonder that great lamentation was made over him when he so suddenly and unexpectedly was taken away. No one seemed to realize that the hale, firm-stepping Dr. Murray was mortal. That he should bury others was expected, but that they should bury him was unthought of. The old men looked back, with mingled emotions of joy and sorrow, to the time when they summoned him from his remote inland charge to take the oversight of them in the Lord; the middle-aged, only a little behind him in the race of life, were proud of the position he held in the Church, and sad that they now should see his face no more; while the young, whom he had baptized, dandled on his knees, and led forward year by year with scarcely less than a father's care, felt that they had lost a friend, in whose animating and guiding voice they had learned to trust with unshaken confidence.

"The day that witnessed the burial of such a pastor, combining so many excellences of head and heart, and so identified with his people in every thing excellent, and lovely, and of good report, can not soon be forgotten."

It has been often said, if there was any one trait of ministerial character in which Dr. Murray excelled, it was his deep and tender appreciation of the trials of his people. The intemperate husband, the erring child, were watched over and often restored to the domestic circle. In his private portfolio were found many pledges solemnly made in his study, and signed after evidence of penitence and prayer by persons, some of whom were, through his instrumentality, restored to usefulness and respectability. In the chamber of sickness, by the bed of death, he was at home. The hearts of all opened to him as he entered with noiseless tread, and in sweet, gentle tones addressed them on the love of Christ. His visits were brief but frequent, and in cases of long-protracted illness looked for as regularly as were those of the physician. A letter from the Rev. Benjamin Cory, whose family, while members of Dr. Murray's congregation, were deeply afflicted, is but one of the many expressions of grateful remembrance made to his services in seasons of sorrow and bereavement:

"Elizabeth, January 28th, 1862.

"MY DEAR MRS. MURRAY,—As a testimony of my ever-affectionate remembrance of your lamented husband, you will allow me to hand you this brief sketch of what I knew him to be as a visitor at the habitations of affliction and mourning.

"As my own family has been visited once, twice, yea, thrice, by painful bereavements, and as on each of those occasions Dr. Murray was with us and officiated, I feel that I can speak from experience upon this subject. Never shall we forget his kind attentions, his warm sympathy, his earnest prayers, his precious words of consolation in our behalf during those trying seasons of our adversity. He was, indeed, all that we could desire in a Christian pastor.

"Nor are we alone in such testimony. Others, I find, who have been in similar circumstances, evidence to the same thing. Wherever I visit among the people whom he served for so many years in the labors of the Gospel, I find he has left his impress upon them in this particular; nor will it be easy to erase it. Frequently have I heard mourners express themselves in this way: 'Oh how good Dr. Murray was in seasons of affliction!' 'how attentive he was to the sick!' 'how excellent he always was on funeral occasions!'

"In this *particular feature* of pastoral services Dr. Murray was certainly pre-eminent. While he meant to overlook none of the families of his flock, he was specially attentive to *mourning households*. There was great faithfulness, great painstaking in his endeavors to serve *such;* and lest, through ignorance of their affliction, he might fail to visit them at the time, he would urge his people not to hesitate to send for him, or inform him in some way of the fact.

"He had often been called to drink of the cup of sorrow himself, and hence he well knew how to comfort others with the comforts with which he himself was comforted of God. As he was a 'Son of Thunder' whenever the occasion called for it, so he was a 'Son of Consolation' to the mourning. He was often tender to weeping; he seemed to be afflicted in the affliction of those who were called to drink of the cup of suffering and sorrow. As a pastor, in respect to tenderness and sympathy in behalf of the afflicted, I can with propriety say that Dr. Murray left no superior, and but few equals behind him."

CHAPTER XIV.

In the Presbytery.—The Synod.—The General Assembly.—Sketch of Dr. Murray in Ecclesiastical Life, by Rev. S. S. Sheddan, of Rahway, N. J., a co-Presbyter, in a Letter to the Author.

THE Rev. Mr. Sheddan, of Rahway, the town adjoining Elizabeth, writes in such words as these:

"REVEREND AND DEAR BROTHER,—In sketching any of Dr. Murray's characteristics, you will appreciate the remark that he owed his commanding position to no one trait of character nor power of mind. Nature had not been sparing in her mental endowments, and they were well-adjusted; but it was no distorted faculty, but a happy combination of all, that made him a man of mark.

"Because of this native equipoise of mind, and a rule of his life that 'what was worth doing was worth doing well,' it were difficult to say what was his *forte*.

"His energy, his large-heartedness, and his systematic working, developed with an uncommon harmony all his powers, and made him great. He was equally the preacher and the pastor, the polemic and the presbyter. His greatest admirers may admit that in each of these departments he had his equals; but all of these, to the same degree blending with high social qualities, and the activities prompted by a generous heart, have been rarely so combined in the same person.

"He took high position in all these varied positions,

because his energy, his systematic arrangement, and diligence accompanied him in every duty. Those traits of nature and habits of life had much to do in making him a noted, and, in some respects, a model presbyter.

"Dr. Murray leaves a record, as to punctual attendance upon our ecclesiastical courts, that is honoring to him, and is a worthy example to others. His connection was always with the New Jersey Synod. Installed as pastor of the churches of Wilkesbarre and Kingston in November, 1829, he first appeared in Synod in 1830 as a member of the Presbytery of Susquehanna. His pastoral relation to those churches was dissolved June 26th, 1833, and on June 23d he was received by the Presbytery of Elizabethtown, and installed pastor of the First Church of Elizabeth.

"His synodical life was thirty years. During his connection with Synod, from the year 1830 to 1860, both included, he was not once absent from the sessions of that body; whether those sessions were held in West Jersey or in the mountains of Pennsylvania, he was always present. Except our worthy stated clerk, Rev. R. K. Rodgers, D.D., Dr. Murray was the only man, according to our records, of whom it could be said that during that generation of years he was not once absent from Synod. The records give the farther good testimony that but twice did he appear late, and that he always remained until the sessions were closed.

"The records of Presbytery will equally testify to his promptness and punctuality, he being only absent when visiting Europe, and from the fall meeting of 1860 because of indisposition. This remarkable faithfulness is almost as marked in the called meetings of Presbytery, when he might often have pleaded the business is a mere formality, and his many other duties were pressing.

"The advice he gave to another was undoubtedly his own rule: 'Make it a matter of conscience to attend the meetings of Presbytery and Synod.' He either shaped or sacrificed other duties and pleasures that he might be faithful to the ecclesiastical courts, there at the opening and at the close of the sessions. In this respect our Brother Murray was a model.

"With him it was not a stern duty; he loved the meetings of his brethren. He enjoyed much both the fraternal and religious character of our Church courts.

"He may have been drawn to like-minded brethren, but he had a cordial greeting for all. As his years were putting him among the fathers, it seemed more his pleasure to give every one the fraternal grasp, and it was doubtful if any left Presbytery saying 'Dr. Murray did not speak to me:' a little act of kindness, but more encouraging to the younger members than the fathers think. His was a cordial greeting, not the chilling two fingers and a heartless word, while the eye looked for another. It was the warm greeting of his heart, which did him good and others felt. And many a young man in the ministry was encouraged by his hearty inquiries and words of cheer.

"Even the casual observer must have remarked

with what interest he heard each brother speak of the state of religion in his charge. He so identified himself with the churches of Presbytery and with his brethren, that I can recall in my ministerial life none more intently hearing the free conversation upon the state of religion than he was; and none more constant upon the devotional exercises, and by his exhortations and adapted prayers adding greatly to their interest. At such times all liked to hear him speak and have him pray.

"Dr. Murray was truly a working presbyter. His nature and his habits made him a stranger to the art of saving himself. In all ecclesiastical duties he very implicitly obeyed his brethren in the Lord. His early life taught him to think and act for himself, and gave him a maturity that fitted him for an early prominence among his brethren. His name soon holds the place of an honored and efficient member of our Church courts. With his willing spirit, there was a promptness, and diligence, and a power to perform, that gave him a frequent place in important committees, in preaching before Presbytery, and in installation services. The frequency of these things is a memorial of his fitness, and how acceptable he was to his brethren and the churches. The frequent question, so often asked, 'Can there be no installation without Dr. Murray?' as often attested his popularity. So frequently was he called, far and near, to the dedication of churches, as to suggest the contrast, the bottles of papal chrism he broke, and the consecrations he performed.

"He rarely excused himself from duties assigned him by Presbytery because overtasked. If he excused himself, it was not so much for saving self as to preserve the parity of the ministry, or to draw out and honor others.

"When he had been a few years in Synod he was elected moderator; and in 1849, the twentieth year of his ministry, he was chosen moderator of the General Assembly.

"As an ecclesiastical jurist, others may have equaled or surpassed Dr. Murray. His feelings were too generous, and his views too comprehensive, to allow him to be a stickler for the mere letter of the law, or to be an adept in knotty points. He studied more the spirit than the letter of the law; and he weighed points more by the question of right than to make a thing right by skillful construction or collocation of chapters and sections. He belonged to the court of equity rather than of technicalities.

"With his natural warm-heartedness there must be strong sympathies; yet personal sympathy would not prevail over a sense of right. Two important cases fell under my notice, where I know intimate friendships and personal endearments were on the side he felt constrained as a presbyter to oppose.

"Young ministers, licentiates, and candidates have lost a friend. The heart and position of Dr. Murray made him important to such. Our young men turned to him for advice as to location and in the straits of their novitiate. His personal intercourse and correspondence with such were cheerful and prompt, although so extensive as to draw heavily upon his time. He was truly a friend to the young ministry. He sought out and encouraged candidates; and many sought an introduction to Presbytery through him.

"His early self-reliance, his brevity, and sometimes curtness of speech, his ready repartee, and the humor of his nativity, may have led some to undervalue his comity as a presbyter. Whatever, at times, may have been the abruptness, or even severity of his remarks, all who knew him well will testify that it was only in the form, and not in the spirit. To what he thought littleness or wrong he might utter a telling rebuke, followed as quickly by his cordial sympathies to the hurt, or confessing one. Those who knew him only in the ecclesiastical forum might not do justice to his heart. His succinct phrases, his humor, his quick reply, with illustration by anecdotes, might fall as wounding arrows, but they never came from a poisoned quiver. In no place did his curtness of speech and uncomfortable anecdotes so prevail as in debate. This was but an element showing his nativity—one strongly inherent, and which he used chiefly in playfulness, and which in later years was greatly subdued.

"None more kindly felt for his brethren than he. As a young man he revered the aged, and as a father he was kind to the young men. Yet it was so natural in him, that it was an effort to withhold the repartee. An example may show this, and the independent thinking of his younger days. He brought some measure before Presbytery which a father of patriarchal name opposed, with a reflection upon youth;

at once young Murray replied: 'No more of that; I am young, but not willing to be taken to the bosom of Father Abraham!'

"Such quick and apt responses were indigenous; not of the corrupt heart, but of the mental structure. They were Murrayisms; but, so far as they were severe, they were not the issues of the heart. I refer to these things to correct misapprehensions that may exist with some who only knew him in the forensic phase of character. This playful severity of debate was no more the heart of our dear brother than a ripple made by the breeze is the deep, pure water beneath.

"Dr. Murray was a Presbyterian, but no bigot. He was an earnest lover of the order and doctrine of our Church; tenacious of the weightier matters, but not a stickler on minor points. Nine years of intimate acquaintance authorize the remark that he was tolerant to those who honestly and fraternally differed, but intolerant to the exclusive. He loved his own denominational home, and held large fellowship with those of different name; but he had no patience with that spirit that ignored all Church existence but its own. For such he had no gentle phrases, and this some tortured into bigotry. And it had its influence until corrected by closer acquaintance.

"He heartily bid God-speed to every man who preached Christ, and cheerfully hailed such as co-laborers. That largely fraternal spirit became more marked with his years, and was perfectly consistent with the remark he made in substance to me in his study: 'With growing years, experience, and observation, I admire and love, more and more, our system of doctrine and form of government.'

"The Presbytery has lost a most efficient and genial member. For nearly thirty years in the Elizabethtown Presbytery; his seat rarely vacant; honored and loved by his brethren; none more quick to mingle his sympathies with a tried brother; none more quick to enter into the personal and pastoral joys of another.

"Our ecclesiastical records are his witnesses that he was a faithful and working presbyter; and those pages confirm the living record upon our hearts how acceptable he was as a leader in our devotions. Sad thought: we shall see him and hear him no more!

"For some time past we marked in Presbytery his growing spirituality, and felt that he gave us an increased stimulus in our devotional exercises and pastoral duties. He was ripening then, but our eyes were holden that we did not see it. He knew it not, but he worked as one whose time was short, and with his increased diligence there was a corresponding gentleness of spirit and heart-desire to do good.

"His closing presbyterial life leaves endearing recollections as we mourn, that in our body and in his wide sphere his work is done.

"No one can wear his mantle; we must divide his duties. In that his race is run we mourn our loss, but rejoice that he has received his crown of life.

"His life and influence will be with us as hallowed and stimulating memories, and his death will remind us, Work 'while it is day,' so that when 'the night cometh,' we may each say, 'My work is done.'"

CHAPTER XV.

Dr. Murray as an Author.—Early Efforts.—At Wilkesbarre.—Origin of the Kirwan Letters.—Sketch of Bishop Hughes.—Systematic Preparation for the Discussion.—Effect of it.—Popularity of the Letters.—Calls for more.—Other Series.—Oral Discussion.

THE first essay of Dr. Murray to write for the press, of which we have any knowledge, was made while he was a student in college. That his early employment in a printing-office had directed his attention to the field of authorship, and stimulated him to efforts in that line of distinction and usefulness, there can be little doubt. In that business he also acquired those habits of precision and method that marked his labors in future years.

Among his manuscripts we find copies of papers prepared while in college for the press, some of which we know were published, and others were, perhaps, never sent away for that purpose. It is certainly remarkable that a youth who had devoted less than a year to studies in preparation for college, having had but common education in boyhood, should so soon enter the lists as a writer for the press, and especially as a controversial writer. The first essay that we find as coming from his pen, and all the early pieces that he has left among his old manuscripts, are tinged with the caustic wit and satire, as well as the genial humor and sparkling vivacity, that grew with his growth, till they became the features of his composition which made him so distinguished among the religious authors of his age.

While he was settled at Wilkesbarre he wrote a series of articles on the measures and doctrines of the Methodists in the Valley of Wyoming. These were published in the monthly magazine, edited by the Rev. Dr. Green, in Philadelphia, and called the Christian Advocate. This periodical was a power in its day. Devoted primarily to the defense of the Calvinistic doctrine and the promotion of evangelical truth, it was supported by the best productions of the best minds in the Presbyterian Church, and it made its mark. The appearance in this periodical of the articles written by Mr. Murray to which we refer, immediately arrested the attention of leading men in the Methodist Church. A deputation waited upon Dr. Green, the editor, and demanded the name of the author. This the venerable editor declined to give, but he assured the gentlemen that his confidence in the correctness of all the facts alleged was such that he would assume the responsibility of the statements as his own, and they could deal with him and them accordingly. He then wrote to Mr. Murray to fortify himself with the most abundant proof of every thing he had or should set forth, and the series was continued with great vigor and effect.

Beyond occasional articles in the newspapers, secular and religious, we have no evidence that he made any contributions to the press until the appearance of his letters to Bishop Hughes. He had now been settled in Elizabethtown fourteen years, and had reached the forty-seventh year of his age. In the maturity of his powers, and firmly established in his charge, he looked back with painful solicitude upon the Church of his fathers and his youth, and his soul yearned, as did the soul of the apostle for his brethren, his kinsmen according to the flesh, who were yet under the bondage of Rome. With an earnestness of purpose and intensity of zeal that few can understand and appreciate, he resolved to make one effort to open the eyes of his countrymen and his former brethren to the danger of the errors by which they were led captive, and, with God's good help, to deliver them. We have the means of knowing that he set himself at this work with prayerful deliberation, and pursued it through months and years of most laborious study. Before putting pen to paper, he unfolded to me the plan and purpose of his work, and the feelings with which he was impelled to its execution. I urged him to go forward, aided him in finding the books that he needed to substantiate his positions, and begged him not to allow any thing to divert him from the holy purpose he had formed.

It was soon determined that his work should take the form of a series of articles in the New York Observer, and for the purpose of more immediately securing attention, and giving them the additional zest of personal correspondence, that they should be addressed as letters to the Rt. Rev. John Hughes, D.D., Bishop of New York. His reasons for selecting this prelate as his correspondent are assigned in the first letter, which opens in these words:

"MY DEAR SIR,—Although an entire stranger to you, I have felt for many years greatly interested in your history and doings, and for the following reasons:

"You are the chief pastor of a very important portion of the Roman Catholic Church in this country, and your ecclesiastical position makes you emphatically a public man. If a bishop in Mexico or Missouri, like many mitred priests, you might live unknown to fame; but as the papal bishop of the commercial metropolis of the Western World, and of the most populous and wealthy diocese of your Church in the United States, this could not be expected. Position, you know, has much to do with our public character. It sometimes gives, even to weak and bad men, an importance out of all proportion to their merits.

"But, in addition to your position, which is one of high influence, you possess the requisite qualifications to fill it. This is confessed by your most ardent opponents. By your genius, tact, and eloquence — by your sleepless devotion to the duties of your calling, you have obtained a position in the very first rank of the ecclesiastics of your Church; and, without saying very much, this is saying considerable.

"Besides, at whatever odds, you have fought like a man with all your opponents. In controversies, religious and political, you have not shunned the hall of debate, nor discussion through the press. You have taken your positions adroitly, and you have defended them with remarkable skill; and even when convinced of the utter fallacy of your positions and defenses, I have yet sympathized with your manly firmness. It is in human nature to respect the man that, with an earnest soul, contends for what he esteems right; and I must confess that, as to some things, when the public voice was against you, your course met with my approbation.

"Besides, if public rumor is worthy of belief, you have raised yourself into your present position by the force of your talents and character, from a social position comparatively humble. To me this is not the least of the reasons why I have felt interested in your career. The *men* of our race have been what is commonly called self-made men. The 'Heroes in History' have been nearly all such. It requires high attributes, both of mind and soul, to rise above the disadvantages of family and fortune, and to take precedence of those who would fain believe that birth and wealth give a patent-right to the high places of influence. Your past history, unless I misunderstand it, must have had a liberalizing influence upon you. You must look at things on a larger and wider scale, and through a clearer medium, than if you had been cradled in crimson and educated in a convent. You know the distinction between prejudice and principle — between what is entitled to belief and what we have been educated to believe—between what is truly reasonable and what is ecclesiastically so; and I therefore address myself to you with a confidence far stronger, that what I shall say kindly and truly will be kindly and truly weighed, than if I addressed myself to a priest from Maynooth or Saint Omer, educated merely in the literature of legends and liturgies, and whose mind only possessed what was distilled into it from others. About such stupid, sluggish minds you must, by this time, know something. I shall address you not merely as a priest or bishop, but as a high-minded and well-educated gentleman.

"Permit me to say that there is yet another reason why I have felt interested in your career. You were born in Ireland—that land of noble spirits and of warm hearts—that sweetest isle of the ocean; and so was I. We are natives of the same soil; and although in principle, by education, and in all my feelings thoroughly American, yet I take a great pride in the high achievements of native Irishmen. America has had its Montgomeries, its Clintons, its Emmetts, its Porters, its Brackenridges, from Ireland. Its sons have adorned the bar, the bench, the pulpit, the army, the navy, the Legislatures, the Congress of these United States. That there are multitudes from Ireland who are no loss to their own country, nor any advantage to this, can not be denied. The evidence is every where present in the ignorance, the squalid poverty of its immigrants. The reasons for this I may examine hereafter. But yet we have many fine illustrations of Irish genius, character, and valor all along our history; and I have regarded yourself as one of them, so far forth as a pushing force of character is concerned, and I have often pointed you out as an illustration of the respectability which Irish character is capable of attaining when relieved from the burdens that oppress and debase it. Hence I have regarded as your eulogy the sneers of those who have addressed you as 'John

Hughes, the gardener.' Such taunts come not from true men."

There are few men now living who exert a more extended or powerful influence than Archbishop Hughes; few who, in a worldly estimate of success, have achieved more than he has done. He is known from Maine to Texas, and from the Atlantic to the Pacific, as the highest dignitary of the Roman Catholic Church on the continent, and as one who by talent, energy, and devotedness is well entitled to the eminent rank which he holds. What Cardinal Wiseman is in England, that Archbishop Hughes is in this country: the leading mind of his Church, the most obnoxious to his opponents, the most idolized by his admirers.

The position which he occupies is in itself a commanding one. That alone would give the one who held it a powerful influence over the minds of millions of his fellow-countrymen. Fill it with a graven image possessed of the mechanical facility for signing documents, and it would still be far from insignificant. But Archbishop Hughes is not the puppet of ecclesiastical machinery. The position he holds does not dignify him more than he dignifies the position. He has risen to it by his own energies. He has fairly earned his promotion by untiring industry and sagacious and successful effort.

Four years before Nicholas Murray, and in the same island, John Hughes was born, and at the present time is 63 years of age. His father is said to have been (like Dr. Murray's) a respectable farmer of moderate means, who emigrated to this country before his son had reached his twentieth year. The first occupation of the latter, after his arrival in this country, was that of gardener. But the zeal of the student was stronger than the taste of the florist, and the young Irishman, devoting his spare time to books, seized the first moment of release from his engagements, and entered the Theological Seminary of Mount St. Mary's, Emmettsburg, Md., where he remained for several years. In 1825 he was ordained priest, and commenced his public career in Philadelphia.

It was not long before he felt himself impelled to come forward as a champion of his Church. His opponent, Rev. John Breckinridge, was a foeman worthy of his steel. The question at issue was substantially, Is Protestantism Christianity? In 1834 he was again engaged in public controversy, maintaining against the same opponent, who challenged the discussion, that the Roman Catholic Church, in principles and doctrines, is not inimical to civil or religious liberty.

The success with which the young ecclesiastic was reported to have conducted the controversy drew public attention to him. In 1837, after five years' labor in connection with St. John's Church, which he had gathered in Philadelphia, he was appointed coadjutor of Bishop Dubois, of New York, and early in the following year was ordained to the episcopate in this city, which has since been his place of residence. The death of Bishop Dubois soon opened to him the succession to the most important see in this country, and, after twelve years of energetic and successful administration of the affairs of his diocese, New York was made an archiepiscopal see, and, at the hands of the Pope, the occupant of it received the *pallium* of his rank.

For the last twenty-three years there has been a steady and even rapid growth of that portion of the Church which has been under the authority of this distinguished prelate. The monuments of his success are too numerous to be specified. Our public-school system was obnoxious to him. It tended to pervert the faith of his Roman Catholic adherents. He did not hesitate to enter the political arena in order to break it down, or to modify it to suit his designs. The property of the churches of his diocese was held by trustees. It was encumbered by mortgages, and, as he declared, altogether mismanaged. He determined, in accordance with the theory of his Church, that it should be vested in himself as diocesan. A bitter controversy subsequently sprang up, and the question was carried into the state Legislature. The archbishop was charged with holding in his hands $5,000,000 of Church property in the city of New York.

But, with a measurable degree of success, the archbishop carried his point. He set himself to the task of clearing the churches of debt, and of buying or building more. Whenever a church edifice of another denomination was to be sold, it was well understood that Archbishop Hughes was in the field. Church after church sprang up under his fostering care. Nor did he neglect the cause of learning or of the priesthood. St. John's College was established at Fordham, with its substantial stone buildings and its beautiful grounds. The Lorillard estate was purchased, and the convent of the "Ladies of the Sacred Heart" was planted on the commanding grounds in the vicinity of Washington Heights. St. John's School at Manhattanville was likewise established; and the Ursuline Convent at Melrose, and another female seminary, possessed of the Forest estate on the Hudson, were added to the training institutions of the Church.

Meanwhile, anxious to secure the most efficient co-operation, and well aware of Jesuit tact and energy, the sagacious prelate determined to introduce the obnoxious order into his diocese. Since 1846 he has availed himself of their assistance. The history of his diocese for the last quarter of a century will be regarded by his admirers as his highest encomium. He found it neglected, dilapidated, and impoverished. He has raised it to a condition of order, prosperity, and efficiency unexampled in this country. St. Patrick's Cathedral has been enlarged, and the foundations of a new Cathedral on Fifth Avenue, which is intended to surpass any thing of the kind on this continent, have been laid. New structures of various kinds in this city and in Westchester County have risen to attest the abundant resources which he has evoked from what seemed at first an impoverished and most uninviting field. He evidently understands all the arts of gathering tribute to forward his plans. No lack of funds seems ever to stand in the way of his designs. Even burial in his cemetery is said to be one source of prolific income.

Archbishop Hughes may lay some claim to literary distinction. He has figured somewhat as a popular lecturer, and has won laurels even in this field. He is unsurpassed, we believe, by any living competitor in reading history backward. He professes the highest admiration for the Dark Ages. He claims that the millions of the Roman Catholic Church are a unit in faith, and that all conform with the precision of stereotyped impression to the same unvarying standard. Blocks of wood, sawn by the same pattern, iron forms cast in the same mould, these seem to be symbols of the unity he admires. Not a few regard him as a masterly strategist of words, which he can so marshal as to break the lines of fact, and carry confusion where he can not conviction.

In his administrative sphere he has achieved what was possible for few. He has brought order out of confusion, silenced disaffection, evoked means to prosecute his plans out of unpromising materials, and we believe that, although he has not accomplished all at which he aimed, he has never been but once forced to beat a retreat. Sagacity, industry, and perseverance have availed to sustain him or relieve him from each dilemma.

In person, Archbishop Hughes well becomes his position. Although of moderate stature, the dignity of his mien and his massive brow give him a somewhat commanding appearance. If not precisely an orator, he is yet an impressive speaker. Nature has either denied him some of the gifts which she has lavished on his countrymen, or his good sense has taught him to restrain their exercise. Grandiloquent he may sometimes be, but he is more sparing than one would anticipate in the pyrotechnics of rhetoric. But for the Latinity of his professional studies, he would, doubtless, have possessed a style less rotund, but more nervous. Yet such as it is, it befits the man. It has something of the "state-paper" element in it. Calm, and for the most part dispassionate, it is adapted to invite confidence or even admiration, rather than excite enthusiasm. It is, moreover, characteristic of the man—a Richelieu rather than a Bossuet—a man who rather writes as a diplomatist than speaks as an orator.

No man in connection with the Roman Catholic Church in this country may more properly be regarded as its "representative man" than the archbishop. The unblushing claims of the Church to the sole title of *Christian* logically require of their advocate an unusual amount of capability. The diverse utterances of the Church authorities in different periods, and the inconsistent and adverse bulls of her pontiffs, expose her assumed infallibility to thrusts from which it requires the resources of a most adroit and ingenious sophistry to defend her. The public opinion of the world has long ago pronounced sentence upon her peculiar moralities, perfected by the arts of her Jesuit casuists, and to veil their absurdities, or garnish their pollution, demands a boldness which is prepared to look public opinion out of countenance, and conquer silence, if not by assent, by the very force of paradox.

But for these tasks, by natural gifts, by tastes, we

might say, perhaps, by instincts, and by peculiar ambitions, the archbishop was fully qualified. Pugnacious enough never to decline, but oftener prepared to give a challenge; the more devoted to his cause for the very reasons that would have led many to abandon it, its difficulties, and its obnoxiousness to popular feeling; a perfect master of all the arts by which an antagonist may be entrapped in his own admissions, or forced into apparent inconsistencies; with a self-confidence which will sometimes supply the place of talent, but which, in combination with it, serves as the intrenchment behind which every gun can be carefully loaded and deliberately aimed; and, moreover, with such supreme reverence for the authority of the Church, that he would make reason, experience, and the lessons of history yield before it, the archbishop was, for the cause to which his life has been devoted, the right man in the right place. Too cool and collected to be led astray by fanatical zeal, or to be chivalrous merely from impulse; too ambitious ever to neglect a tourney of controversy where he could hope to win the coveted laurels; too astute not to perceive that the very readiness with which the lists are entered created an impression in favor of the combatant, and one often more extensive and abiding than the argumentative issue itself, he combined the qualities which designated him as *facile princeps* among his compeers, and as the leading Roman Catholic champion in this land. A modest man would not have answered. A learned man merely would have been too timid, from the consciousness of the weak points of his cause. A man more cautious would have encouraged his opponents and disheartened his friends by the very manner he would have assumed; but neither by modesty, too profound learning, nor excessive caution was the archbishop disqualified for his task. Adroit, unscrupulous; if scholastic, never cramped by his scholasticism; if well read, not overburdened by the lore of mere ecclesiasticism, and with a conscience precisely adjusted to papal decisions, he could perceive, with a clearer eye than most, just what the Church needed to have done, and was enterprising and self-confident enough to undertake it without the least hesitation.

In these circumstances, he was regarded by others, and might justly look upon himself, as the champion of the Church. In successive encounters in defense of his faith he bore off a fair reputation as an intellectual pugilist.

Such a man Dr. Murray selected, not as an antagonist, but as the person to whom his argument against Romanism should be addressed. The choice was sagacious. The boldness with which the letters were written, the force with which the theological was often made a personal question, and the pertinacity with which the sharp points were pushed against the bishop, as if he were an adversary in danger of the blows that were struck, intensely excited the interest of the reader, and gave a novel attraction to the papers as they appeared from week to week. But so cautious was the writer, that he did not venture upon this attack until his ground had been thoroughly examined and the consequences well weighed. Though he was to publish one letter each week, he did not begin the publication until nearly the whole series was carefully written out for the press. This became his habit. That he might not be tempted to hasty execution if he depended on the leisure that each week should offer, he uniformly anticipated the time, and completed the work before the first number of any series of papers was committed to the press. Only a man of method could master himself so far as to enforce such a self-imposed rule. But it was invaluable. The letters were signed KIRWAN, the signature being the name of an Irish clergyman, Dean Kirwan, whose conversion from Popery to Protestantism made his name peculiarly appropriate for Dr. Murray's use.

Walter Blake Kirwan, of Killalo, was born in the year 1754, in the county of Galway. His parents were wealthy Roman Catholics, who designed to rear their son to the priesthood of that Church, for which purpose he was educated in the College of English Jesuits at St. Omer's, in France, but afterward received priest's orders, and was soon after promoted to the chair of natural and moral philosophy. But at the early age of twenty-four he accompanied the Neapolitan embassador to the British court as chaplain, an appointment which, it is thought, laid the foundation of his subsequent oratorical fame. His residence at London gave him the opportunity of attending those exhibitions of public speaking by which the English Senate and bar were at that time eminently distinguished.

While in London he seems to have begun to entertain doubts as to the infallibility of his Church, and whether it had any claim to be considered as the only Church of Christ on earth. These doubts continuing to increase, he resigned his chaplaincy and retired to the bosom of his family, where he remained two years before he formed the final resolution of breaking away from the bondage of Popery.

Mr. Kirwan attached himself to the Established Church, and his first sermon in the capacity of a Protestant minister was preached June 24, 1787, in the church of St. Peter's, Dublin. He preached here for some time, and afterward was made Dean of Killalo. His sermons were chiefly on works of beneficence; finally he was reserved for charity sermons almost entirely, such was his great power over the purses of the people. His popularity as an orator rose so high, that when it was known he was to preach, the entrance of the church had to be defended by guards and palisades. Even in seasons of national distress, one of his sermons repeatedly drew contributions to the amount of a thousand or twelve hundred pounds. Mr. Grattan said in Parliament that Dean Kirwan had wrung sixty thousand pounds out of the people by preaching, and stopped the mouth of hunger with its own bread. His great labors wore him out, and he died at the age of fifty-one.

Dr. Murray's letters to Bishop Hughes became suddenly and widely popular throughout the country. Inquiries were made in various quarters for the name of the author, but this was carefully concealed. The letters were attributed to various distinguished writers, but the facts of personal history which were necessarily embodied in them soon narrowed the question of authorship; and those who were acquainted with Dr. Murray's early career soon fastened upon him without any doubt as the author. As the series was continued, the interest of the public in them increased. They were eagerly and widely copied into other newspapers, in this country and Great Britain and Ireland. Roman Catholics read them with avidity. Scores of instances were reported of the intense interest with which Catholic servants in Protestant families sought the letters and devoured them. A meeting of Roman Catholics was held in the city of New York once a week, in secret, at which these letters were read aloud by one of the number. They were the heart and life experience of one who had felt and believed as they themselves were feeling and believing now. They had the stamp of sincerity on every line, and the Roman Catholic who read them knew that every thing said of his religion in them was literally true. Unlike the most of controversial writings, there was no bitterness in them. There was not a line that the author "dying would wish to blot." The sprightly humor spread so pleasantly over every page was welcome to an Irishman, and opened his heart to receive the force of an argument and admit the truth of a fact. Every Romanist, certainly every Irish Romanist, would appreciate such passages as these. He is speaking of the tendency of Popery to impoverish the people.

"It meets them at the cradle, and dogs them to the grave, and beyond it, with its demands for money.

When the child is baptized, the priest must have money; when the mother is churched, the priest must have money; when the boy is confirmed, the bishop must have money; when he goes to confession, the priest must have money; when he partakes of the Eucharist, the priest must have money; when visited in sickness, the priest must have money. If he wants a charm against sickness or the witches, he must pay for it money. When he is buried, his friends must pay money. After mass is said over his remains, a plate is placed on the coffin, and the people collected together on the occasion are expected to deposit their contribution on the plate. Thus pounds are collected for burying the poorest of the people. Then the priest pockets the money, and the people take the body to the grave; and then, however good the person, his soul must go to Purgatory; and however bad, his soul may have stopped there. And then comes the money for prayers and masses for deliverance from Purgatory, which prayers and masses are continued as long as the money continues to be paid. Masses are yet said for people who died hundreds of years ago. Now, when we remember that seven out of the nine millions of the people of Ireland are papists, and of the most bigoted stamp, and that this horse-leech process of collecting money, whose ceaseless cry is '*give, give,*' is in operation in every parish, and that, as far as possible, every individual is subjected to it, can we wonder at the poverty and the degradation of Ireland? Can we wonder that its noble-hearted, noble-minded people are every where hewers of wood and drawers of water? Shame, shame upon your Church, that it treats a people so confiding and faithful so basely! Shame, shame upon it, that it does so little to elevate a people that contribute so freely to its support! O popery, thou hast debased my country—thou hast impoverished its people—thou hast enslaved its mind! From the hodman on the ladder—from the digger of the canal—from the hostler in the stable—from the unlettered cook in the kitchen and maid in the parlor —from the rioter in the street—from the culprit at the bar—from the state prisoner in his lonely dungeon —from the victim of a righteous law stepping into eternity from the gallows for a murder committed under the delirium of passion or whisky, I hear a protest against thee as the great cause of the deep degradation of as noble a people as any upon which the sun shines in the circuit of its glorious way!"

The first series consisted of twelve letters, and were published between February 6th and May 8th, 1847. Their immediate publication in book form was demanded. They were printed by John F. Trow, in a neat little unbound volume, and tens of thousands were sold with great rapidity. Orders came in for them to be distributed gratuitously in distant parts of the country. One edition followed another in rapid succession. They were translated into the German language, and sent by colporteurs in great numbers among the people speaking that tongue. They were speedily republished on the other side of the water, and were exceedingly popular and greatly useful there.

More than a hundred thousand copies were soon in circulation; and, adding to this number those that were circulated in the newspapers, we shall make up an aggregate scarcely exceeded by any publication of the day. And it is certainly safe and just to say that no writings on the Roman Catholic question have excited so much attention since the Reformation, or have been so widely read by the masses of the people.

Bishop Hughes preserved a silence equally discreet and profound. Perhaps he considered the letters quite beneath his notice. An answer might give them notoriety. Let alone, they might soon pass out of mind. The Roman Catholic newspapers assailed them with great virulence. Anonymous writers attacked the author, whose name had now become identified with the letters, and, without any authority from himself, they were freely spoken of in public and private as Dr. Murray's.

He was called on repeatedly, and through various channels, to continue the letters. One of these calls may be cited as an indication of the esteem in which the first series was held, and of the public desire that Kirwan would resume his pen.

"*To the Author of the Letters on Romanism, lately addressed to Bishop Hughes over the signature of Kirwan.*

"SIR,—Though you have chosen hitherto to keep in the shade in reference to the authorship of these letters, I suppose you are not buried in so deep obscurity as not to have some knowledge of what is passing in the world around you. But, lest you should chance to be less knowing than might be presumed, I beg to state to you through your own channel of communication, that the letters to which I refer have been read by the religious community at large with a degree of interest that has rarely been felt in reference to any similar publication. If I mistake not, the judgment of the world is, that they are characterized by a simplicity and perspicuity that bring them fairly within the scope of any comprehension—by a force of thought and expression which no reflecting and impartial mind will find it easy to resist—by an amount of good nature and Christian charity which must prevent any reasonable opponent from taking offense; and last, though not least, by an unwonted pungency, which is likely, ere this, to have vibrated in a note of terror to the innermost heart of Rome. I believe, in common with a multitude of wiser and better men, that these letters have as yet only begun to fulfill their mission, and that those who live at the ends of the earth, and who are destined to live in coming years, will look upon them as having had much to do in lifting from the world one of its heaviest curses.

"But my object in addressing you is something more than to inform you of that of which, I dare say, you need no information. You are aware that it is only a portion of the ground of the Romish controversy which your letters have occupied. There are many points of equal moment with those already discussed which you have left untouched. Allow me to say, yours is the hand to sweep through this whole domain of error. It would be an occasion of deep regret if you should not carry forward to its completion a work which you have so happily begun. The Christian public expect—may I not say, demand it of you. The multitude who are yet in the same spiritual thralldom from which you have escaped demand it. Your country, whose political as well as religious interests are threatened with deadly invasion, demands it. The cause of an enlightened Christianity, of a sound and evangelical Protestantism, demands it. There is a requisition upon you, Kirwan, which I am sure you can not resist without offending against the mercy that hath taken your own feet out of the miry clay, and established your goings. May the Head of the Church enable you suitably to appreciate your obligations and responsibilities. Keep in the dark if you will, only lead others into the light of life and into the liberty wherewith Christ makes his disciples free. Be assured that in making these suggestions I am

"One of Many."

These repeated and urgent calls were not needed to induce Dr. Murray to resume and pursue the work he had undertaken. His heart, and mind, and hand were in it. He was working with a will. It was a labor of love for his countrymen, for Christ, and the world. The first letter of a second series appeared October 2, 1847. In the Introduction he sets forth with great dignity and felicity the reasons that impelled him again to address the bishop:

"My dear Sir,—When I closed the letters I had the honor of addressing to you during the last spring,

I fondly hoped that my part in the thickening controversy on Romanism in our country had closed also. As those letters formed my first, I designed that they should also form my last appearance before the public on that topic. So I expressed myself to you in my closing letter; but the unexpected 'ripple' has been 'excited on the current of my feelings,' and, whether wise or otherwise, I have concluded again to address you.

"My reasons for so doing, and thus departing from my original resolution, are briefly these: The public, who have so kindly received and so widely circulated my 'Letters,' have called for another series, embracing the reasons which I have omitted to state, and which, together with those stated, forbid my return to your Church. At least one of the papers devoted to the interests of popery in this country calls upon me, in a semi-serious manner, to give my views on certain points which it raises; individuals of your communion, who have given my letters a candid perusal, have asked what Kirwan had to say upon this and that point not considered by me; and last, though not least, is a desire to put into the hands of every inquiring Roman Catholic a complete manual of my objections to your Church, candidly and kindly considered. These, reverend sir, are the reasons and motives, and not a love of controversy for its own sake, which induce me again to address you. Controversy, for its own sake, is not desirable, but it is necessary so long as error resists the progress of truth.

"While yielding to these reasons and motives, I yet

confess to you that I deem the present series of letters, which will be brief, a work of supererogation. If you have never performed such a work, you know what it means. My conviction is, that the reasons given in my former letters for refusing to return to your Church are sufficient—sufficient to induce any sane mind to withhold its faith from your teachings, and every sane man to abandon your Church. This, you will say, is a partial decision; it may be so. But as a tree may be held in its place by a few weak roots after the main ligaments that bound it to the earth are cut, and when the weakest wind that blows may cause it to totter, so a mind, when the power of an ancient superstition over it is broken, may yet retain a connection with it, influenced by reasons which seem unworthy of consideration. I know this to be the case. The belief in 'witches and warls' was early impressed on the mind of David Hume; and it is said of him that, after he reasoned matter and mind out of existence, he could not hear the rustling of a leaf after dark without starting as if a witch were upon him. The taste and smell of a sour liquid remain long in the emptied cask; and if any mind, rejecting the great outlines of your system, is yet held to it by some reasons which I have not considered, and whose absurdity I may be able to expose, I feel anxious to relieve it. I must not withhold from you my deep conviction that popery is an evil tree—that its fruits are only evil. I believe it to be a falling tree. Its branches are withering in the air, and the axe, wielded by an Almighty hand, is cutting its roots; and if I can assist in cutting a few more of its roots, and thus hastening its fall, I feel that I will be conferring a benefit upon our race, and contributing to the emancipation of millions of men from a slavery in comparison with which that of the Pharaohs was freedom. Hence these additional letters; and all I intend doing is to state to you some farther reasons which forbid my return to your Church.

"Before entering upon a statement of these reasons, permit me to say a few things which I can better say in this preliminary letter than any where else.

"The question has doubtless suggested itself to your mind and to the minds of others, Why do I address these letters to you? Some of my reasons I have already given you. I believe you to be a man of sense and of fair character, which can not be said of all papal priests. You are put forth, now that Bishop England, also one of our countrymen, is no more, as the Achilles of your party in these United States. If any man in the country can refute my reasoning and obviate my objections, it is thought you can do it. In the absence of the higher qualities of mind, you are considered as quite smart; and as my sole object and aim is the truth, I have selected the man, in my opinion, best fitted to correct me when in error; when false, to show me the fallacy of my reasoning; and if he should reply, who would reply as a gentleman. If you can not confute me, no man of your Church in these United States can. Nor will I consent to notice what may be said in the way of reply to or abuse of these letters by any man save yourself. I have, as they say, a drawing toward you as an Irishman; I respect your open and manly bearing; and sadly as, in my opinion, you prostitute your talents, I have respect for them. Hence I pass through the ranks of soldiers and by inferior officers, and go up to Achilles himself.

"But you have not answered my former letters! I confess to you, sir, that I had no expectation that you would answer them, and for these reasons: First, because they are anonymous; and as I like not myself to contend with a masked opponent, so I judged of you. The text is capable of wide application: 'As face answereth to face in water, so the heart of man to man.' I prefer, for the present, to stand behind the curtain; and for this, among other reasons, that you and all men may decide upon what I say simply upon the merits of my statements and arguments; and for the additional reason, to prevent a *personal* controversy. It is an old trick of your Church to leave the argument for the man. And, secondly, because of their matter. I speak to you of what my eyes have seen, of what my ears have heard, of what my heart has felt. Facts are stubborn things. How can you make a man believe that to be sweet which, from actual taste, he knows to be sour? It is hard to reason against a man's experience. On these grounds I expected from you no reply. And although, unless I mistake you, not one of the little men who seek to put the more abundant honor on the part that lacketh by a mock dignity, by an assumed superiority, yet you know when to be wisely silent. If, sir, without compromising your crosier—if, during some hours of leisure from your varied and manifold duties, you would consent to answer some of the reasons and considerations which I have stated, and will state in the following letters, which forbid my return to your Church, there is one, at least, that will read your reply with great pleasure. I am not, sir, among those who impute your silence to your inability to reply to my statements; but if I can only gain access to the public ear—if I can only obtain from candid Roman Catholics a careful consideration of what I say, your silence will give but little troublo. You may play dumb as long as it suits you; my object will be attained."

After such an introduction, Kirwan went forward with his second series of letters. In these he discussed the doctrines and practices of the Roman Catholic Church with more freedom of language, and, if possible, with more vigor than in the first. He assailed the "sacrament" of extreme unction with arguments from Scripture, and closed with the following exclamation and incident:

"And what a tremendous use your Church has made of it! Gaining access to the dying beds of kings, princes, and barons in past days, with your olive oil, you have extorted millions of money from those who believed in your ghostly power. You have thus enriched the Church and impoverished the people. You have built palaces for your bishops, and reduced the people to beggary. What will a dying sinner withhold from a man, who, he believes, has the power to lock him up in hell, or, by a little olive oil rubbed on with his thumb, can conduct him to the port of eternal happiness?

"The man yet lives who narrates the following scene, of which he was an eye and ear witness. The chief of one of our Indian tribes, a man of great sagacity and decision, was on his dying bed. Many of his people, by a French Jesuit, were converted to the faith of your Church. He knew the wiles of your missionary, and forbade him admission to his dying bed. The priest came with his olive oil, and pressed so hard for admission to him that it was granted. 'Stay,' said the dying chief to the man who relates the story, 'stay outside the door, and if I knock, come in.' The priest entered, and the door was closed. Soon a violent knock was heard, and the man entered the room. 'Take him out,' said the dying chief; 'take him out—land—land—give me land.' The priest would put on the olive oil, but wanted first a grant of land.

"Reverend sir, your Church must annul this sacrament of extreme unction before I can return to its embrace. To my mind it is extreme nonsense. Should not incantations over dying men be left to Hottentots? I implore you to seek some other market for your olive oil than the chambers of the dying. You sell it there at too dear a price, and very often to the deep injury of the widow and the orphan. Often do your wretched priests carry away the last dollar of a poor man in pay for their olive oil, and leave the victim of their delusions to be buried as a pauper!"

Next, he took up the system of penance, and this he disposed of with masterly skill, and in the happiest style. He exposed its unscripturalness; and when he came to its use and abuse by the priesthood, his invectives were withering, as his illustrations were overwhelming. He says to Bishop Hughes:

"Of confession I have already spoken. I have shown it to be a priestly device of the most fatal influence upon human liberty; its tendency to the corruption of morals is acknowledged. There is on my table a book, called 'The Garden of the Soul,' bearing on its title-page your own name; and such a garden! Now, conceive yourself sitting in your confessional, and whispering through the little hole in its side in the ears of a modest or immodest young girl of eighteen, or an amiable young wife of twenty-one years, the questions on pages 212 and 214! Sir, I dare not quote them here. I strove to read them to a friend a few days since, and before I got half through he cried out, 'Stop! I can hear no more.' The polluting confessional is a part of your sacrament of penance."

What can be more convincing to an unsophisticated mind than such an illustration as the following from the same letter:

"Take another case: the man bound by the curate may be loosed by the parish priest. I take the following illustration from a book before me: A penitent is enjoined to abstain from breakfast every morning until his next confession. Christmas day intervenes, and he eats breakfast, not thinking that that day could be included. On confessing this at his next confession, the curate drove him from his knee, declaring that he would have no more to do with a person that so trifled with his commands. On the borders of despair, he went to the parish priest, telling him the whole story. 'Do not mind it, my child,' said the kind-hearted father; 'I will confess you.' He did so, and absolved him. Here one priest binds sin on his soul, and another unbinds it. He dies in this state. What becomes of him? Does the binding of the curate send him to hell, or does the loosing of the parish priest send him to heaven? What becomes of him? Is he suspended somewhere between heaven and hell? Do explain this matter to our comprehension."

And again:

"The penances enjoined by the priest are optional and multiform, and are modified according to his own prejudices and the dignity of the confessing penitent. Some of the voluntary austerities are curious enough. St. Dominic, when a child, would leave his cradle and lie upon the cold ground. I have seen many an urchin do this whose name is not yet, and is not likely to be, in the calendar. St. Francis used to call his body Brother Ass, and whip it as badly as Balaam did his. Saint Francis Loyola put on iron chains and a hair shirt, and flogged himself thrice a day. He deserved it all! St. Macarius went naked six months in a desert, suffering himself to be stung with flies, to atone for the sin of having killed a flea! Now, is it not a wicked burlesque upon the religion of God to make ignorant people believe that in these and similar ways they secure an exchange of eternal punishment? Language supplies no words in which I can express to you my deep abhorrence of your sacrament of penance."

And having in this style exposed the folly and

wickedness of the whole system of penance as taught by the Romish Church, he says: "Before closing my letter, let me ask you one question: Do you believe that none go to heaven from New York but those to whom you and your priests, with your keys, open its gates? It takes a hard heart and a soft head to believe this. I charge you with neither."

The miracles of the Church furnished the finest possible theme for the display of Kirwan's peculiar skill in attack. He cites from authors of renown among the Romanists a long catalogue of miracles, the most absurd and incredible, and some of them irresistibly ridiculous. And then he says, "In Ireland your priests are constantly performing miraculous cures on men and cattle. Even your common people there work miracles. When a thunder-storm is raging, they kindle a fire, and heat the tongs red-hot. This preserves their cattle from the lightning. If they are killed notwithstanding, it is in chastisement for some sins not confessed, or some penances not rightly performed. Perhaps, sir, it may astonish you when I tell you that I myself, while yet in your faith, wrought two or three. Near my father's residence was a wood in which a man was once killed. His ghost was regularly seen after dark. I never passed through that wood without crossing myself, and saying Hail Mary; and I assure you I never saw the ghost! After dusk, in the spring of the year, I was sent on an errand to a neighbor's house, which was separated from ours by two or three fields. As I ran along, I saw through the magnifying twilight what was obviously an evil spirit. I stopped suddenly, and the sweat commenced pouring. Naturally of a resolute spirit, I thus reasoned: If I run back, he can catch me; if I go forward, he can but catch me. So, after saying my Hail Mary, and crossing myself, I went forward with a trembling step. As I advanced, the horns of the fiend became perfectly obvious. Almost dead with fear, I rushed forward and caught hold of them; and, marvelous to narrate, those fiendish horns were instantly turned into the handles of a plow! Now I submit it to you, sir, whether these miracles wrought by myself are not as great as those wrought by St. Mochua or St. Columbanus? And yet I fear my chance for canonization is exceedingly small."

Kirwan closes this letter with a characteristic paragraph:

"You must give up your lying legends and your claim to miraculous power before I can return to your fold. I feel as did our fellow-countryman with the bad asthma, who exclaimed, 'If once I can get this troublesome breath out of my body, I'll take good care it shall never get in again.'"

In the same vein he pursues the marks of the Papal Church being the true Church, and examines its unity, its sanctity, its catholicity, its apostolicity, and its infallibility, and the conclusion he reaches is summed up in these few words:

"If a boat were as rotten as I believe your Church to be, I would not trust it to carry me across the North River; and yet it claims the entire monopoly of carrying to heaven all the souls that ever enter it, and for no reason, human or divine, that I can see, unless it be for the freight and the toll!"

Kirwan's denunciations of the traffic of the Church in relics and indulgences is worthy of Luther or any of the old Reformers. He rises into a vehemence of righteous indignation that sweeps away the whole system as infinitely unworthy the countenance of a rational, much more of a Christian man; and he concludes:

"But you will say all this was the abuse of the thing. My dear sir, your doctrines of relics and indulgences have no use—they are all abuse. Guard them as you may in your catechisms and books, practically they are all abuse. Millions have prayed at the tombs of your saints who never offered an intelligent prayer to God through his Son; millions have worshiped your relics who never worshiped God in spirit and in truth; and millions have sought deliverance from sin by your penances, and extreme unctions, and indulgences, who never sought it through the blood of Jesus Christ. And at this hour, many of your churches in Rome are nothing but splendid spiritual shops for the sale of indulgences.

"The frauds which your Church has practiced on the world by her relics and indulgences are enormous. If practiced by the merchants of New York in their commercial transactions, they would send every man of them to state prison. For frauds amounting to about two millions, a man of the name of Schuyler has been banished from society, and has fled the country. How many millions, think you, by their pious frauds, have your priests raised from the poorest of the people of New York during your episcopate? Fraud is not the less fraud because committed under a religious garb, and by a man in vestments blazing with crosses!

"By your doctrine of relics, you lead the people into idolatry on the one hand; by your doctrine of indulgence, you give them a license to commit sin on the other; at least, this is their practical effect. It is said of the holy Sturme, the disciple of St. Winifred, that in passing a horde of unconverted Germans as they were bathing in a stream, he was so overpowered by the intolerable stench of sin that arose from them that he nearly fainted away. Similar is the effect of the odor of your relics and indulgences upon me. Your Church must abandon them utterly before I can return to her communion."

The next letter brought to a close the specific reasons which Kirwan assigned for not being willing to return to the Church of Rome. In it he exposes the unmeaningness of the Romish doctrines and ceremonies. He is very severe in its strictures on the mass, and even more so when he comes to the unwillingness of the Church to allow the free circulation of the Scriptures among the people. In another, he contemplates the destiny of the papacy, denies that its reformation is possible, and anticipates its total extinction.

"It is my strong conviction that God has ordained the total extinction of your Church. I will not detain your, sir, nor my readers, with any dissertations upon the prophecies bearing on this point; this would be aside from my object. John, when rapt in vision in Patmos, informs us that Babylon 'shall be utterly burned with fire,' and calls upon God's people to 'come out of her,' that they might not be partakers of her sins, nor receive of her plagues. And Paul tells us that the Lord shall consume 'that wicked' with the spirit of His mouth, and destroy him with the brightness of His rising. And by 'Babylon,' and 'that wicked,' I believe Paul and John meant the papal Church. It has already lost its civil power. Once she could dethrone kings, and absolve subjects from their allegiance: now, in a civil point of view, there is no weaker power on earth. Metternich can send his Austrian troops into the States of the Church without fearing the least injury from the successor of Gregory the Great! How is the mighty fallen! Ronge, in Germany, excited to opposition by the impositions of the 'Holy Coat of Treves,' has led out one hundred thousand from the yoke of your Church, and all that his Holiness can do is to bear it. Even in the city of New York, the resolute Germans are flocking out from the care of Holy Mother, and all that you can do is to flourish your crook, your keys, and your crosier around the altar of St. Patrick's, without the least power to stop one of the wandering sheep; and the more you strive to stop, the more determined are they to leave your fold. The temporal power of your Church is gone; the spiritual is fast going after it; and the time will soon be here when the pen of the historian will write, THE CHURCH OF ROME WAS, BUT IS NOT.

"How this is to be done is a question of some importance, and upon which I have my own opinions. A careful looking at past providences may cast some light upon the future, and inspire hope or fear, according to the relation we sustain to God and his Church. You know, sir, the way in which God treated Pharaoh and the Canaanites, and how he blotted out the nations that opposed the progress of his people. You know the way and manner in which he broke up the Jewish Church and state for their opposition to Christ and his Church. You know how the Reformation progressed, from small beginnings, until it opened a new epoch in the world's history; from what was considered a little ecclesiastical gladiatorship, until kingdoms were shaken; until thrones, cemented by ages, were convulsed, and tottered to their base; until hostile armies met in deadly combat, and fattened the earth with the blood of the papist and the Protestant. God has the control of all agencies to accomplish his will. Much will be done for the extinction of your Church by education; much by the general influence of learning; much, very much by the circulation of the Bible; much more by the simple and fervent preaching of the Gospel to the masses, as did Luther; and much by the direct agency of Him in whose sight the nations are as a drop in the bucket, and who will overturn and overturn until He shall come whose right it is to reign.

"These, reverend sir, are, in brief, my reasons for believing that your Church is destined to utter extinction. No reasons can be drawn for its future continuance from its continuance until now. If your people had not been papists, they might have been pagans or infidels. The Canaanites remained a long time in the land to perplex the Jews. Paganism continued for ages in the Roman world after its conversion to Christianity; yet both became extinct, save as paganism has been perpetuated by your people. Nor can any argument be drawn from the occasional conversions to your communion which are now occurring. You know that in ages past some Christian ministers relapsed into idolatry; and that, during the French Revolution, some of your bishops, and many of your priests, went over to infidelity. You must lay no flattering unction to your soul from arguments like these. Your Church is opposed to the truth of God, to the people of God, to the will of God. The shed blood of the martyrs is crying to heaven against it. Its extinction is certain, and may God hasten it in His own time and way.

"With the most sincere prayers for your spiritual and eternal welfare, I remain, with respect, your fellow-countryman and fellow-sinner, KIRWAN."

This was the last of the second series of letters to the bishop. Two letters followed in the same series, but they were addressed to the people of the Church. They were full of tender expostulation and affectionate appeal. With the earnestness of one who had been in all the darkness and bondage of the system in which they were still lying, he called upon them to turn from their priests to the Lord Jesus Christ. "These," he cried out, "are the reasons, Roman Catholics, why I turn to you, and why I would implore you, by all that is to be desired in a mind free to think, in a soul free to love and to act—free in its access to God, without priestly taxes and interferences; by all that is to be desired in the social and religious elevation of your children, and in the moral regeneration of your race, to rise, and to fling from around you the chains forged in the Dark Ages, and with which priests would bind you to their footstools in this age of light."

"My dear Roman Catholic friends, I once suffered just as you now do because of my utter ignorance as to the way of forgiveness with God. I was taught all about confession, and confirmation, and penance, and saints' days, and fasting, and holy water, and saying 'Hail Mary.' I looked upon the priest as the door-keeper of heaven, without whose permission there was no admittance; but I knew nothing about the Bible, and was taught nothing about the work of Christ for the sinner, nor about the work of the Spirit in him. In great mercy, and in the way stated in my letters to Bishop Hughes, I became a reader of the Bible; and, to my utter amazement, I found there taught, with perfect plainness, the way of salvation, which the priest had wrapped up in mystery inextricable. The wayfaring man, though a fool, may understand the way in which a soul may be saved as taught in the Bible—it is beyond the comprehension of Gabriel as taught by your priests."

And then he appeals to his countrymen with Irish fervor, and with touches of pathos that can not fail to reach the Irish heart, as he exclaims:

"Irish Roman Catholics! would that I could induce

you to look at this great subject in the light of the Bible. It is intimately connected with your temporal and eternal interests, and with the interests of unborn generations. When a boy, I often heard, and never but with burning indignation, of the magistrate, the tool of British power, entering the houses of the Irish suspected of disaffection, and tearing from its frame the speech of Emmett, made in reply to the question of the bloodthirsty judge who tried him, 'What he had to say why the sentence of death should not be passed against him according to law?' The British ministry felt that that speech fostered the spirit of nationality in the Irish bosom, and made every man who read it to resolve, at whatever expense, to be free; and they destroyed every copy of it that could be found, and forbade its publication. As my kindred were among the disaffected ones, I felt it to the quick. And what, think you, must be my feelings now, in the vigor of my manhood, when I see, in this free land, the descendants of those who fought at Vinegar Hill and at Tara permitting individuals calling themselves the priests of the religion of God to enter their houses and take away their Bibles, and to forbid them, by the terrors of eternity, to think for themselves on the most important of all subjects connected with their being! It is the very feeling that prompted the British spies to destroy the speech of Emmett that now prompts your priests to destroy your Bibles. The one fostered the spirit of civil, the other of religious freedom. The British ministry wished to suppress the breathing of your fathers after their civil rights; your priests wish to suppress the breathings of you, their children, after religious rights. And will you, the sons of noble sires, submit, in a land of freedom, to wear the galling chains of spiritual bondage? Will you submit to have these chains clanking around you to the grave, and, when you die, to have them bound upon your children; and for no earthly purpose but to sustain a priesthood and a hierarchy for whose utter overthrow the civil and religious interests of the nations, and the temporal and eternal interests of our race, are calling aloud to heaven?

"If so, with a slight variation, mine will be the language of the pious Jeremiah, who had the civil and the religious welfare of his people equally at heart: 'O that my head were waters, and mine eyes a fountain of tears, that I might weep day and night for the blindness and folly of my people.'

"My letters are ended. I commit them to you, Roman Catholics, and to the blessing of Almighty God."

When Dr. Murray here laid down his pen, he had no thought of resuming it in this department of literary and religious labor. But the bishop was now roused, and resolved to make an attempt, at least, to stay the power of Kirwan's attack upon the faith of his Church. The first series of letters he had treated with silence. That was wise. The second series, less popular with the Protestant community, was more effective among the Roman Catholics than the first. They were frequently and freely criticised by the author's friends as wanting the delicacy and finish of the series that introduced the discussion, and made it so widely famed in the religious world. But, if there was any foundation in truth for this criticism, the author knew the class of men for whom he was writing too well to be diverted or deterred from his purpose, and the event justified him in the opinion that he must adapt his weapons to the enemy against whom he was directing his charge. He wrote so as to be understood, and he wished his words to be felt as well as read. The effect of this second series was more powerful than that of the first. The newspapers of the Catholics assailed them with virulence quite unusual even with them.

The bishop himself was at last compelled, but most reluctantly, to take them up. They were anonymous, and he could therefore have been justified in treating them with silent indifference. But the pressure of public sentiment was too great to be resisted. To refuse to reply seemed to be a tacit admission that they were unanswerable. The mass of readers would not admit the validity of the excuse for silence that the writer was unknown to the bishop. "Every body" was supposed to know, and the bishop could know as well as others. Yielding to the pressure, the bishop at last entered the field, and in a series of ten letters in the "Freeman's Journal," a newspaper under his own control, he addressed his people with arguments to counteract the force of the Kirwan Letters.

These were followed by a series of letters to Kirwan himself; and in the midst of the series, after having published six and promising more, the bishop left the city for Halifax on official business, and brought his letters suddenly and abruptly to an end. Universal disappointment was caused by the matter, the manner, and the termination of the bishop's correspondence. The close was so much like a retreat, that it was discreditable to him and disheartening to his friends.

In Dr. Murray's reply to Bishop Hughes there was more learning, logic, and real ability than in both the former series, but less vivacity, less satire, less anecdote, and incident; and the letters were, therefore, less popular, and less read. In some of them he introduces his favorite Irish characters, and plays them off against the bishop with great effect.

"'Bishop Hughes,' says John Murphy, 'what is the meaning of that text (James, v., 16), "Confess your faults *one to another*, and pray *for one another?*"' 'Why, John,' you reply, 'it means, confess your sins to the priest, and ask the priest to pray for you.' John believes and makes an act of faith. I, a little more cautious, look at the text, and thus reason about it. 'One to another'—that looks very much like the priest confessing to me if I confess to the priest, and I praying for the priest if the priest prays for me. I look a little farther after 'one another' or 'one to another.' I find in Heb., iii., 13, the following words: 'Exhort one another.' Does this mean that the priest must exhort me, but not I the priest? Very well. I find the following words in Eph., iv., 32: 'Be kind one to another, tender-hearted, forgiving one another.' Does this mean that the priest must be kind and tender-hearted to me, and not I to the priest? that he must forgive me, but not I him? What say you,

Bishop Hughes? Yet John Murphy believes you, and makes an act of faith, and goes to confession, and pays you, and goes to heaven; I, a 'private reasoner,' conclude you pervert the Scriptures to make a gain of godliness, confess my sins to God, and for my opinion —go to hell!

"John Murphy again asks, 'Bishop, what is the meaning of Matt., xxvi., 26, 27?' You reply, 'Why, John, it means that Christ transubstantiated the bread and the wine into his own body and blood, and that then he multiplied himself into twelve, and that then he gave himself to be eaten to each of the apostles, and after he was thus eaten he was not eaten; he was yet alive, and spoke to them.' With his eyes wonderfully dilated, he asks, 'Bishop, is this done now?' 'Oh yes, John,' you reply, 'daily in the mass.' He again asks, 'Bishop, why not give the bread and the wine now to the people?' 'The reason, John, is,' you reply, 'that, as the wafer is changed into the real body and blood of Christ, there is no need of it; for if we eat the whole body, we of course eat the blood with it.' John is satisfied, makes an act of faith, and is saved; I, looking a little farther into the Scriptures, soon conclude that the passage means that the broken bread represented his body broken, and the wine in the cup represented his blood poured out. John Murphy, for his act of faith, is saved, and I, poor Kirwan, for my opinion, am damned!!

"Such, sir, is the way your rule works as to texts. Let us now see how it works as to some important truths.

"John Murphy again approaches you and asks, 'Bishop, how can I be saved?' 'Why, John,' you reply, 'the Church makes that very plain; you must be baptized, and go to mass, and perform penance; you must go regularly to confession; when dying, you must receive extreme unction; then you must go to Purgatory, from which you are to be delivered by the efficacy of masses, and by the alms and suffrages of the faithful; and then you go to heaven.' Amazed at the tedious, roundabout process, poor John makes an act of faith and is saved; I turn to the Scriptures, and preferring the word of God to yours, believe that 'he that believeth in the Lord Jesus Christ shall be saved.' John Murphy believes you, and is saved; I believe God, and am damned. And so on to the end of the chapter. Why, Bishop Hughes, all this has not even the redeeming quality of being good nonsense, an article in whose production our countrymen are not usually deficient, even when their power as private reasoners is at low-water mark—an article in whose manufacture even you yourself are sometimes quite clever!

"Here, sir, I will close my review of your reasons for adherence to the Roman Catholic Church, as given in your ten letters to 'Dear Reader.' Never were reasons more baseless, or weaker, presented to the human mind to justify either opinions or conduct. The way in which you state them obviously shows that you never examined them; that you received them as true, as a good son of the Church, without ever asking why or wherefore in reference to them. Your reception of them was obviously an act of faith, and not an opinion formed in the usual process of a private reasoner. And to ask me, or any sensible, thinking man, to believe in the Catholic Church for the reasons presented in your letters, is on a par with asking me to believe that the little wafer, made of flour, which you lay upon the tongue of a papist bowing before your altar, is transubstantiated by a miserably mumbled ceremony into the real body and blood of Christ. You might almost as soon ask me to believe in all the miracles of the good St. Fithian or the holy St. Bridget.

"Balaam's ass would never have had a name or a place on the page of history were it not for the whipping which his master gave him; and were it not for that whipping, never would hairs from his tail have been preserved amid the sacred relics of Rome. Similar, I fear, will be the effect of this review in bringing up to public notice letters which have neither sense, truth, wit, logic, or even 'clever scurrility' to recommend them, and which, if let alone, might have reached the very depths of oblivion by the massive weight of their dullness."

The bishop's six letters to Kirwan were disposed of in a single letter, and this closed the letters of Dr. Murray to Bishop Hughes. Whatever may have been, and may be hereafter, their influence on the great controversy with the Church of Rome, we know that their immediate effect was to give vast popularity to their author, and to bring him prominently before the Protestant public as a champion of the faith.

Not long after the completion of these letters, Bishop Hughes delivered a discourse in the city of New York on *the decline of Protestantism.* Its artful perversions of history, its subtle philosophy, and plausible eloquence were well fitted to mislead the hearer. It was published in the daily newspapers, and in pamphlet form, and widely diffused. So greatly excited was the public mind on the questions it discussed, and so sensitive were the friends of truth to the effect of this discourse, that a written memorial was circulated and signed by a large number of distinguished citizens inviting the Rev. Dr. Murray to review it. With this request he promptly complied. The "Broadway Tabernacle" was then the largest hall for public meetings in the city of New York. On the evening of Wednesday, January 15, 1851, it was thronged to its utmost capacity; and long before the hour of meeting, hundreds were obliged to go away, unable to gain an entrance. These crowds had assembled to hear a discourse by Dr. Murray on "THE DECLINE OF POPERY, AND ITS CAUSES." For nearly two hours they listened with intense attention, while the speaker, in probably the ablest public effort that he ever made, gave a condensed account of the progress of corruption in the Church of Rome, and the evidence that she is now in the days of her decay. Thousands will remember with what thrilling earnestness he said:

"In wealth, in enterprise, in rational liberty, in literature, in commerce, in all the elements of political and moral power, Protestant are to papal nations as the sun and moon in the heavens are to the fixed stars. That you may see this, blot from the map of

Europe all that it owes to Protestantism, and what is left for the people to desire? Blot from those nations all that they owe to popery, and it would be like Moses lifting up his wonder-working rod heavenward, and rolling back the darkness that enshrouded Egypt. If this does not picture our idea, stop for a month or a year all that Protestantism is doing to civilize, enlighten, and bless the earth, and the world is moved and astounded from its centre to its circumference; even old Austria, the Sleepy Hollow of the world, would spring to her feet and ask, What is the matter? Stop for the same time all that popery is doing for the same ends, and it would be no more missed than is the light of the lost pleiad from the sky."

And in the midst of what applause he concluded in these words:

"Popery has rapidly and is rapidly declining. There was a time when, if it was not respected, it was feared. But it is not so now. The force of its fanaticism is spent and unfelt. While all other institutions are rising with the progress of society, this continues petrified. It is like a vessel bound by a heavy anchor and a short iron cable to the bottom of the stream, while the tide of knowledge and freedom are rising around it. Its spiritual tariff—its restrictions on the commerce of thought—its taxes on the Bread of Life—its efforts to bring seats in heaven into the priestly market—its mimic immolations of the Son of God—its sacrifice of the people for the sake of the priest—its nameless exactions and endless tyrannies, are not much longer to be borne. The Lord will consume it with the breath of His mouth, and will destroy it with the brightness of His rising.

> 'Though well perfumed and elegantly dressed,
> Like an unburied carcass tricked with flowers,
> 'Tis but a garnished nuisance.'

"From every tower of Zion the watchmen should lift up their voices together, and cry to the people that they have nothing to fear. The world is not to be educated back again to the intelligence of the Dark Ages. While popery may be compared to a decrepit, nervous, and wrinkled old man, whose hearing is obtuse, and whose memory is short, and who, heedless and forgetful of the events passing around him, is always prattling about the past, Protestantism is strong, and active, and zealous, and enterprising, and attractive, and looking to the future. The mind of the world is with it. Reason is with it. The literature of the world is with it. The Bible is with it. God is with it. The entire current of civilization is with it. And all these are against popery. The combat may be protracted, but the victory is certain. Nor, in the conflict, will the cause of popery be much aided by the support, nor will the cause of Protestantism be any weakened by the assaults, of those whose chief aim and grand ambition it is to wear a fillet made from the wool of holy sheep."

Dr. Murray's next essay against the Church of his fathers and his childhood was in the form of a series of letters addressed to the Hon. Roger B. Taney, Chief Justice of the United States. These letters contained the results of his observations and studies in the city of Rome, and were appropriately entitled "ROMANISM AT HOME." They were published in a volume in the year 1852. Terse, lucid, pungent, and powerful, more grave and elevated in their style than the letters to Bishop Hughes, they were read with deep interest by men of thought and intelligence, and added materially to the high reputation which Dr. Murray had now attained as an author.

We have already referred to his practice of gathering into note-books the most remarkable incidents of pastoral experience, and from these we have made extracts in this volume. These incidents were published in a book—"PARISH AND OTHER PENCILINGS." Some of the events recorded are in themselves of the deepest interest; while even the least interesting are invested with a charm well-nigh irresistible, from the freshness and originality with which they are related. There is scarcely a chord strung in the human heart which will not vibrate to something to be found in this volume.

We shall anticipate the order of time, but here is the proper place in which to speak of his "MEN AND THINGS AS I SAW THEM IN EUROPE." Familiar as the scenes here described are to most readers, this volume is too much like its author to be lost in the crowd of foreign travels. All that he saw takes its distinctive hue from his own mind, and old things seem to become new in the garb with which they are presented. Many of the descriptions are strikingly beautiful, and some are even gorgeous. But the greatest value of the work, perhaps, is derived from the heavy blows which it deals upon Romanism. This, as might be expected, was always present to the author's mind; and it was impossible that he should travel, especially in his native country or in Continental Europe, without gathering material for a fresh onslaught upon this foe of a pure Christianity.

"THE HAPPY HOME" is a little book well fitted to be an auxiliary to domestic happiness in every dwelling to which it finds access. It is not only characterized by great good sense, and discrimination, and practical wisdom, but it is pervaded by a tender, genial, loving tone, that shows how much the author was at home in writing on such a subject. Judging from all our observation, we should say that the ideal of the happy home which he has so vividly portrayed was found in his own dwelling; though it is sad to reflect how the inroads of death have reduced the number of its inmates, and yet delightful to think of the yet happier home to which they have been removed.

"PREACHERS AND PREACHING" was the last volume that Dr. Murray carried through the press. Its design is to render the ministry more useful and effective by increasing the sense of responsibility, by defining with great accuracy the course of ministerial duty, especially in the pulpit, and by inducing a hearty and vigorous co-operation on the part of those to whom the Gospel is preached. In short, it is adapted to make better preachers and better hearers, while it is especially fitted to accomplish good in our theological seminaries, by fixing in the minds of those who are soon to enter the ministry a proper standard of preaching, and guarding them against mistakes essentially prejudicial to their usefulness. It would be a fitting exercise of a beneficent spirit to take measures for putting this book into the hands of every theological student in the country.

"A DYING LEGACY TO THE PEOPLE OF HIS BELOVED CHARGE" consisted of several discourses prepared by Dr. Murray shortly before his death, but never preached, thus indicating his habit of remarkable industry in anticipating the demands of his pulpit. They are full of impressive truth on the most momentous of all subjects, and are characterized by simple and natural arrangement, by pungent appeals to the conscience, and an all-pervading solemnity, showing a deep sympathy with the powers of the world to come.

Dr. Murray's occasional discourses, published in pamphlet form, were numerous, and are distinguished for their striking adaptedness to the circumstances which called them forth, for simplicity and strength of style, for the absence of every thing like pretension, and for the manifest desire and design to give to the providence of God its legitimate effect on the minds and hearts of men.

CHAPTER XVI.

Dr. Murray as a Preacher.—Habit of Sermonizing.—System in Study.—Style of Speaking.—Contrast between his Sermons and Published Letters.—Calls to various Fields of Usefulness.

THE first great business of Dr. Murray's life was to preach the Gospel. All his energies were summoned to the work. All his ambition had its aim in its accomplishment. That he was eminently successful as a preacher, the fruits of his ministry are the most precious as well as abundant testimony.

In his earliest ministerial life he began to take great pains with his sermons. They were invariably written with deliberation, and method, and completeness, in a style of penmanship and general finish that seem scarcely consistent with the earnest mental activity that distinguished him. In later life, this habit of neatness, order, and *preciseness* grew upon him, so that his manuscript sermons would not have been more handsomely prepared had he expected to deposit them in a public library for inspection. The text is often written in English and Hebrew, or Greek, and neatly defined with black lines underneath, showing the particularity with which his paper was prepared before he proceeded to write his discourse.

He devoted the first part of every day in the week to his sermons, until his week's work upon them was done; and so systematic was he in this habit, that he always kept his work ahead of him, frequently having from five to ten sermons on hand that he had not preached; and this diligence was continued and increased even when he was able to avail himself, in an emergency, of the sermons that he had written twenty and thirty years before, which would, of course, be new to most of his hearers, and acceptable to all. When he was suddenly called to rest from his labors, the series of five fresh sermons on "A Future State" were found in his study, which have since been printed as a legacy to his people.

He was not a pulpit orator. He spoke with earnestness, solemnity, energy, and power, and he never failed to secure the fixed and interested attention of his hearers. But he was not eloquent in the sense which modern usage has given to the word. When he went into a new congregation, even in a distant city, his fame, preceding him, would draw together large numbers; but they had heard and read so much of the Irish wit, the satire, the pungency and point of KIRWAN, that they were disappointed when they heard the solid, methodical, instructive, and able discourses of DR. MURRAY. Very rare, indeed, it was that a flash of his native humor enlivened the page of one of his sermons. Seldom did he tell a story, or even introduce an anecdote, to illustrate his subject, though he would scarcely write a paragraph for the press without bringing them in with striking effect.

His sermons were always very serious, his writings for the newspaper were always very lively.

Few men have received more frequent and more

pressing invitations to take the pastoral charge of important congregations. And these invitations were given to him after full proof of his ministry, and many of them before he had acquired fame as an author. So frequently was he called on to preach at the dedication of new churches, and at ordination and installation of ministers, that he playfully sometimes styled himself the Bishop of New Jersey. But those calls often took him far beyond that diocese, even to Canada and Nova Scotia, where his visits were attended by demonstrations of great respect.

The progress which Nicholas Murray made, and the position which he occupied in the Church, may be seen at a glance by the summary of his course prepared from authentic documents:

1802, he was born in Ireland.

1819, he was in the employment of Harper & Brothers, Publishers, New York.

1826, graduated at Williams College, Massachusetts.

1829, finished his course of study at the Theological Seminary at Princeton, New Jersey.

1829, called to Wilkesbarre and Kingston, Pennsylvania. Also to be Secretary of the Presbyterian Education Society. Also to be General Agent of the American Tract Society for the West.

1833, called to Elizabethtown, New Jersey.

1834, called to the Presbyterian Church of Charleston, South Carolina. His acceptance of this call was strongly urged by some of his best friends in the North, but he declined.

1835, elected Secretary of the Foreign Missionary Society (for New York, Baltimore, Philadelphia, etc.), but he declined.

1836, called to the Park Street Church, Boston; a call that gave him great uneasiness. He declined it, and it was renewed and pressed upon him by a committee who visited him at Elizabethtown. He again declined, and a *third* effort, equally unsuccessful, was made by the same Church to transfer him to the metropolis of New England.

1837, called to Natchez, Mississippi, to succeed the Rev. George Potts, D.D., who came to New York; declined.

1839, called to Brooklyn, N. Y., to the Church of which the Rev. M. W. Jacobus, D.D., was afterward the pastor. To this Church he was nearly *driven* by the counsel and entreaties of his fathers and brethren in the ministry. He declined the call, and for ten years afterward steadily refused to allow his name to be presented to vacant churches, though *often* solicited for this purpose. He insisted that he would not be a "coquette."

1842, he was called, for the second time, to the Church in Natchez which had invited him in 1837, and again he declined the call.

1849, called to the Central Presbyterian Church in St. Louis; declined.

1850, called to the Seventh Presbyterian Church, Cincinnati, and to a professorship in the new Theological Seminary opened in that city. He was strongly tempted to go, that he might enter on a new field of labor in the West, but he finally, after great hesitancy, declined.

1852, called to the same Church in Brooklyn, N. Y., whose call he had refused in 1839. I was one of the committee who went to Elizabethtown and urged this call upon his attention. In the committee and in private, personally and by letter, I sought to induce him to leave Elizabethtown and go to Brooklyn. I set before him the obvious fact that being now just fifty years of age, he must move soon, or consider it a fixed fact that he must spend his days in Elizabethtown. But it was all in vain. He felt as Dr. A. Alexander did, who said "he had never known an instance of a minister going out of the general region where he had spent the energies of his youth, after he was fifty years of age, who did not repent it to the day of his death. His motto to ministers was, 'Go down hill where you went up.'" Subsequently Dr. Murray was called to secretaryships in the Board of Education and the Board of Domestic Missions, but he preferred to live and die among his own people.

Such a record is rarely to be made in the life of any minister.

CHAPTER XVII.

First Visit to Europe.—In London.—Meeting of Bible Society.—Distinguished Men.—Tract Society.—Rev. Dr. Hamilton.—Dr. Cunningham.—France, Italy, and Switzerland.—Returns to Ireland and Scotland.—Visits his Birthplace.—Reflections.—Second Visit to Europe.—Letter from George H. Stuart, Esq.

To revisit the land of his birth, but still more to see the system of Romanism at home, had long been a passionate desire of Dr. Murray. Coming from his native land, not in childhood, but in youth, and having undergone so complete a transformation of character and condition as to be able scarcely to recognize himself as the wanderer from Ireland of thirty years before, the greater was his *curiosity* and anxiety to look upon the scenes of his childhood and the land he had left.

But a stronger motive than this which urged him to cross the ocean was the duty and importance of studying the workings of popery in Ireland, France, and in other countries, especially in Italy. He was writing of Romanism constantly; he was often called on to speak and to preach in relation to it; he was justly regarded as the most popular writer on the subject, and he felt deeply the necessity of seeing for himself the form and fashion of the system in the land of its birth. Just before going abroad he visited the city of Washington, and was received with the highest marks of respect by the most distinguished members of the government. Mr. Webster, then the Secretary of State, understanding that he was about to visit Europe, gave him letters, and made him bearer of dispatches to Rome, that by this merely nominal appointment he might be saved from some annoyances, and enjoy some facilities of travel.

He left New York April 3, 1851, in the packet ship Montezuma, Captain De Courcy. His friend and neighbor in Elizabethtown, Dr. Chetwood, was his traveling companion, and among the cabin passengers were the Rev Dr. Wm. L. Breckinridge, Mr. Sayre, and Mr. Dolan, of Lexington, Ky.

Dr. Murray's habits of industry and system are shown in the regular, complete, and comprehensive diary which he kept of the journey. It was his habit, daily, to enter in his journal a brief mention of every occurrence, with the reflections awakened. These notes are less available for use in this volume than they would have been had he not designed them for immediate service for his letters, which he sent back, from week to week, to the press, with which he constantly corresponded. He often makes brief allusions, which would be easily understood by himself, and would serve as hints to be elaborated hereafter, but they are so obscure as to render the manuscript diary of little service to us. But we find him on shipboard, as at home, always the soul and centre of the social circle, ready for every pleasure or labor, the genial companion and the useful man.

On his arrival in Liverpool he was met by his early

friend, Daniel James, Esq., whose kind hospitality he enjoyed while there. His first Sabbath in England was spent in Liverpool, and in the morning of that day he preached for the Rev. Dr. Raffles, and for the first time in his life in gown and bands. Of this day he says:

"I met Dr. Raffles, previous to the service, in the vestry, surrounded by his deacons. The sexton was there to put on the gown and bands, which are universally worn by all classes of ministers in Europe. The Bible and Hymn-book are taken to the pulpit before the preacher enters it. The minister then passes into the church preceded by the sexton, who opens the pulpit door for him and shuts him in. Then the services commence, and are conducted in form and fashion as in our best-regulated Presbyterian churches. On this occasion the doctor conducted the introductory services with a propriety, solemnity, and unction which made them deeply impressive, mingling with his supplications a devout thanksgiving for my happily-ended voyage, and for my merciful deliverance from the perils of the deep. The services ended with the administration of the Lord's Supper, in which I was permitted to unite. I deemed the whole service a merciful beginning and a happy omen of my subsequent Sabbaths and rambles in Europe."

Dr. Murray arrived in London May 5th, in the midst of the religious anniversary meetings. He writes:

"*May* 6. Went to the Bible Society Buildings, and was most kindly received by its secretaries. Saw the Rev. Mr. Jewett, brother of the celebrated missionary in the East, a middle-sized man, gray, and perfectly blind. I said to him, 'We shall soon be where we can both speak to and *see* one another.' He instantly replied, 'We shall see *Him* as he is—Christ, which is far better.'"

May 7, he attended the anniversary of the British and Foreign Bible Society as the representative of the American Bible Society. He says nothing of the speech that he made on that occasion, but his descriptions of the men whom he met and heard that day are graphically characteristic of his pen.

May 8. Dr. Murray attended and addressed the London Religious Tract Society, and formed the acquaintance of a large number of the most excellent and distinguished men in this and other departments of Christian benevolence. He shared their liberal hospitalities so far as his time would permit, but he was obliged to decline far more invitations than he was able to accept.

His journal is full in its notes of men and things that he met, and some of his characteristic strokes in sketching the glimpses he saw of the various phases of character in public and private life may perhaps as well be suffered to rest in his manuscript. Many of his notes he afterward wrote out more fully and sent them home to the press, but they are less free and easy than the lines he drew to preserve vividly in his own mind the images of all that passed before him. Of the next Sabbath he writes:

"*May* 11. This is the Lord's day. I declined all invitations to preach in London, that I might spend a

Sabbath in hearing and seeing for myself. As a good Presbyterian, I went to the church on Regent Square, to hear the Rev. Dr. Hamilton, so favorably known in our own country by several attractive, popular, and truly evangelical works. This is the church in which Irving once preached with a popularity which has never been equaled—when prime ministers, dukes, and nobles were willing to enter by a window to hear him. The church is plain, but substantial and large. I entered it before service commenced, and was shown to a backless bench in the middle aisle! I had the consolation of seeing others, male and female, treated with equal politeness. After the service commenced we were invited to empty pews, of which there were several. Others accepted, but I declined the honor; and, partly out of ill humor with their way of treating strangers, I kept my backless seat through the service. Instead of Dr. Hamilton, my old friend Dr. Cunningham, so widely and favorably known in America, rose in the pulpit and performed the entire service. It was a missionary sermon from 2 Cor., v., 14, 15; full of matter, sound, long, and exhaustive of the text. It was Scotch throughout. After service I was introduced, in the vestry, to Dr. Hamilton, with whom I went to dinner, in company with Dr. Cunningham. Dr. Hamilton is very like his books—pleasant, imaginative, free in conversation, full of information, cheerful, with face, accent, and manner which would prove his north Tweed origin if met in the moon."

May 15. Dr. Murray, with his friend Dr. Chetwood, left England for the Continent of Europe, and, making a rapid tour through France and Switzerland, visited Italy, and sat down in Rome to study "Romanism at home." The results of this visit have been already noticed in connection with the volumes that he gave to the world on his return. Coming back from the Continent, he made a visit to his native IRELAND, and to the spot where he was born, and the graves of his parents. From his diary, every page of which would add to the interest and value of these memoirs, we copy the record of his feelings when he reached the scenes of his childhood.

EXTRACT.

"In going on board the boat for Belfast, the steward pointed me to a room in which I could have the upper berth. Anxious to know who would sleep under me, I asked him who would be my room-mate. 'Dr. Cook, of Belfast,' was the reply; the very man of all others in Ireland I wished to see most. Finding out who he was, I eyed him. He was anxious to know who I was. Finding out my name, and I finding out his, we each commenced making gradual approaches, until finally we announced each other. I complimented him, and he me; and having tickled each other in Irish fashion, we went to bed and talked until the claims of sleep became irresistible. The night was fine, but the sea was unquiet; yet, while others were sick through the cabin, I felt perfectly well; and, amid a glowing sun, a refreshing air, and the kind invitation of Dr. Cook to dine with him, etc., I stepped my foot upon my native soil, exclaiming in heart,

"'My foot it treads my native soil,
I breathe my native air!'

Oh, how changed in years, in mind, in heart, in all the circumstances of my being, from what I was when, a youthful wanderer, thirty-three years ago, I took my departure to seek my fortune in the New World of the West! God be praised for all the goodness and all the mercy which he has caused to follow me; and may this visit to my native land be blessed to me and to it.

"*July* 22. Took a car at six this morning for Castletown, Delvin. Every thing seemed strange and new. Thence rode to BALINASKEA. Remembered the turns in the road, but all else seemed new. Old houses all gone, old roads laid out in fields, old fences removed, and new houses, roads, and trees every where confounding me. As my arrival was expected, the moment the car stopped all knew who I was. On reaching my old home, *that* was gone, and a new one had taken its place. If dropped from the skies upon the spot, I would not have known where I was. My brother met me, now an old man, who was a joyous boy when we parted. I would not have known him. His wife and children I never saw before. Save in name, and some of these almost faded out from memory, all that thronged around me were entire strangers. Not one that I left in midlife remained. Not a trace existed of entire families. And, save a few persons a little older or younger than myself, who remembered me when going to school, and who said they would recognize me any where, the correctness of which was questionable, there were none who had any remembrance of me. The feeling induced was more than I could bear. With my brother, I started in the afternoon on a visit to the house of an aunt, where I spent two years in going to school to Master White, but so materially was the neighborhood altered that I did not recognize the house or the place. Aunt, uncle, and all the neighbors were gone, and as my two cousins were absent, not a person did I recognize. One old lady said she remembered me as a 'fine, bright chap going to school.' And that was all the remembrance I could eke out. Thence I rode with my brother, older than myself, to the youngest member of my family, James, who lives near Castlepollard. He came to the car and spoke to my brother, but had no remembrance of me, nor I the least of him. We three were the only survivors of a large family of children, and we spent the evening together in seeking to refresh each other's memory as well as we could. Feeling quite sick, I went into Castlepollard in order to have the accommodations of a hotel, and doctor if sick; and it was well I did, as through the night I had a most violent attack of illness, which kept me awake all night.

"*July* 23. Ordered the car at six this morning to breakfast with my brother Thomas, but was unable to leave my room until eleven. Rode with my brothers to the old homestead—met many of the children of old neighbors, who came some distance to see me. About four o'clock, rode to the grave-yard at Castletown, Delvin, and there, over the graves of my parents, preached Christ to my two brothers, and pointed out to them the way of life, and the terrible delusions of Romanism. They rode with me toward Athboy, and there, in a secluded part of the road, I bid them good-by, probably forever. My riding through Castletown made quite a sensation, as somehow or other the fame of me got among the people of the village, and they gazed on me as the representative of the New World."

In the year 1860 Dr. Murray revisited Europe in company with George H. Stuart, Esq., of Philadelphia, a distinguished philanthropist, an Irishman by birth. The special object of the visit was to observe and enjoy the remarkable revivals of religion then in progress in Ireland. Commissioned as a representative of various religious societies, Dr. Murray attended the anniversaries in London, and the Presbyterian General Assemblies in Edinburgh, and then passed over into Ireland. His traveling companion, Mr. Stuart, has kindly furnished a sketch of the tour, which is here presented:

"Philadelphia, Aug. 9, 1862.

"In compliance with your request, I now subjoin a few fragmentary memoranda of a memorable and happy visit made to Europe in 1860, with our beloved departed friend, Dr. Murray.

"I saw him first in 1837, and watched his course with interest, but did not make his personal acquaintance till 1851, in London, while attending the May meetings in Exeter Hall. During this visit to Europe we both made the acquaintance of that eminent servant of God, Rev. Alexander Duff, D.D., and his memorable visit to America was one of the results of that visit and acquaintance. Dr. Murray took a special interest in promoting the immediate object of Dr. Duff's visit. Being appointed chairman of the Business Committee of the Missionary Convention which met in New York, his influence was still more powerful in guiding, encouraging, and cementing that spirit of Christian love and evangelical alliance which was so signally manifested on that occasion. The New York train, in which Dr. Duff was traveling to Philadelphia, having been delayed by a heavy snowstorm, the clergy of the city, who had been invited to welcome him at my house, spent the evening in forming and cultivating acquaintanceships, which have continued to grow and strengthen with farther knowledge of each other's virtues; and when, at a late hour, Dr. Duff arrived, they were prepared to join heartily with Dr. Murray in his address of welcome to the distinguished missionary in Concert Hall—one of those impassioned outbursts of Christian feeling which it were vain to attempt to describe or report, but which those who have heard him, in his happiest moods, can perhaps imagine. The whole assembly was deeply moved, and from that hour the cause of foreign missions has been inseparably united to the progress of evangelical alliance.

"I need hardly say that my acquaintance with Dr. Murray deepened into an esteem and friendship which he was pleased to reciprocate, and which led me to advise with him, on matters of grave importance, as with a most intimate friend, and which resulted in our being associated in several matters of deep concern to the Church of God. He united with me in extending an invitation to the Irish General Assembly to send a deputation to America, which, being accepted, resulted in the visit of Dr. Edgar, and Rev. Messrs. Wilson and Dill, in 1859. Co-operating with him in promoting the object of this deputation, the evangelization of our dear native land, tended still more to deepen our friendship, and induced us to carry out, in concert, a desire which each had long entertained to revisit the scenes of our childhood, chiefly for the purpose of declaring the Gospel of the grace of God. For this object the season of the year of grace furnished a most fitting occasion.

"On the 14th of April, 1860, we set out on this journey, and returned on the 11th of August following. It was the most interesting of the many trips I have made to Europe. The general benevolence, lively wit, and earnest piety, so remarkably mingled in Dr. Murray's character, and which made him the most agreeable of companions in travel, speedily arrested the attention and commanded the respect of all our fellow-passengers on board the Adriatic.

"We arrived in time to attend the May meetings in London, at two of which, those of the British and Foreign Bible Society, and the Tract Society, he spoke as the representative of the corresponding American organizations, making on these occasions the ablest addresses I have ever heard him deliver. We were hospitably received by the noble patrons of these great national societies, and on such occasions Dr.

Murray's native politeness and urbanity toned naturally in harmony with the courtliness and kindness of these aristocratic circles.

"In Edinburgh he appeared and spoke before both the assemblies, the subject of his address before that of the Free Church being, What constitutes a Blue-stocking Presbyterian? We were invited to the public breakfasts of both the moderators, and were honored with an invitation to dine in Holyrood Palace, by Lord Belhaven, her majesty's Lord High Commissioner to the General Assembly of the Church of Scotland. The hospitality with which we were received by the Christian friends of America in Edinburgh was so universal as to forbid any attempt at enumeration or record of our hosts; and through the special attentions of Messrs. Nelsons, the well-known publishers, we were introduced to all the scenes of historic interest in that classic city and vicinity. In connection with a mission to the masses, we addressed a large meeting in the Royal Theatre, Dr. Murray entering with all his soul into the great movement, since so successfully prosecuted there, for preaching the Gospel to the poor.

"The only Sabbath we spent in Scotland was in Glasgow, where Dr. Murray preached in the pulpits of Dr. Buchanan, Rev. Jacob Alexander, and that formerly occupied by Dr. Chalmers, St. John's. While there, we attended the annual soiree of the Sabbath-schools of Mr. Alexander's Church, and of course Dr. Murray addressed the audience.

"Through the kindness of the Rev. Thomas Phillips,

the efficient agent of the Bible Society in Wales, who accompanied us, we were permitted to witness the progress of the revival with our own eyes in that country, where the whole face of society has been transformed by the power of the grace of God. We held four large meetings, at each of which a sermon was preached in Welsh by Mr. Phillips, and was followed by addresses by Dr. Murray and myself, in which we endeavored to give an account of the work of God in America. In the slate quarries of Port Penrhyn, near Bangor, we found more than fifty daily prayer-meetings held in the huts of the 2700 quarry-men, during the dinner-hour. Our guide, when asked why he did not give himself to God, replied, 'Indeed, sir, I had a hard job to get rid of it.' At our departure from Wales, while taking our tickets at the railway station, one of the porters, who recognized us, took us to the lamp-room, and showed us the box of Bibles and Hymn-books used by the railway men in their daily prayer-meeting. These and other signs, which met us on every side, showed that the work had penetrated the working-classes, and gone down to the very bottom of society in Wales. Their congregational singing was indescribably solemn and impressive. The architecture of their meeting-houses and their forms of worship are very simple. The prevailing form of religion is Calvinistic Methodism, nearly identical with Presbyterianism.

"But the most interesting part of this visit was that to Ireland. Dr. Murray had a double object in view: to behold for himself the progress of the mission work of the Presbyterian Church in the north and west, and of the great revival, and to procure materials for a history of our native land, which should disabuse the minds of the people of America of the ignorance and prejudice consequent on the want of any accessible impartial history of that much calumniated country. This history, the fruit of great research, was in a state of considerable forwardness, and possibly may yet be given to the public by some person inspired with the like ambition of doing justice to Ireland, though it will be hard to find one worthy to handle the pen of Kirwan. In carrying out these designs, we were indebted to many clergymen and gentlemen for the kindest attentions and the most warm-hearted Irish hospitality; but our acknowledgments are specially due to Dr. Edgar, of Belfast, who invited a large company of ministers, professors, and leading Christians of Belfast to meet us at breakfast at his house the morning of our arrival, placed his extensive knowledge and influence at our service, accompanied us to many scenes of interest, and introduced us to the friends of Christ all over the north and west, and thus enabled us to see much which otherwise would have been utterly impracticable, and to form and express, on our own observation, the conviction that, of this great work of God the half has not been told.

"Our first visit, as arranged by Dr. Edgar, was to the mission field of the Athlone Presbytery, in the west of Ireland, and in the very midst of Romanism. Here we had an excellent opportunity of contrasting the influence of the Gospel of Christ in improving the temporal condition of the people, with the effects of popery, manifest in the filth, poverty, ignorance, and vice of the unevangelized districts. We had an opportunity of visiting and addressing every congregation of this Presbytery save one, and of witnessing the progress made by these little mission stations, in a few years grown into respectable congregations, with substantial meeting-houses, settled pastors, large worshiping assemblies, and a people who, for their zeal, and love to the people and ordinances of God, will bear comparison with any in the world. During his visit to this Presbytery, in whose bounds he was born, and where he spent the years of his childhood and youth, he preached the dedication sermon at the opening of a new church in the town of Athlone—the very centre of Ireland—more American in its style of architecture than any thing we had seen in Europe, the pulpit being literally American. While we were received by all the ministers and people of this Presbytery with the greatest kindness and hospitality, we were laid under special obligations by the Rev. Messrs. Adair, Edmonds, Whigam, Mawhinney, Fleming, and Watson, and by Captain Burd, and Messrs. Digby and Campbell, and their families, who bestowed on us the kindest attentions and the most generous hospitalities.

"In the neighborhood of the Ballinasloe congregation we visited the farm of one of its principal supporters, Mr. Allan Pollock, a farmer from Scotland, of the class which has produced such a revolution in Irish farming since the year of famine. This gentleman farms 32,000 acres in fields of 50 to 100 acres each, inclosed by over 100 miles of stone wall. He feeds 32,000 head of cattle, 20,000 sheep, and 400 horses. He employs 2000 hands, to whom he pays $7500 wages monthly, and who are lodged in neat, comfortable cottages, which he has erected instead of the hovels he found on the estate. His sales are principally of cattle, though he sells grain annually to the value of $7500, and imports guano by cargoes. We counted seven tall chimneys, driving as many steam-engines, employed in doing his farm-work. On the very border of his estate was a little heap of bushes, projecting over a miserable hovel, dug out of the side of the ditch, into which I entered, to ascertain by personal inspection whether human beings dwelt in a hole unfit for hogs, and found a woman and children living there in filth and misery, enabling us at a glance to see the immense elevation of social condition produced in Ireland by Protestantism and its attendant industry. Before leaving, we addressed a crowded meeting in one of the neat school-houses he has built on the estate for the children of his working people.

"We spent a night in Limerick with the Rev. David Wilson, and saw there a little of the work of God under his ministry—a work which is already beginning to affect the state of society in that important city.

"On our way from the Presbytery of Athlone to the north, we spent some time in Dublin, where the Presbyterian Church has made a rapid advance in the last ten years. Here Dr. Murray preached to large congregations, and addressed two public meetings; at the close of one of which a professional gentleman, well known in Dublin, waited to thank the author of Kirwan's Letters as the means of his conversion. We met with several other instances of the same kind during our visit to Ireland. In company with Mr. Hugh Moore and Rev. John Hall, we made an excursion to the Wicklow Mountains, and spent the greater part of the day in exploring the scenery on foot. In the intercourse of Dr. Murray with the peasantry on this occasion, the peculiar mingling of humor and wisdom which marked his character had ample field for exercise, and furnished a perpetual fountain of enjoyment to himself and his companions. The hospitality and kindness of Mr. Moore, and Mr. Hall, and many other friends in Dublin we can not soon forget. On the morning of our departure, we found, on coming down stairs, fifty-six ministers and laymen assembled for breakfast in Mr. Moore's dining-room to bid us God speed. Here Dr. Murray, wholly overcome by his feelings, as he referred to the portrait of his sainted daughter in heaven which hung against the wall of the hospitable mansion where she had been received with so much kindness when seeking health in the land of her fathers, was, for the first time in his life, unable to express the thoughts he designed to utter, and could only sit down and weep.

"Leaving Dublin, we proceeded at once to visit Ulster and the scenes of the revival. At Belfast, the metropolis of Presbyterianism, we were honored with a public breakfast, presided over by the distinguished Dr. Cook, who, though far advanced in life, was still as vigorous in mind and body as ever. We had there an opportunity of visiting several of the daily prayer-meetings, conducted very much like those in America. One of these was held near one of the large factories, the hands employed in it coming in to spend a portion of their dinner-hour in prayer and praise. Here, also, Dr. Murray preached to large, and often crowded congregations, and assisted in laying the corner-stones of two new churches, which, with three others, were needed to accommodate the additions made to the Church; speaking on both occasions in the open air, to large assemblies, with extraordinary animation and unction.

"Our crowning privilege, however, in Belfast was the great prayer-meeting in the Botanic Gardens, where over 40,000 persons from the city and vicinity assembled for worship on Monday, July 2d, 1860. About fifteen different stands enabled the principal speakers and leaders of the meeting to be heard by the crowds surrounding them. On one of these stands stood the rector of the Episcopal Church, and just opposite, a large crowd was addressed by the Ballymena weaver. At the principal stand, where Dr. Murray spoke, might be heard the voice of the coach-maker of Coleraine, whose remarkable conversion has been published to the world. The vast assemblage was pervaded by the spirit of devotion, and the greatest order and solemnity prevailed. When the multitudes lifted up their voices in singing the hundredth Psalm, in the old Scotch version, the sound was as the voice of many waters. This meeting will live in the memory of all who attended it. It was one of the most extraordinary assemblages for the worship of God on earth since the great congregations in the wilderness and at the dedication of the Temple.

"Rev. Dr. S. M. Dill, and Revs. Messrs. Simpson, M'Clure, and Moorehead, directed us to more of the same interesting scenes of the revival in the counties of Antrim, Down, and Derry. Though the progress of the work through a whole year had taken away the excitement of novelty, we had abundant opportunity of witnessing the ingathering of the rich harvest of the year of grace. One of its most remarkable features, to one acquainted with the previous condition of the churches, was the revived ministry, with whom the work of conversion was the great subject of conversation on all occasions. Religion was, indeed, the great subject of public interest, and of conversation in railway-cars and places of concourse. We often saw walls placarded with texts of Scripture, and the stands at railway stations filled with religious books. It is impossible, in the brief space of a letter, to chronicle all the blessed results of this revival; for a full account of them, I must refer my readers, who take an interest in the Kingdom of God, to the authentic record given by Professor Gibson in his well-known book, *The Year of Grace*, and that by Dr. Weir, of London, *The Ulster Revival.*

"At Ballymena, the focus of the revival, near which it originated, we met the ministers and principal inhabitants of the vicinity at a public breakfast, presided over by Mr. Dickey; and through the kindness of Dr. Dill, through whose influence large assemblages were brought together, we were permitted to see much more of the fruits of the revival than would otherwise have been possible. Dr. Murray lectured in Dr. Dill's church before the Young Men's Christian Association, and preached there also to a crowded congregation. Here we witnessed one of the most interesting assemblages of children and adults our eyes ever beheld. At the close of a lovely Sabbath evening in the month of June, on the verdant carpet of a newly-mown lawn, and under the spacious canopy of the blue heaven, twenty-one Sabbath-schools assembled to commemorate their anniversary, and to unite in those exercises of prayer and praise which seemed to be the principal delight of the whole population. As he beheld the crowds flocking past the window of Dr. Dill's house, in which we were guests, to the place of meeting, Dr. Murray was overwhelmed with the responsibility of addressing such multitudes of awakened souls, and said to me, as I sat at a distant part of the room, 'Look here, Mr. Stuart, this is fearful;' nor could the agitation of his soul be composed until after repeated approaches to the throne of grace and peace. His speech on that occasion will long be remembered, and many will bless God for it through eternity. At this meeting several cases of prostration occurred, the first Dr. Murray had witnessed, but I do not recollect any expression of his opinion on that subject. He notes in his diary, 'This is one of the marked Sabbaths of my life.'

"Dr. Taylor, of Ballymoney, came all the way to

Belfast to invite him to deliver a lecture in Rev. Mr. Parks's church, which was crowded. Here also he was received with the most unbounded enthusiasm and generous hospitality.

"At Londonderry he preached for Dr. Dunham and Rev. William M'Clure, to congregations measured by the capacity of the meeting-houses, and was deeply interested in the ancient walls and bastions, and other monuments of its defense under its brave Presbyterian minister and governor, Walker, whose monument is an auspicious landmark to all travelers approaching the city. But the city itself, with its thriving factories, its noble schools, and Magee College, and its multiplying Presbyterian churches and Sabbath-schools, is the best monument of the vitality of that form of the Gospel of the grace of God.

"On the invitation of Francis Watson, Esq., we visited Lurgan, and addressed two simultaneous meetings, rendered necessary by the incapacity of any single building to receive the multitude—a Young Men's Society of the Episcopal Church, in the Mechanics' Institute built by the liberality of William Watson, Esq., of New York, and a public meeting in Rev. Mr. Berkeley's meeting-house; Dr. Murray giving the opening address there, and proceeding immediately to address the meeting in the Institute, where I made the opening address, and then, on his arrival, went over and addressed the other meeting. A very solemn feeling pervaded both these large assemblies.

"Of several other scenes of deep interest I omit any mention, as the subject of this letter did not accompany me to them; but the kindness and love of the Christian friends by whom I was received, and the tokens of the presence of God among them, I can never forget. This letter has already extended to such a length that I must also forbear reference to many deeply interesting incidents, and to many dear friends whose hospitality and attentions were lavished upon us both, merely stating the fact that, during the six weeks of our stay in Ireland, we only slept three times in a hotel, at the Giants' Causeway and the Lakes of Killarney.

"In England we held meetings on behalf of the Evangelical Alliance, at the request of the Committee of the British Branch in Manchester and Brighton; and Dr. Murray preached in Liverpool and Birkenhead, and at the latter place attended a tea-party given us in the lecture-room of Rev. Mr. Tower's church. Our last meeting in Britain was that above referred to in Brighton; and while all his public addresses there were marked by increasing earnestness, this last address in the Royal Pavilion, in the very room where George the Fourth held his bacchanalian orgies, was characterized by an indescribable energy and unction, and produced the most marked and solemnizing influence on the audience. He felt, and expressed the feeling, that these were the last addresses he should ever make to these vast assemblages, to whom he ministered the Gospel as the savor of life unto life, or of death unto death.

"We made a hasty visit to Paris, where he preached in the American Chapel for Dr. M'Clintock, and spent one of the last hours of our stay in a visit to the grave of Napoleon. Taking the steamer Adriatic at Havre for home, we touched at Cowes for the mails, and went ashore to spend the last moments of our stay in Europe in visiting the grave of the Dairyman's Daughter, and reflecting on the contrast between the growing glory of her immortal usefulness, shining undying as the stars, and the fading honors of the destroyer of nations. In God's sight, the humble Christian peasant is more truly heroic than the conqueror of Europe.

"In these journeys I had ample opportunities of observing Dr. Murray's prudence, cheerfulness, zeal, piety, and readiness for every good work, and my esteem for his character daily increased. It does not become me to attempt any delineation of his character; that duty has been performed by an abler hand; but I feel that by his departure I have lost a confidential friend, to whose judgment, on matters of delicacy and importance, I was frequently permitted to refer, and in every instance had reason to acquiesce in the wisdom of his conclusions. His departure is a large subtraction from the society of the excellent of the earth, and should be an additional incentive to hasten to that better land where, with congenial and worthy companions, he is showing forth the glories of our Divine Redeemer, which he loved to exhibit here below.

"Taken away, as he was, from the evil to come on our afflicted country, it will be interesting to his many friends to know that one of the last conversations I had with him was on the subject of our national dangers, on the occasion of the fast proclaimed by President Buchanan. He read me an extract from the sermon he preached on that occasion, in which he strongly protested against the continued encroachments of the slave power, and the growth of a seditious spirit among the politicians of the South, and against the cowardly relinquishment of free discussion by the churches and people of the North; indicating that, had he lived to take part in the great conflict now waging, his heart, and voice, and powerful pen would have been engaged for God and liberty. But his work was finished—let us bless God for it—in happier times, and now he shall no more see the storm of battle, or hear the alarm of war. He has entered into peace. May we, by God's grace, be enabled to follow those who, through faith and patience, inherit the promises. Man's chief end is to glorify God and to enjoy Him forever was his favorite motto.

"I remain, reverend and dear sir, respectfully yours,

"GEO. H. STUART."

CHAPTER XVIII.

Sorrows.—Joys.—His Family.—The Sickness and Death of six Children.—Letters from Drs. A. Alexander, Miller, and J. W. Alexander.—Effects of these Afflictions.

GREAT trials make great saints. Dr. Murray was so prospered and successful in his career that he needed afflictions, many and often, to make him humble and dependent. From the time that he gave himself to God and the ministry of the Word, all went well with him. His course through college and the seminary was a constant success; and his entrance on the pastoral life was attended with circumstances well calculated to exalt him above measure. His services were sought for so many different fields of labor, that he might be easily tempted to believe that he was more than an ordinary man. And his popularity grew on him rapidly. The calls that he received to various churches, and positions of responsibility and honor were so many, that it would have been no strange thing had he come to think of himself more highly than he ought to think. And as he advanced in his career, he became so marked a favorite with the public, and in so many circles of society he was courted and flattered, that he needed, as Paul needed, a constant admonition of his dependence on the grace of God.

He was singularly happy in his domestic relations.

Mrs. Murray, the wife of his youth and his life, combined in a degree, as beautiful as rare, the various graces that, when blended, make the wife of a pastor her husband's crown. Dr. Murray often said to me, "What a blessed thing it is to have a wife who has common sense!" With a strong and well-cultivated intellect, Mrs. Murray united the tenderness of an affectionate disposition, the gentleness and delicacy of a refined and amiable woman, with a practical business talent, that made her literally a help meet for such a man as her husband. She doubled all his joys, and more than shared his cares; for, in a measure quite unusual with the wives of ministers, she took upon herself the burden of domestic life, regulating the household, providing for its wants, and relieving her husband of the necessity of seeing many who called upon him in hours of study, answering multitudes of letters for him, and in a thousand nameless ways lightening the labors that were laid upon him. He appreciated all this wealth of service, and loved to speak of it as the help without which he would have been utterly unable to accomplish the work which he was performing for his own Church and the world.

His domestic circle was the scene of his highest and most complete enjoyment. In the sports of his little ones, frolicking with him in the wildest glee, or in the pleasures of the children as they grew to be his companions in his hours of relaxation, he found the sweetest relief from the toils of study. His children were never afraid of him, but they always loved him, and enjoyed nothing more than to play with him when it was his time to play. Eminently companionable among men of his own age, calling, and culture, he was even more fond of the society of the young, who were always at home with him, as if he were a father, a brother, or a warm personal friend.

It was necessary to develop these domestic and social traits of character to prepare us to understand the nature of those domestic trials through which he was made to pass, in the midst of his arduous and absorbing labors. These trials were the *deaths of six beloved children.* Few parents are called to drink so many cups of sorrow. Few find so much consolation and draw so much profit from the lessons of affliction.

His first-born son lived but a few weeks. Its death was a sore disappointment, and a sad memento of the frailty of earthly expectations. After prayer by the father in the chamber where the mother was still sick, the infant of days was buried in the rear of the new church at Wilkesbarre. The affliction had a very softening and subduing effect upon his spirit. He preached a sermon immediately on the gift of God abounding to them who had not sinned after the similitude of Adam's transgression.

On the day that this first-born son was buried, his daughter Elizabeth, then two years old, was attacked with scarlet fever, and for many weeks was so ill as to require constant watching for her life. The mother was sick, and the father hung with double solicitude over their only surviving child. It pleased God to spare her life; but when health returned she had forgotten how to walk and to talk. And "it was amusing," says one who observed him, "to see her fond father giving her daily lessons, and sharing, for her encouragement, in her blunders."

A second son was born in Elizabethtown, December 29th, 1833. He was a child of uncommon personal beauty, and, if not sanctified from his birth, he was, from his earliest developments, a religious boy. Because of his implicit obedience, his parents often called him their "Casa Bianca;" his name was William Wilberforce. For eight years he lived the joy of a father's heart and the light of his eyes, growing constantly in knowledge and in favor with God and man. The first time that I ever saw Dr. Murray, he came to my house with this son in the summer of 1841. The memory of the boy is fresh in my mind this moment, so deeply was I then impressed with the loveliness of his person and the sweetness of his temper as he mingled with my own children.

In a note to me respecting this period of Dr. Murray's life, Mrs. Murray says:

"Thanksgiving day, 1841, was one of the happiest of our lives. Our five lovely children in fine health, and the pastor as beloved as he was useful among his flock. Our children, as a thank-offering to God for His goodness, formed a family missionary society. Willie presided, and Lizzie was secretary; and out of this grew the Juvenile Foreign Missionary Society of our Church, which has contributed from year to year, for the past twenty, an average of over one hundred dollars to educate heathen children. Several of the children educated were hopefully converted, and died in the faith of the Gospel. It was at this time, before death had desolated our happy home, that a friend, after recalling many pleasant early recollections, asked if childhood was not the most joyous season of life. 'I never,' replied my husband, 'knew what true happiness was until surrounded by my children.'"

A few days afterward this noble boy, the only son, sickened of scarlet fever and died.

Among the many letters of sympathy to the afflicted parents, received from numerous friends, are two or three of permanent and general interest, and the names of the writers are so fragrant in the Church that I shall copy them here:

Letter from Archibald Alexander, D.D.

"Princeton, Dec. 16th, 1811.

"REV. AND DEAR SIR,—Before I received your letter of yesterday, I had heard of the heartrending affliction with which it hath pleased our heavenly Father to visit you, and ever since you and Mrs. Murray have been much on my mind. Last night I waked in the middle of the night, and almost the first thought which occurred was your sore bereavement. Well did the sacred writer understand the poignancy of human grief when he compares the bitter anguish of the mourning penitent to the sorrow of one who has lost a *first-born* or *only son.* I knew that this must be a desolating stroke to your feelings, as I observed that your affections were strongly twined around the child, so that your life seemed to be, as it were, 'bound up in the life of the lad.' Perhaps, indeed, without knowing it, you made him too much of an idol, and therefore he was snatched away from you. He was, indeed, a lovely child; but such are so far from being exempt from the shafts of death, that they are more frequently the objects of his relentless stroke. Precocious children, who are at the same time susceptible of tender religious impressions, seldom are permitted to grow up to manhood. They are taken away from the evil to come. They are carried into a purer and more salubrious atmosphere to complete their education. Christ says, 'Suffer little children to come unto me, and forbid them not, for of such is the kingdom of heaven.' Thus spake He when on earth. And now, methinks, He loves to have the dear little ones who believe in Him where He is, that He may take them in His arms and bless them. He delighted to hear their young voices singing *hosannah* when He made His royal entry into Jerusalem, and still He delights to have a choir of such to 'perfect His praise' in the temple above. You would not have hesitated to give up your son to be under the tuition of the best earthly teacher; and, whatever natural affection may say, faith says it is far better to be absent from the body and present with the Great Teacher. While his life hung in jeopardy, and you knew not what your Father's will might be, deep anxiety was natural; but now, since the child is dead, and the will of God is manifest, *do* like David under a similar stroke: when he 'perceived that the child was dead, he arose from the earth, and washed and anointed himself, and changed his apparel, and came into the house of the Lord and worshiped; then he came to his own house, and when he required they set bread before him, and he did eat. Then said his servants unto him, What thing is this that thou hast done—thou didst fast and weep for the child while it was alive, but when the child was dead thou didst rise and eat bread? And he said, While the child was yet alive, I fasted and wept; for I said, who can tell whether God will be gracious to me, that the child may live? But now he is dead, wherefore should I fast? Can I bring him back again? *I shall go to him, but he shall not return to me.*'

"Read Cowper's hymn, 'God moves in a mysterious way,' etc. Christ seems to say, 'What I do you know not now, but you shall know hereafter. All things work together for good to them that love God.' But I need not cite texts; you know them. Yet sometimes, when proposed by another, they take effect. I have sent you a little book, in which nearly all the texts suited to the case have been classed and arranged by J. W. A. when he had suffered under such a stroke.

"I regret that I am unable to visit you in this time of sorrow, but I have made an engagement to preach at Lawrence, where there is more than usual seriousness. James expresses tender sympathy—seemed at first to be willing to go—but he is unwell, and has just now *double* duty in college, which he can not leave without deranging their whole system. He says he will write. I sent your letter to Dr. Miller. I have just received his answer, saying, 'I deeply sympathize with Mr. Murray, and would willingly go to Elizabethtown, but expeditions of this kind at this season of the year are particularly perilous to me.' You perceive, then, that though you can have our sympathy and prayers, you can not have our aid in the pulpit. But you will not need it; the Lord will strengthen you. His promise is, 'As is your day, so shall your strength be; my grace is sufficient for thee, and my strength is perfected in thy weakness.'

"With kind respects to Mrs. M., I am your affectionate brother, A. ALEXANDER."

Letter from Samuel Miller, D.D.

"Princeton, December 16th, 1841.

"MY DEAR BROTHER,—Mrs. Miller and myself, with our whole hearts, sympathize with you and your excellent companion in your late heavy bereavement. We had heard of the illness and death of your beloved boy before the arrival of your letter. We know how to feel for you. Our first-born son, nearly of the same age, was taken from us nearly thirty years ago. We found it hard to say from the heart, 'The Lord gave, and the Lord hath taken away; blessed be the name of the Lord;' yet I hope we were enabled, in some degree, to say it sincerely. And now, when we think that that dear boy has gone before us to glory; that he escaped the toils and sorrows of this corrupt, insnaring world; and that he is now far above us in knowledge, and in conformity to Him who loved us, and gave Himself for us, I trust we can more than acquiesce in the Divine will—that we can cordially rejoice that our beloved Edward is infinitely better off than if he had been permitted to live, as we then wished. I do not expect, dear brother, to stop your flowing tears. Nature will feel, ought to feel; and we, as well as other friends, feel with you; but is not your dear son with his and your Father? Can you *long* weep when you recollect what he has *escaped* and what he has *gained?* May the Lord pour into your heart, and that of your companion, those rich consolations which I know you recognize and love, but which, alas! the pleadings of nature often prevent our viewing at once in all their unsearchable riches.

"Dr. Alexander sent your letter to me, being himself under an engagement, and his son James not being well, and also under an engagement. I should be glad to spend the next Sabbath with you, at once to weep with you, and rejoice in hope of glory. But my growing infirmities, my exceedingly delicate health, and the perils which now attend my undertaking any such expedition at this season of the year, all conspire to forbid my venturing on the journey.

"I am, my dear afflicted brother, with sincere regard to you and Mrs. Murray, your affectionate brother, SAMUEL MILLER."

Letter from James W. Alexander, D.D.

"MY DEAR BROTHER MURRAY,—I have heard of your great bereavement, and you will believe me when I say I sympathize in no ordinary degree with you and your dear wife. The heart of a father I know, but the heart of a mother surely I pretend not to understand. And now what shall I say to you? What can any one but God say to you? You have already found the voice of human condolence all vain, yet there is a satisfaction even in the pressure of a brotherly hand, and this is all I have to offer. May the God of our children, and our own God, stanch your wound, and pour in the balm of Gospel comfort! I have been in these waters, my dear brother and sister, 'And I said, my strength and my hope is perished from the Lord; remembering mine affliction and my misery, the wormwood and the gall. My soul hath them still in remembrance, and is humbled in me.' Your sweet boy has escaped this, yea, every sorrow. What an escape! His salvation is no more a matter of doubt or prayer; an everlasting smile is upon his angelic countenance. Oh, let us not wish him back on this sea of tempest and shipwreck!

"Let me quote a few sentences from the letters of heavenly Samuel Rutherford: 'Your Lord may gather His own roses and shake His apples at what season of the year He pleaseth.' 'The child hath but changed a bed in the garden, and is planted up nearer the sun, where he shall thrive better than in this out-field moor-ground. You must think your Lord would not lack him one hour longer, and since the loan of him was expired (as it is, if you read in the lease), let Him have His own with gain.' 'Something of yours is in heaven besides the flesh of your exalted Savior, and ye go on after your own.' 'If he hath cast his bloom and flower, the bloom is fallen in heaven in Christ's lap.'

"Oh, my friends, be comforted with the views, which I am sure are the life of your souls, and which show you the face of a tender Father behind this chastising power. How greatly I regret that it is impossible for me to be with you. A mere inconvenience should not detain me; but our arrangements in college are such that I should lose the only exercise I have in the week with the Senior class, and a still more important service on Monday morning. I am also quite unwell, and should not dare to go unless the weather changes.

"Be assured of the affectionate interest we all feel in your trial. Present me kindly to your suffering wife, and believe me yours in Gospel bonds,

"James W. Alexander.

"Princeton, 17th December, 1841."

This was his first great bereavement, to be followed by sorrow upon sorrow, until, in deep humility, he was heard to ask, "Wherefore contendest Thou with me?" The lovely boy, so suddenly snatched from the family circle, had given, in his dying hours, expression to a strong faith in God, and loving preference to be with Him, well calculated to soothe the anguish of his father's heart, and prepare him for still greater trials of faith and patience. One after another of his children and servants sickened with the dreadful disease then passing like a scourge through the land. On the 14th day of January, 1842, one month after she had followed her brother to the grave, Anna Rhees, aged six years, died. She had inherited from her father a large share of his Irish character, frank, and full of mirthfulness, and was warmly loved in the congregation. On the same day her father writes: "Our beautiful, eccentric, and ethereal Annie has left us, singing, as she ascended to heaven to unite with Willie in the unending song, 'Unto Him who hath loved us, and washed us in His own blood.'" Thus faded on earth another of the beautiful buds of promise God had so graciously given His servant. The Rev. Dr. Archibald Alexander, very tenderly affected by the multiplied afflictions of his young friend, came to Elizabethtown to preach the funeral sermon. Dr. Murray often said he owed much to that visit; it taught him how little need be said to persons in affliction. After a warm pressure of the hand, the venerable man sat down, silently seeming to enter into the feelings of the afflicted parents. He then remarked that although Job's friends were very foolish in their speeches to him, they were wise in their silence. God speaks at such a time, and man need not.

This was a dark and trying hour. The hand of God seemed to be resting heavily on the house of his servant. To preserve the health and lives of the rest of the children, it was thought prudent for the family to go to Philadelphia for a season. They went. Mr. Murray remained, and gave himself with intense devotion to his work. Soon the darkness gave way to dawning and advancing light. The Spirit of God was poured out upon the Church, and many souls were converted. The seriousness was generally attributed to the deep sympathy of the people with the pastor in his sorrows, and, without doubt, it was the fruit of his increased spirituality and zeal in the ministry of the Word. He could now comprehend the design of the afflictions that had come with such fearful frequency and power. Always afterward he was wont to say to others and to himself, in seasons of great sorrow, "Work—work for God and man. Pour blessings round you. This will soothe your woe."

In the month of March ten new converts were added to the Church; at the next communion season in July, forty-four, and in September, eighteen; making seventy-two conversions as the result of a good work that had its beginning in the sorrows of the pastor's house and heart.

Margaret Breckinridge was born in August, 1843, and for seven years was a bright and beautiful star in the heaven of this home. She died of croup, January 2, 1851. This was the fourth child that Dr. Murray had laid in the grave; but his cup was not yet full. These trials were all doing good, working out the sanctification of the bereaved father, and fitting him for still greater usefulness. Yet the Lord had other and still greater trials in store, and they came in their order, increasing in severity, as he had grace to bear them and improve them.

In the year 1847, a daughter, Catharine Loxley, was born. As she grew in years, she seemed to her loving father to include all that he thought lovely and promising in William and Anna who had been taken away. Perhaps the traits which she developed, reminding him of those who had gone before, drew his heart with peculiar tenderness of affection toward this child, and made him dote upon her more than on any other one in his little flock. And so she died early. Only six years she lived and gladdened the house with her love, and then Death came and took her to the family, now rapidly becoming the most numerous, in heaven. It was this blow that dissolved the ties that bound him to the world. Henceforth he was emphatically another man. His grief was great beyond expression. I remember how he fell on my neck, and wept like a child, when I entered his house, while the lamb was waiting its burial. It was heart-breaking to see a strong man so crushed in grief.

Mrs. Duncan, of Edinburgh, whose visit to this country will be remembered with delight by many friends, and whose name is imperishably associated with that of her accomplished daughter, Mary Lundie Duncan, wrote to the family on the occasion of this bereavement, and I venture to copy a few lines from her letter:

"7 India Street, Edinburgh, February 12, 1852.

"MY VERY DEAR FRIEND,—I do not know in what strain to address you, yet I can not stay. Ever since dear Miss L.'s letter, so touching and so descriptive, has reached my hand, I have been thinking, and dreaming of, and praying for you all. That bright sunbeam of the sweet dwelling, with her considering critical eye, her shrewd observations, her ready kindness, I see her before me. One that I thought would forget me presently, but whom I should not forget. So her dear light is quenched to you! I can not forbid you to weep, for I too am weeping. Yet how far has she got before you all! The guiding parents, in whose words she had such implicit faith, are but babes in knowledge to her now. How soothing and sweet has she found the verification of His word, who gathers the lambs in His arms, and bears them in His bosom! She has not shed one tear for want of her own beloved mother, however many you may have shed for her. Precious revelations are they to which our hearts greedily hold in times of separation and sorrow. My dear friends, I entreat you not to spend time in pitying yourselves as bereaved. We are apt, when we have had trouble and pleasure in our offspring, and have laid hold on them with strong appropriating affection, to be inclined to say with David in his perplexity, 'Surely Thou hast made all men in vain.'

"But let our darkened spirits be hushed, and let us reason on His wisdom, and love, and purposes. Looking out of our own rifled nest, let us, by faith, behold the store-house where our God treasures up His jewels. How many have you and I there? Who ransomed and placed them there? Who made them so bright? Could we have won crowns and palms for them? We would, if our will had been done, have detained them to struggle, to sin, and repent, and weep, and hope, and fear as we do. And we would have left them behind us to mourn for us. Is it not safer for them to sin never again—to weep never again? We are not going to be selfish parents; our love for them forbids it. I have sometimes said I could bear to part with them all if I knew they were with Jesus. One knows not what they could *not* bear, the Lord sustaining. Yet, while I think of little, beaming, sincere Kate, with her clear eye and her chestnut curls, my tears run down for you. She was not born in vain. She has been taken 'home to heaven,' and she has not still to die as all of us have. Holier, safer, happier far than any of us, we *must not* mourn, but give thanks about her and for her. Are you not rich to have so many in heaven? Feeling flies out and will have its way, but reason calmly weighs it down, while the Comforter tells you all is well with the child.

"With ourselves there is much to be done, and much depends upon the uses made of affliction. My mind flits from the very affectionate father, bowing to the blow, and saying, 'I shall go to them—the will of the Lord be done;' to the dear, shaken, trembling mother, with her weary frame, her imagination full of images of hours of pain, and her heart full of sorrows; to the young group looking at the desolation, and wondering who shall go next. When our God wounds a Christian family, He has a right to expect fruit of His stripes. Ah! dear children, I have been trying to join the petitions of your beloved parents, that the death of the darling's earthly part may be the life of your souls. Do not pass this dark mark in your journey without turning to the Lord with all your hearts. Let it be said, the little sister is dead, but the elder three and the brothers are alive. They have found the life of their souls. * * * *

"*April* 16*th*. Your *little* ones. Oh, how gladly would many mourning parents have parted with theirs when they were little! One looks around on the griefs of Christian parents, and sees what afflictions far heavier than death are in the wilderness. Then, if the death of one is the new life of another—if the *perishing* loses its worth in the eyes of one dear child by reason of the quick removal of another, is there not cause of much joy and praise? I often fancy dear Kate. There was something of deep thought and feeling between her eyes and hair, simple, yet most unlike a child. Do you not often observe that children early removed have an aspect of feeling quite peculiar? Such was hers. Her simple confiding in our God, so little cause to shrink by sin on her conscience, her certainty of being safe and at home with Him whom she only regarded as a higher Father, all that was about her so fit to touch the hearts of the young people.

"I trust a great blessing will fall on that peaceful study and these young seekers for truth, and that your newly-adorned Church will be quickly filled with songs of praise more humbly joyful than you ever had before."

This prayer was answered by the refreshing which continued throughout the coming year, and which brought into the communion of the Church, among many other spiritual children, the pastor's daughter.

Yet a greater sorrow was still in reserve. All these had died in early childhood; the first but three weeks in life, and none of them more than eight years. Elizabeth was the first-born child; she had grown to be the companion and counselor of her parents, the pride and joy of the social and domestic circle, and the delight of a host of admiring friends. From a child she had been in delicate health. Her complexion was so white, and contrasted so vividly with the brightness of her beautiful eyes, that no one could see her without being at once interested in her appearance. Hopeful, cheerful, and patient under sufferings painfully acute and long endured, her very feebleness had made her a loving burden on her parents' hearts, who, year by year, watched her with fond solicitude. To personal attractions she added the charms of a highly-cultivated mind, and manners polished by wide associations with the most refined and accomplished society. In the hope of finding benefit from the voyage and foreign travel, she accepted an invitation from Daniel James, Esq., of Liverpool, a life-time friend of her father, to visit him in the Old World. She traveled in England, Scotland, and Ireland, spending much of her time in the enjoyment of social intercourse with some of the best people on the earth. With the family of Mr. James she visited the Continent, and rejoiced among the beauty and grandeur of the Rhine and Switzerland. Returning home with health improved, she devoted herself to the duties of a daughter in her father's house, gladdening all his days, and ministering as she could to lighten his labors. Having known her well and long, I speak thus freely and confidently of the treasure which Dr. Murray had in this beautiful and precious daughter. But it was a treasure in a very frail vessel. She was so *spirituelle* to look upon that she seemed to be rather of heaven than earth. And it was strange that she lived with us so long, rather than that she died so soon. It was the first day of the summer of 1858, when, just as the sun was rising, she breathed out her spirit on the breast of her Redeemer; and those eyes, so long closed to external objects, were opened "to behold the King in his beauty." It was a solemn hour of mingled peace and joy with the bitterness of bereavement when Dr. Murray knelt by the side of his first-born and long-cherished child, to thank God, who had given her the victory over death, and for all the precious memories connected with her life. This was his last offering to Heaven.

We have accompanied the father to the grave with six children. Four only out of ten survived. Repeated and dreadful were these bereavements, but they were, doubtless, just the sorrows that Infinite Wisdom, in infinite love, devised for Dr. Murray's personal advancement in the life divine, and his highest preparation for the work he was called to do.

These afflictions softened, humbled, and purified him. God put forth His hand and touched him just where he was most tender and exposed, and the fruits of gentleness and love, of increasing spirituality and devotion, bore witness to the virtue of the affliction with which it pleased his heavenly Father to visit him.

CHAPTER XIX.

A new Baptism.—Words of Cheer.—Extracts from his Journal.—Exposure to Cold.—Paroxysms of Pain.—Faints and revives.—Farewell to Friends.—Dying Prayer and Benediction.—Funeral.

THE close of Dr. Murray's life was in keeping with its steady onward, upward course. During his last visit to Ireland, amid scenes of revival, he received a new baptism of the Spirit, and returned home with a burning desire to see among his own people, and in this country, the Word of the Lord glorified as it was in Ireland and Wales. For this end he labored, and prayed with increased zeal and love.

Earthly cares were no longer a hinderance to him; and to a friend laboring under their burden, he said, "Look up; your treasures are not here; where Christ lives, we live; our children are with Him in heaven; soon we shall have finished *our work*. I am a working-man as well as you, and I do not go bowed down, looking into the grave. Your daughter is not there; mine is not there. Be cheerful; let us work for God, and soon we shall be with them." And these words, spoken in the street, were blessed to a bereaved, weary pilgrim, who, leaving his burden at the foot of the Cross, went on his way rejoicing, and continues to bless God for that casual meeting.

Dr. Murray had been often heard to say "he would rather wear out than rust out," and "that he hoped to lay aside his armor only on the brink of the grave." That wish was literally fulfilled; for so brief was the sickness that terminated his useful career, that we pause but a moment to listen to the words of the dying before we hear the song of the redeemed.

Dr. Murray's systematic habit of jotting down the *little things* of each day affords us a glimpse of his active, busy life for a few weeks previous to its close. To show how many and varied were his engagements, and the effect of such constant exposure on his health, we copy a few extracts from his Diary, from January 1st, 1862, to February 1st, when he laid aside his pen for the last time.

Jan. 1. A beautiful day. A good congregation. Many calls. A glorious meeting in the First Church to-day. The first time in all its history it was declared out of debt, with a balance in the treasury, with a yearly income to meet all its expenditures, and about four thousand dollars in funds for the poor, and to keep the grave-yard in repair.

Jan. 2 and 3. [He notices the arrival and departure of friends, and many calls made among his people.]

Jan. 4. National fast held with great solemnity. This is a memorable day—the nation in convulsions! South Carolina has seceded, and secession seems the order of the day, and the prevailing sentiment of the Southern people. President Buchanan appointed this as a day of fasting and prayer as to the affairs of the nation. The day was remarkably kept here. The various churches met by themselves in the morning, and there was a crowded meeting in the Second Church in the afternoon. If the day was kept all over the country as here, it must have been a remarkable day of prayer.

Jan. 5, *Saturday*. Very pleasant. Commenced a series of sermons on "Things unseen and eternal."

Jan. 6. A beautiful Sabbath. Preached twice. Good monthly concert.

Jan. 7. Very unpleasant day. Good ministers' meeting. Union prayer-meeting in the Baptist Church. Not many present, but good and solemn.

Jan. 8. Pleasant, though cloudy. Excellent Union meetings in the First Church afternoon and evening.

Jan. 9. Went to New York in a snow-storm. Attended a good meeting in the Methodist Church in the evening.

Jan. 10. Fair. Union meetings in the Third Church.

Jan. 11. Meetings in the Second Church. Well attended.

[This week of prayer was one long to be remembered in the Church of Elizabeth. The earnest tenderness of Dr. Murray's manner, and the faithfulness of his addresses to the people, and solemnity in prayer, were frequently spoken of.]

[On Saturday, the 12th, he left home, at no small personal sacrifice, to meet an engagement for the American Tract Society in Hartford. He then remarked, "They were among my *first* friends, and I can not refuse them their *last* request." The visit was in every respect pleasant, and gratefully remembered. His own brief record says, "Left home at 9 A.M. Called at the Tract and Bible House. Took cars for Hartford at 12 15. Reached there at 5 P.M. Went to Mr. Childs's. Mr. Eastman and Nixon called in the evening."]

Jan. 13. Preached in the morning for Mr. Childs; afternoon for Mr. Beadle. In the evening, spoke at the Tract meeting in the Central Church. A very cold day.

Jan. 14. Left Hartford at 1 P.M., and reached home at 7½. Cold and snowy.

Jan. 15. Went in the afternoon to Bergen. Took tea at Mr. Parker's. Lectured in the lecture-room at 7½ P.M. Returned home in the night train. The evening very unpleasant.

Jan. 16. Very stormy. Rev. Mr. Crittenden here. Made some calls —one at the Orphan Asylum.

Jan. 17. Very fine. Went to Trenton, to meeting of the Historical Society. Pleasant meeting. Presided in the afternoon. Returned in the evening train.

Jan. 18. In the study all day. Very stormy. Wrote letters in the afternoon.

Jan. 20. Pleasant, though cloudy. Preached twice, and, not feeling well, staid at home in the evening. Congregations full and solemn.

[His text on that day was from Isaiah, 55th chapter, 11th verse: "The word of the Lord shall not return unto Him void," etc. He extemporized in these sermons a very affecting view of his ministry for nearly twenty-eight years, its success and its failure; leaving the fruit to depend on the assured promise that God would accomplish what He pleased, and that it should still "prosper in the thing whereto He sent it."]

Jan. 21. Bright day. Visited the sick. Had a good prayer-meeting. Dined with my family at Mr. De Witt's.

Jan. 22. Had many calls. Left home at half past two; lectured in Brooklyn Institute, and returned home by 11 P.M.

Jan. 25. Pleasant. Wrote all the morning; then attended the funeral of Miss Mulford, who died in Tennessee; then made some visits.

Saturday, 26*th*. Wrote all the morning. Miss Slater came to see about Miss Spaulding's school. Great snow-storm in the afternoon; merry sleigh-ride.

27*th*. Pleasant; fine sleighing. Preached twice. Union service in the Third Church.

[His text on this last Sabbath was appropriately chosen from Numbers, 10th chapter, 29th verse: "We are journeying unto the place of which the Lord said I will give it you. Come thou with us, and we will do thee good; for the Lord hath spoken good concerning Israel." There was such an earnest solemnity in his manner, and tenderness of appeal to his people as "dearly beloved and longed for" in these discourses as can not soon be forgotten. He was affected to tears at the close of the afternoon service in trying to persuade some who were almost Christians to decide at once to come with the people of God and secure the blessings promised to Israel. This led a friend, after the service, to remark to him, "If your people are lost, their blood will not be required at your hands."]

Monday, 28*th*. Pleasant. Wrote all the morning. Judge Savage called as to orphan children. Executive Committee of the Bible Society met. Called on the sick.

29*th*. Pleasant. Visited the sick during the afternoon. Excellent prayer-meeting in the evening.

Jan. 30. Cold. Rode to W., in our neighborhood, with Mrs. Hotchkiss, to see a poor family. The mother very ill. Baptized three children. Visited a member of my Church deeply afflicted. Attended Mr. Lore's lecture in the evening.

Jan. 31. Fine day. Attended Mr. Moses Ogden's funeral at 11 A.M. In the afternoon Pastor Fisch and wife came. He preached in the evening.

[At 10 o'clock P.M., just before leaving his study, he wrote his *last* memorandum.]

Feb. 1. Pastor Fisch left for Philadelphia. Dr. Blakeman's child buried to-day. Visited the sick.

[He had met Pastor Fisch in Paris during the summer, and very cordially welcomed him to this country. In October he had introduced him to the Synod of New Jersey in a manner that secured the kindness and benefactions of many present. On Friday, before they left, he had called with them at Dr. Magie's and Mr. V. S. Wilder's, arranging with them more fully for their enjoyment and success on their return in the last week of February. In parting with them at the cars, he said, "Give my love to my friend Mr. Stuart, and tell him I had not time to write, but I send him two living epistles."]

Friday, Feb. 1. Returning from the funeral alluded to in the grave-yard of the First Presbyterian Church, at two o'clock P.M., Dr. Murray was first seized with a pain in his side. So severe was it that he paused for a moment in crossing the street to recover his breath, and on reaching the house of a friend he again paused, holding on to the door until sufficiently recovered to ring the bell. This call was one of the many errands of love and mercy he had yet to fulfill, and he hastened through them in expectation of leaving home early the next morning, to spend the Sabbath in Albany. The sympathy and prayer offered on that afternoon are spoken of as peculiarly sweet.

At family worship, which it was his habit to observe immediately after tea, and which, in this way, was made a means of grace to many casual visitors, he was unusually sad, and tender in his petitions for the bereaved, and earnest in seeking a blessing on his family, particularly the child who was sick. "The foreshadowing of care in reference to that dear boy," he said, and his "own indisposition, clouded the prospect of the happiest visit he made in the year." To his little son he related the circumstances connected with the happy death of Dr. B——'s son, and tried to impress on him the great need there was that he, at the same age, should begin to love and serve the Lord. He then went to his study to select his sermons for Dr. Sprague's people, and arrange his papers to be absent until Thursday of the next week, intending to spend a day or two with his son in Williams College.

Interrupted at nine o'clock, he was found reading his Bible. His sermons were ready to be packed, and written directions for his pulpit left on his study table. He soon joined the family circle, and, resting on the sofa, desired to have a speech on the times read to him. But a few minutes after he was seized with pain so severe he could not speak. After the application of active remedies, he so far recovered as to retire and rest tolerably well through the night. Early in the morning of Saturday, he said he should have slept but for anxiety as to his duty about going to Albany. He said he could not bear to disappoint Dr. Sprague a second time, and *must* go. When dissuaded from doing so by the exposure to cold in traveling, and danger of being sick from home, he consented to wait until noon and try his strength, and then, but for another severe attack of pain, he would have gone. Never to give up until fairly conquered, was his rule to the last. Then he cheerfully yielded, and, without any misgivings as to the past or future, rejoiced that he had not had his own way.

He dictated a dispatch to Dr. Sprague, saying, "Violent rheumatism prevents my coming—will write." This was done, as he desired, by express; and he sent word, as the Rev. Mr. Breed, of Philadelphia, was to preach for him on the next Sabbath, he would then be in Albany.

His physicians were now sent for, and his disease was pronounced neuralgia of the intercostal muscles. The pain was acute, but spasmodic, and the interval one of almost perfect rest. He described it, when dying away, like the strains of music vibrating on a sensitive ear. He expressed his intention of going out to hear Rev. Dr. Schenck preach the next day, but the physician persuaded him it would be better to rest for a few days. During the afternoon Dr. Schenck arrived, and he spent some time in conversing with him on the interests of the Church. Dr. Crane, calling in the afternoon, found him so comfortable as to say he needed little more than good nursing. He bade his daughter residing in Paterson a very cheerful good-by, desiring her to ask Dr. Hornblower to exchange with him very soon.

After he decided not to attempt going to Albany, he frequently, through the day, congratulated himself on being at home. A spirit of thankfulness pervaded his whole sickness, and he often said, "How good it is to be at home"—"no place like home." And, referring to parts of a favorite hymn, "Unnumbered comforts to my soul," etc., "Nor is the least a *cheerful* heart, that tastes these gifts with joy." "A cheerful religion," he said, "ought to be more cultivated by the people of God."

Saturday night. Although sleepless, he was not so distressed as to require any service, and in the morning he requested to see Dr. Schenck before church, that he might remind him that his people liked short sermons. He also saw Mr. Nutman, one of his elders, and mentioned to him the series of sermons he had been writing on "Things Unseen and Eternal." He said "he had seldom written sermons that afforded him more comfort; his mind had been full of the subject, and that he intended a week from the next Sabbath to begin and go straight through the series."

When the bells for church had ceased ringing, he requested to be read to. The selection made was from the crucifixion and ascension of our Lord, in connection with the commentary of his friend, Judge Jones, of Philadelphia.

After the morning service Dr. Schenck came to his room, and they were left alone. Returning to the room after some time, he was heard saying, in a subdued tone, "There was never a cup of sorrow that might not have in it one more bitter drop." The conversation had evidently been one of tenderness and spirituality. Soon after this he became restless, and desired Dr. Schenck might go to his study to rest for the afternoon service. While at dinner, the paroxysms of pain were so severe that he groaned aloud.

The doctor was immediately sent for, and succeeded in so far alleviating his sufferings as to leave him to go to church.

He was much exhausted for want of sleep, and, when longing for it, was reminded who it is "that giveth His beloved sleep." Not in that sense, he said, or many would be discouraged. He was unable to bear reading, and spent much time in ejaculatory prayer, thanking God on the cessation of every pain that one more had gone. Sometimes he exclaimed, "Fearfully and wonderfully made!" "Strange that a harp of a thousand strings should keep in tune so long!"

He took his tea as usual, though he could retain nothing but *ice*, for the blessing of which he often expressed his gratitude. After tea, the doctor, to divert his thoughts from suffering and lull him to sleep, kept up a cheerful conversation in the room, in which he joined, relating little incidents in his pastoral experience. The effect was soothing, and when the doctor rose to bid good-night, he affectionately pressed his hand, and spoke of the many obligations he was under to him for his unwearied kindness. On another occasion he said, "Doctor, do not wear yourself out on me."

He also remarked to those around him how pleasant it was to be blessed with loving friends in his kind and skillful physicians. At this time no fears were entertained but that he would soon rally from an attack induced by exposure to cold storms during the past month.

After the doctor left he desired to be read to sleep,

and the most familiar and comforting passages of Scripture were selected, on which he remarked, "That keeps me awake, as my mind anticipates every word." The morning and evening hymns from the Christian Year were then read. "Very beautiful," he said; "but I want nothing but sleep." He desired all the family might enjoy rest, and was only watched *this*, that *last* night on earth, by eyes that could not sleep. Very early in the morning he complained of feeling exhausted, and wished a cup of tea. He was refreshed by it, arose, washed as usual, and changed his room. He wished, he said, to speak to Dr. S. before he left, and then he kept very quiet through the day. His mind had been very much exercised as to the dark clouds hanging over our country, and the foreboding of secession in the Church, as well as state, gave him great pain. Conversing with his friend in that last interview, he said, "Give my love to the brethren of the New Brunswick Presbytery, and tell them to send Dr. Hodge to the General Assembly." When asked if he would be a member, he said "No; but I would like to make one more speech there;" and, laying his hand on his heart, "*I have it all here.*" Emphatically, and, as it proved, prophetically, he once said in a social prayer-meeting, "I feel sure we can not, in this enlightened age, among a Christian people, united as we are North and South by the closest ties, go to war." And again, "I shall never live to see *civil* war or the dismemberment of our Church."

The day passed as the night, sleeplessly, with no increasing symptom to alarm but his exhaustion and feebleness of pulse, which was constitutional, and on that account less feared, though it led to some change of treatment and the sending for consulting physicians. During the afternoon he was so bright, when free from pain, that it seemed impossible he could be dangerously ill. To the doctor he told some pleasant anecdotes —a ruling passion strong in death.

About five o'clock P.M. he desired just such tea and toast as he had early in the morning. When it was brought, he said pleasantly to the servant, who had waited on him for more than twenty years, "You know how to make it!" and then, in recognition of the fact, he added "that he had reason specially to be thankful for faithful domestics. So happy were they always in serving him that his wishes were anticipated." After tea his restlessness increased; and frequently passing from one room to another, "he changed (he said) the place, but kept the pain." "This restlessness—intense restlessness," he often said, "what does it mean?" During the absence of the doctor, a new symptom induced the sending for him, and he begged his friends might not be alarmed. He had some difficulty of breathing, and directed how a free circulation of air might be admitted; was fanned; felt comforted, he said, by the remedies, but they did not last long. When the doctor returned, he retired to a dark room, and desired to be left alone there, hoping to sleep. Very soon the pain, that had been for some hours lulled, returned to finish its work. It was excruciating around his heart, so that he groaned aloud; and, after wiping the cold sweat from his face, he asked the doctor, "How much of *such* pain do you think a man could bear?" On being answered, because of its character, a great deal, he replied, "But nature can not bear every thing; she must some time yield." A few minutes after, he said, brightly, "Now the pain is all gone." A short time before he had walked with a firm, quick step from one room to another; had listened to the news of the day, and directed how letters of business should be answered in the morning. From the passing away of that last severe pain his restlessness ceased, and his countenance became sweetly serene.

So quiet was he at this time that it was hoped he was about to enjoy the sleep he so longed for. The doctor sat fanning him, and his wife bathing his head, when suddenly he turned to ask for something, and fainted. As he had before, in previous illness, fainted from debility, the danger was not even then recognized. The family were called, and all were for some time hopeful in assisting the doctor in the use of restoratives; and it was not until after some minutes of unconsciousness, when no pulse could be found, and his faithful physician said "*I fear*," that the knell of death was sounded.

Then there was agony in prayer—beseeching God, "if *this* cup might not pass," His servant might be permitted to speak *a word*, that his family might know he was conscious of this *great reality*, and receive his parting blessing.

Slowly he opened his eyes; and the doctor, seeing that he recognized his wife, offered him some brandy, which he refused, saying, "No more brandy. My work is done." He was then reminded of a promise he had made to take any thing the doctor wished, and urged to take the brandy, that, if his life might not be spared, the stimulant would enable him to speak to his family. "No, wife," he repeated, "no more brandy. Let me not die as the drunkard dies, with the taste of brandy on his lips. You know how I abhor it. My work is done! I want my mind unclouded! I want to pray!"

The language of that prayer can never be recalled, nor the pathos of those tones. So deep and calm was the stillness, the light of heaven so visible as it beamed upon his face, that all felt surely "the Lord is in this place," and "this is the gate of heaven." Raising his hands, he earnestly confessed his own unworthiness, and his simple faith in Christ as the Savior of sinners. "Washed in His blood, sanctified by His Spirit," he thanked God He had not left him to *this hour* to prepare to meet Him. He then, with unwavering faith in the promises of a covenant-keeping God, committed his beloved family and his domestics to His care; and, in brief sentences, he added, "Bless my beloved Church and people;" "My dear elders, may they all be men of God;" "Bless the trustees and deacons: may they all be men of God;" and then, as if gathering new strength of utterance in the recollection of his *young* men, he added, "My young men, young merchants, young mechanics, may they be God-fearing men, and *hating covetousness.*" He asked that the words he had spoken might not be forgotten, but bear fruits to the glory of God. He then prayed for his "brethren in the ministry, the Church universal," his country, and the world.

At the close of this prayer, he said, again lifting his hands, "Receive the blessing;" and repeated, "The grace of our Lord Jesus Christ, and the love of God, and the communion of the Holy Ghost, be with you all." He then repeated the Lord's prayer, and added, "Father, into Thy hands I commend my spirit." "*No more—no more.*" But, emboldened with holy confidence to ask yet another blessing, his children were presented, and those present and absent alike received his dying admonition, instruction, and blessing. And there are sorrows, as well as joys, in which others may not intermeddle; scenes in the chamber of the dying that may not be unfolded to the world's view. Loving ties were sundering, and the full heart gave vent to its warm affections in earnest, tender, and ever-to-be-remembered expressions.

After a pause, he was reminded of the series of sermons on "Things Unseen and Eternal" he had never preached, and asked if they should be given to his people as a legacy. "Yes," he replied, "my dying legacy." To one of his physicians he said, "Doctor, you have treasures laid up in heaven; live so that you may win them."

The friend nearest to him, catching some glimpses of the glory to be revealed when the mortal had put on immortality, spoke to him of that exceeding and eternal weight of glory, "which eye hath not seen, nor ear heard, neither hath it entered into the heart of man to conceive." "I give unto them eternal life." "Father, I will that they also whom Thou hast given me be with me where I am, that they may behold my glory." "In my Father's house are many mansions." "Blessed mansions, and six precious children all hastening to meet you." A favorite doxology was then named: "'Tis Jesus the *first* and the *last*;" when he faintly added, "Whose Spirit shall guide me safe home;" "We will praise Him for all that is past;" and, looking tenderly at his wife, "*You* must trust Him for all that's to come." As he still continued conscious, he was asked if he had had any premonition that this was his last sickness. "Not at all," was the reply. And then to his family, when asked to direct as to the *future*, his last words were, "Let the world go; it will all be right." And so he departed as calmly as for the night. Like his Divine Master, he seemed to have led those nearest him to Bethany, "and while he blessed them he was parted from them, and carried up into heaven."

"Death was swallowed up in life, and we worshiped Him who had given him the victory through our Lord Jesus Christ. So undisturbed was the dying saint by any physical suffering, so radiant with the light of heaven was the expression of his face, that even the shadow of the King of Terrors was not seen; and it was long after that warm, loving heart had ceased to beat ere we could resign to the power of Death, for a time, that mansion, beautiful in ruins. Then, with the eye of faith, we followed the immortal soul, 'unclothed, that it might be clothed upon,' to the gates of the celestial city; and when the gates were opened, we saw that he was transfigured, and had raiment put on him that shone like gold. There were also shining ones that met him with harps and crowns of gold, spiritual children, seals of his ministry, and stars in the crown of his rejoicing. Then it seemed to me that all the bells of the city rang for joy, and that it was said unto him, 'Enter ye into the joy of your Lord;' and 'I saw, as it were, a sea of glass, mingled with fire, and them that had gotten the victory over the beast, and over his image, and over his mark, and over the number of his name, stand on the sea of glass, having the harps of God; and they sing the song of Moses, the servant of God, and the song of the Lamb, saying, Great and marvelous are Thy works, Lord God Almighty; just and true are Thy ways, Thou King of saints.'"

So died NICHOLAS MURRAY, on Monday, the 4th day of February, 1861, in the 59th year of his age. His funeral was attended by a vast multitude on the Friday following. The clergy from New York, Princeton, Newark, Elizabeth, and the surrounding country gathered in great numbers to testify their sorrow and their love of him who had been so suddenly and unexpectedly taken away. The remains were laid in the parlor adjoining the study, where his Bible, yet open, showed the subjects which had there last employed his mind. His white, massive head, his bland and noble face, his manly form, were yet so like to life, it was hard to believe that the soul was gone.

Rev. Thomas L. Janeway, D.D., offered prayer at the house, and then the procession was formed to follow the body to the church.

The bells of the churches of various denominations tolled in concert as the sad procession moved through the silent streets. Silent indeed they were; for the places of business, even the shops of Roman Catholic citizens, were closed, and the entire community, by simultaneous consent, yielded themselves to respectful expression of sympathy and grief. A neighbor, a pastor, a brother, a friend, was dead. The church was thronged, and more were unable to gain admittance. The pulpit and columns were hung in mourning, but no signs were needed to speak the sorrow of the smitten flock in the house where they had so often listened with gladness to the voice of their shepherd. Over the pulpit and against the wall were inscribed the pastor's dying words: "MY WORK IS DONE."

The services were conducted and addresses made by the Rev. Dr. Rodgers, of Boundbrook, Rev. Mr. Rankin, of Baskingridge, Rev. Dr. Ogden, of Chatham, Rev. Dr. Hodge, of Princeton, Rev. Dr. Magie, of Elizabeth, and Rev. Mr. Sheddan, of Rahway. The body was then borne to the cemetery adjoining the church, and there buried among his children and people who had preceded him to the grave.

On the Sabbath following the funeral sermon was preached by the Rev. William B. Sprague, D.D., of Albany, between whom and Dr. Murray an intimate friendship had existed for many years. His text was, "Wonderful in council," and the sermon presented the wisdom of God in raising up the men He needs for the accomplishment of His purposes on the earth. The sermon, which was in all respects worthy of the occasion, the author, and the theme, gave an admirable outline of the life and character of Dr. Murray, and was heard with profound sensation by a great concourse of people from the city and the surrounding country.

The newspaper press, various religious and literary societies, boards of the Church and ecclesiastical bodies, gave expression to their respect for the memory of the deceased, and their sense of the loss which religion and learning had sustained.

CHAPTER XX.

Outline of Character.—Usefulness.—Activity.—Lectures.—A Citizen.—A Pastor.—Social Qualities.—Anecdotes.—Liberal Feelings.—Sketch by his friend, Dr. Sprague.

In following our friend and brother through his ministerial and literary career, we have neglected to observe the various yet important labors in which his heart and mind were actively employed for the general good of the community in which he lived, the Church at large, and the world.

Usefulness was emphatically the object of his life.

Few men in the Church were more efficient and successful in advancing the interests of her boards of benevolence, and her Theological Seminary at Princeton. An active director in these institutions, he was punctual in attendance, and vigilant and sagacious in counsel. At the same time, so catholic was his spirit, and so wide the range of his labors, that he gave to the great national societies for the circulation of Bibles and Tracts, and for various other noble works, his warm support.

He was sent for, and he went as a lecturer, from the farthest East to the Mississippi, and from Canada to the South; and the lectures that he delivered are among the most able, learned, and brilliant productions that he left behind him.

As a citizen he was ever foremost in every enterprise that promised to advance the welfare of the people. Among the memorials of his leading influence are the Lyceum and the Orphan Asylum, the monument to the Rev. Mr. Caldwell, near now to his own, and schools public and private, in whose establishment or support he took the liveliest interest. The cause of common school education in the State of New Jersey occupied a large place in his affections, and his exertions were felt in the Legislature and in the remotest county. He was among the founders of the New Jersey Historical Society, and at his individual request the meeting was called that resulted in its organization.

So much time and labor did he bestow upon these extra services, that his own vineyard might have been neglected but for that high principle and thorough system which made his pastoral duties paramount to all others. Of his own people he was never forgetful, and his success is the best proof of his ministry.

To those who knew Dr. Murray in social life, any sketch of his character will appear unlike him that does not reflect the constant sunshine of genial humor, and the flashes of wit that illumined and enlivened the circle around him. Yet it is quite impossible to preserve and reproduce these most characteristic passages of his history. He could make no record of them; no one else has recorded them; and they can not be recalled. But those who heard him in Synod, when in his happiest moods, will remember such hits as this. He was remonstrating against the course of an inferior court that had tried a man while absent.

"Why, Moderator," said he, "I agree with one of my own countrymen, who said he would not hang a dog unless he was present!"

Every year he spent a few weeks in summer at Saratoga for the benefit of the waters. Then he was the animating spirit of a group of friends, who loved to get within the charmed circle of his conversation and his sunny smiles. A young sprig of divinity had been ventilating his Puseyite ideas to the great annoyance of the company, who had been disgusted with his affectation of clerical dignity and dress. As he left the piazza, some one remarked, "He is a miniature edition of Romanism." "Yes," added Dr. Murray, "bound in calf."

He was liberal in his feelings toward Christians of other names than his own; and it is to his honor, as well as to the praise of Divine Grace, that he was charitable to the Church which he abandoned in his youth. He abhorred Romanism, but he loved all men, Roman Catholics especially, his brethren and kinsmen according to the flesh. When I learned that he had subscribed and given money to aid in building a Roman Catholic church in Elizabethtown, I ventured to question the propriety of such an act. He replied that he desired to testify his kindly feelings toward those whose errors of faith he was bound to oppose.

Among the many sketches received since these memoirs were commenced, there is none more complete than the letter which is here given, from the pen of the Rev. Dr. Sprague. No man is so well fitted, by intimate knowledge of the subject, to portray the life and character of Dr. Murray.

"Albany, 2d July, 1861.

"MY DEAR DR. PRIME,—You could not have asked a service of me more grateful, in every respect, to my own feelings, than to record my recollections of our much loved and lamented friend, Dr. Murray. There are two reasons why I can perform it with the utmost alacrity. One is, that I loved him so much that my heart warms at every remembrance of him; the other is, that I knew him so well that I can speak of him with perfect confidence in the correctness of all my statements. I confess, however, to a degree of disappointment in regard to the amount of material which I have for such a communication as you have asked for. My first impression was, that there were lodged in my memory facts and incidents enough, which had fallen within my observation, to make a larger part of your forthcoming volume than could reasonably be appropriated to me; but, now that I have set myself to an effort at recollection, I find that I am much richer in impressions than incidents—the former remaining in all their vividness, while the latter have, for the most part, become confused and shadowy, or faded away altogether. I will endeavor, however, as faithfully as I can, to portray the man as he now lives in my memory and my heart, taking care to say little or nothing for the truth of which my own personal observation is not the voucher. In doing this, it will be impossible to avoid a substantial repetition of some things contained in the discourse I delivered on the occasion of Dr. Murray's death (already published); and, instead of suffering myself to be embarrassed by any attempt to do this, I shall just write what occurs to me, as if this were the first offering I had made to the memory of our friend.

"I first heard of Dr. Murray in connection with his settlement at Elizabethtown as the successor of Dr. M'Dowell; and the very favorable account which I had of him, coming, as it did, from one of Dr. M'Dowell's own family, created in me a strong desire to make his acquaintance. After the death of Dr. Griffin in 1837, it devolved upon me to write a brief memoir of his life; and as Dr. Murray had been one of his pupils at Williams College, Dr. Griffin's gifted and excellent daughter, Mrs. Dr. Smith, then of Newark, requested him to write out his recollections of her father, to be incorporated in the memorial of him which I was then forming. He readily complied with her request, and, in doing so, gave me the first definite idea I had of his character. The letter he wrote me was marked by great clearness, discrimination, and point, and showed me that he had a thorough appreciation of the character of the great man whom he had undertaken to describe. Two or three letters passed between us at that time, but the first time I met Dr. Murray was in April, 1839, on the day that John Quincy Adams delivered his celebrated oration on the Jubilee of the Constitution. Some one of our mutual friends brought us together that morning, and we went together to the North Dutch Church to hear the oration, and then went to a hotel (I think the City Hotel), where there was a large gathering of gentlemen, and, among others, Major General Scott, to whom Dr. Murray introduced me. When we had seen enough of the magnates there assembled, we strolled off on a long walk, which, so far as I was concerned, had no other object than to secure to me an opportunity of making farther observation upon my newly-made acquaintance. The moment my eye first rested upon him I was strongly impressed by his frank and generous, as well as decidedly intellectual expression of countenance; and, as I conversed with him, I felt sure that the face was but a faithful reflection of the mind and heart, and before we parted I resolved that it should not be my fault if our acquaintance, thus commenced, did not ripen into an enduring friendship. And this was actually the result. Before many months I went to Elizabethtown and passed a Sabbath with him, and shortly after he came and passed one with me, and thus commenced a course of mutual annual visiting that was terminated only by his death. *His* Sabbath was the second in January, and *mine* the second in September; and so regular was this exchange of labors, that it came to be regarded in both our congregations quite in the light of an institution. As his return from Europe last summer was only a little prior to the stated time for my visit, I felt unwilling to occupy his pulpit, while I knew that his own voice would be so much more welcome to his people than any other, and therefore postponed my visit for three or four weeks; but when I did go, it seemed to me that there was not wanting a circumstance to render my enjoyment complete. I never saw him more bright, or genial, or active, or with better prospects of a long-continued course of usefulness. Having just returned from his foreign tour, his mind was exuberant in interesting reminiscences, illustrative at once of his own close and accurate observation, and of the cordial welcome which had every where been extended to him. I do not remember that so much as a single moment of that delightful visit was imbittered by the reflection that possibly it might prove the last in the series that had continued so long. About the beginning of the year I received a letter from him, stating that he had reluctantly yielded to an earnest request from the American Tract Society to present its claims at Hartford on the second Sabbath in January, in consequence of which he should be obliged to suffer another invasion of the established order of our visits, but that the delay would be for only a week or two. After a few days, another letter from him informed me that his arrangements were made for being at Albany on the first Sabbath in February; and he subsequently consented not only to occupy my own pulpit in the morning and afternoon, but to preach for our new State Street congregation in the evening. On the Sabbath preceding I had, as usual, given notice of his intended visit, and much interest had been awakened in the prospect of it. On Saturday, two or three hours before we looked for his arrival, a telegraphic dispatch came, announcing that, owing to a sudden attack of rheumatism, he was unable to leave home. The same evening a letter from Mrs. Murray came, informing me that all his arrangements had been made the night before, even to the packing of his valise, for coming to Albany, but that a recurrence of a difficulty in the chest, to which he had before been subject, led her to dissuade him from attempting the journey, though she seemed confident that it would be only the delay of a single week. The next intelligence, which came in a letter from his daughter on Tuesday morning, was that he continued quite ill, and had suffered much from restlessness during the preceding (Sunday) night, but it conveyed no intimation that his illness was deemed of an alarming character. Immediately after reading the letter I went out for an hour or two, and on my return found lying on my study table the following heart-rending telegram: 'DR. MURRAY DIED AT ELIZABETH LAST NIGHT." The tidings, as they spread through my congregation, and through Dr. Murray's wide circle of friends in this city, seemed to me to awaken a feeling of sorrow scarcely less intense than if he had lived and died in the midst of us.

"Dr. Murray's annual visits to us, always including a Sabbath, gave me a good opportunity to judge of the general character of his preaching; for, while I always heard him preach twice, I sometimes read one or more of the manuscript sermons which he brought with him; and I can truly say that I have known few clergymen whose sermons were so uniformly of a high order of excellence. Some, indeed, produced a stronger impression in the delivery than others; but the difference was generally to be traced to the subjects rather than to the mode of treating them. His text always pointed directly to his subject; and his thoughts were so consecutively and logically arranged, and so clearly and forcibly expressed, that it must have required an uncommonly obtuse or wandering mind either to have withheld attention or to have resisted impression. He always led his hearers in a perfectly open and luminous track, and no one ever hesitated a moment as to the import of what he was saying; but he was as far as possible from being commonplace, in any proper sense of that term, either in matter or manner; his thoughts, though always flowing naturally from his text, were sometimes exceedingly striking, and he would often condense into a single sentence what it might take hours of reflection in the hearer to digest. His manner, though entirely free from every thing like awkwardness, was characterized rather by force and dignity than grace. He retained enough of the Irish accent to betray his nationality, but not enough to offend any American taste, or to impair in the least degree the effect of his utterance. And I may add that, while his services in the pulpit were usually characterized by much more than ordinary solemnity and impressiveness, so natural to him as his breath was his wit, that an occasional and apparently unconscious flash of it would sometimes brighten the countenances of his audience into a momentary smile, though the next sentence would be pretty sure to restore the accustomed gravity even to those who had approached nearest to a laugh. I never heard him preach except from a manuscript, and therefore can not speak from personal knowledge of his extemporaneous efforts in the pulpit or the lecture-room, though I should suppose that the exuberance of his wit would have been more likely to discover itself in his unstudied than in his written productions. His written discourses were all framed and executed with the utmost care; and so thoroughly had he trained himself to precision and accuracy in writing, that it was a rare thing that he ever had occasion to erase or substitute a word. I have heard him say that it was a rule with him to begin his sermon (he rarely wrote more than one a week), at least so far as to choose his subject and arrange his thoughts, on Monday, and then he gradually proceeded, giving to it the best part of each day, until Friday, when it was completed, leaving to him Saturday as a day of rest preparatory to the labors of the Sabbath. I do not know exactly the number of his written sermons, but my impression is that it somewhat exceeds a thousand, all accurately numbered and dated; and if another equal number of sermons can be found written with equal care, and accuracy, and legibility, as if each one was intended to be placed in the hands of the printer, I know not where to look for them.

"Dr. Murray was, in principle and practice, not only a thorough Presbyterian, but a thorough Old-School Presbyterian, and he never hesitated, when occasion required, either to avow or to defend his denominational preferences. But no man was farther than he from every thing like sectarian bigotry. Though not a particle of *Roman* Catholicism lingered either in his mind or heart, in true *Christian* catholicism — that quality that promptly recognizes and cordially welcomes the image of Christ amid undesirable and even revolting associations—I may safely say that he yielded to none of his brethren. I have more than once heard him say that he could not possibly sympathize with that spirit that could find nothing to fellowship outside of its own denomination; and I have heard several clergymen of different communions, who were thrown into his immediate neighborhood, render a most cordial and cheerful testimony to the uniform Christian courtesy and kindliness which marked his intercourse with them. Every body knows that, in his controversy with the Roman Catholics, not only his clear, strong intellect, his vast stores of information, and his dark and sad early experience were put in requisition, but also the power of scathing sarcasm, in which it was not easy to find his rival. But those who knew him well knew that his heart yearned with sympathy for the great mass of the Roman Catholics, knowing, as he did, that their ignorance was hereditary, and fortified by influences which, under ordinary circumstances, they could not be expected to resist. Whenever he was brought in contact with them he always evinced toward them the utmost good-will, and they could not be long with him without becoming sensible that he was their friend. On one occasion, as he informed me, just as he was getting into the car to leave Utica, a young girl entered alone, whose appearance indicated her Irish extraction. He took a seat by the side of her, and quickly found that she was a Roman Catholic, and was on her way to Rochester, where she expected to meet her brother. As she was traveling without a protector, he made himself as agreeable and useful to her as he could during the journey, while she, in turn, was by no means sparing in her expressions of gratification and thankfulness. As the train entered the depôt in Rochester, her brother, who seemed a very decent man, was waiting to receive her; and then it was that she first learned that the friend who had devoted himself so much to her during the day was no other than KIRWAN, Bishop Hughes's great antagonist.

"In no relation do I think of Dr. Murray with more interest than that of a companion and friend. With intellectual powers of a very high order, with great freedom and facility of communication, and that remarkable aptness which enabled him always to say the right word at the right time, he combined as much of frankness, and kindliness, and generosity as we can expect ever to find in this imperfect and erring world. His very extensive general information made him at home on almost every subject, and in all practical matters he was fruitful in wise and seasonable suggestions. At the same time, his coruscations of wit kept all listeners and lookers-on in good humor, and often supplied material for pleasant recollection and conversation for a good while afterward. When he came to us on his annual visit, he usually not only passed the Sabbath, but remained over Monday, and on Monday evening we had generally a small circle of friends to exchange salutations with him. On those occasions nothing could exceed the bright actings of his mind and the genial actings of his spirit toward every body with whom he came in contact. Without the least attempt at any thing like self-display, or the assumption of what did not belong to him, he was always the centre of attraction to the whole circle; and all seemed to feel—ladies as well as gentlemen—that the nearer they got to him, and the longer they staid by him, the better was the object of their visit accomplished. And I have heard some members of my congregation, who have been accustomed to meet him at Saratoga Springs, say that his presence there was always greeted as a benediction; that not only ministers, but judges, and lawyers, and doctors, and last, though not least, ladies, were always delighted to find themselves in his society.

"But no one could fully appreciate the strength of Dr. Murray's affection, or, I may add, the dignity of his character, who did not see him in his own 'happy home.' My visits there, which gave me an opportunity of seeing what he was in the tenderest relations, come up to me now in sorrowful but grateful recollection, as having marked some of the brightest spots in my life's journey. With a companion whose noble qualities both of intellect and of heart he perfectly appreciated; with children full of love, and life, and promise, to whom his smile was sunshine, and who knew no earthly bliss above that of making him happy, and with the ability to enjoy and communicate as much of domestic happiness as any one I have ever known, he was certainly pre-eminently blessed and pre-eminently a blessing in his own endeared circle. His eldest daughter, his much-loved Lizzie, who preceded him to the grave by a year or two, possessed almost matchless attractions. In the progress of her decline, I knew how his heart had been kept bleeding, and how, for months, he had been alternating between hope and fear, until death finally made the decision. I was unable to be present at her funeral; indeed, knowing the unusual pressure of my engagements at the time, he very considerately sent a request that I would not come. I met him not long after, and was prepared to see him saddened and bowed by his affliction; but, instead of that, he evinced all his accustomed cheerfulness. He talked freely of the loved one who was gone, and walked with me into the grave-yard, and we stood together beside the spot where they had laid her; but his mind was evidently flying off to the glorious habitation of her ransomed spirit. And what I witnessed on that occasion, I have been assured, was but a specimen of his conduct on all similar occasions. While his children were spared to him, he cherished them with the strongest parental affection; but when it pleased God to take them away, he reverently recognized His superior right to them, and, instead of yielding to despondency, only found in their removal a fresh motive to a more earnest and cheerful devotion to his work.

"I must say a word of the eminent Christian character of my lamented friend; for, though I am well aware that none who knew him well would need any other assurances on this subject than have been supplied by their own observation, yet I can imagine that some, who have only had a glance at the exterior of his life, while he was relaxing from his severe duties, may have formed an inadequate estimate of his spirituality. The grand palpable evidence of the strength of his religious character was his steady and consistent course of devotion to his work. But those who were brought near to him, and especially his intimate friends, knew that his heart was ever awake to those themes which have the most vital bearing upon Christian experience. He had, indeed, a great abhorrence of every thing like cant and vainglory in religion; and it is believed that he very rarely, even in the most confidential intercourse of Christian friendship, said much of his own private religious feelings; but the tone of his spirit was easily inferred from the deep interest he took in conversations of a decidedly experimental character. He always showed himself interested in whatever involved the spiritual well-being of any of his fellow-men, or the general prosperity of Christ's kingdom, and, what was still more, he was always ready to put forth vigorous efforts in aid of either whenever it was in his power.

"Scarcely any thing in Dr. Murray's character has impressed me more strongly than the interest which he took in every body around him, and the facility with which he could turn his hand to the aid of any benevolent or useful project. I have been struck with the fact, when walking with him in the streets of Elizabeth, that every body whom he met seemed to be in the most friendly relations to him; and when I have inquired whether such and such persons, who have seemed remarkably cordial, were members of his congregation, the answer has often been that they were Episcopalians, or Methodists, or perhaps belonged to one of the other Presbyterian churches. I have been assured that no object of public utility could present itself in the town of which he did not at once stand forth as the advocate and supporter; if judicious counsel was wanted, he was ready to render it; if efforts and sacrifices were demanded, he did not hesitate to make them; and by this prompt and unsolicited exercise of public spirit, he identified himself with the entire community in which he lived. On the day of his funeral, it was manifest that we were in the midst, not of a mourning congregation only, but of a mourning city. The first bell that tolled, after the procession began to move, was the bell of a church which is, perhaps, as far from any denominational sympathy with Dr. Murray's as is consistent with both being Protestant; and the rector of that church, to his honor be it recorded, addressed to Mrs. Murray a letter of condolence, paying a just and beautiful tribute to the memory of her departed husband. I heard it stated that even Jews and Roman Catholics closed their places of business during the hour of the funeral solemnities.

"There is one point more on which I wish to say a single word, because I happen to know that Dr. Murray's views in respect to it have been, to some extent, misapprehended—it is the matter of slavery. A friend of mine, and a gentleman of great worth and respectability, residing in Illinois, wrote me, shortly after Dr. Murray's death, that while he had a very high estimate of the ability and general character of my friend, he had been pained to learn that he had given the aid of his name, if not of his pen, to the cause of slavery; and, if I have been correctly informed, the same impression has prevailed, to some extent, in other quarters. I have heard him express his opinion on this subject so often that I think I can not have fallen into any mistake in respect to it. He was, indeed, far from having any sympathy with the party technically termed "Abolitionists" at the North; on the contrary, he believed that theirs was a mission of unmixed evil; and this opinion he never hesitated to express on either side of the Atlantic. But he considered slavery, as it exists in our country, not merely in the light of a calamity, but as involving great national guilt; and he wrote me, only a few weeks before his death, that he had just preached a sermon in which he had protested against human beings being bought and sold as "chattels." It pleased a gracious Providence to call him home before the present reign of terror and distress throughout the country was fairly inaugurated; but he lived long enough to see the clouds begin to gather, and to deliver, on more than one occasion, the most earnest and impressive testimony in favor of the government which he saw threatened with formidable attack, and even utter extinction.

"I fear, my dear sir, that this communication may prove of an inconvenient length, and yet knowing, as I do, how cordially you respond to every effort to honor and embalm the memory of our dear departed friend, I have no doubt that you will be tolerant of any error I may have committed in that direction. As Dr. Murray was a man, he must, of course, like all other men, have had his infirmities, but what they were I leave it to those who looked at him with eyes different from mine to describe. I will only add, that I heartily rejoice that the writing of his life has devolved upon the person whom, of all others, I should have selected as the one who is in every respect best qualified to do justice to his memory.

"I am, my dear sir, with great regard, faithfully your friend, W. B. Sprague."

CHAPTER XXI.

Letter from Rev. Dr. Edgar. —Rev. Prof. Gibson. —Mrs. Duncan.— Mrs. Jones. —Rev. Mr. Reinhart. —Rev. Dr. Chickering. —Rev. Dr. Childs.—Rev. Dr. Janeway.—Rev. Dr. Schenck.

Rev. Dr. Edgar to Geo. H. Stuart, Esq.

"Belfast, June 27th, 1861.

"MY DEAR MR. STUART,—In furnishing for Dr. Prime's work reminiscences of our dear departed friend, Dr. Murray, I desire to associate them with you, not only because his love for you was enthusiastic, but be-cause I am anxious that he should be in death, as he was in life, a bond of union between me and one for whom my love can never die.

"One of my first links of connection with him was my republishing the Kirwan Letters, which first made him eminently great. Having written a preface, and added notes by the late Dr. Samuel O. Edgar, I issued, in 1850, an edition of five thousand copies of the first series, one thousand of which were purchased by an eminent lawyer; and the good effected by them verified a statement of the preface, that they were republished in unhappy Ireland, not chiefly because of the talent and eloquence which distinguished them, but because, being brief, clear, practical, and characterized by genuine good-nature and politeness, they are well qualified to be a useful manual for all, especially the ignorant and young.

"When, next year, I issued the second series, my

distinguished fellow-helper, author of *Edgar's Variations of Popery*, was no more; and in a preface I said, 'Had his life been a little prolonged, he might have formed a personal acquaintance with him whom he had favorably known by his writings; for the Rev. Dr. Murray has visited the Old World, and been enthusiastically received by many who had formed a high estimate of the convert from Romanism, who had done as much as any other in the Western World to breathe Protestant life and spirit into the masses of the people. His Letters have commanded in America an enormous circulation. A chief feature of their popularity here is the eagerness with which they are read and circulated by Roman Catholics in districts blessed with scriptural schools.'

"Of his visit on that occasion he has published an account in his work, '*Men and Things as I saw them in Europe*.' He accompanied me in a part of my annual missionary tour, visiting our schools, preaching in our missionary stations, received as an honored guest at the houses of landed gentry—every where delighted by interesting scenes and society, awakening the liveliest sympathies, making happy friendships, and leaving impressions never to be forgotten.

"Some time after he sent to this country a loved and cherished representative, who, first for her father's sake, and then for her own, was received with extreme kindness. She was one of the most intensely interesting of beings in female form I ever saw. So fascinating, so talented, so full of activity, genius, wisdom, kindness—and beautiful withal; but, alas! so delicate, tiny, worn—the victim of many a disease, and yet with an elasticity, buoyancy, and a large-hearted scriptural piety and devotedness rising above all, and throwing over all a soft and heavenly radiance. Her likeness is here with me now; her spirit is with her God. He who loved her best could keep her from His fond bosom no longer. 'Come up hither,' He said, and she was not, for God took her. Her dying expressions of gratitude and love endeared to the heart of her father and mother some, like our friends the Moores, of Dublin, and Miss Holmes, of Clogher, for whose noble missionary institution in Connaught both raised munificent contributions.

"The effects of missionary effort shown him by Miss Holmes and others gave deep intensity to his zeal for our Presbyterian mission to Roman Catholics; and I need not say how often or earnestly he and you pressed me to undertake a deputation to the United States to obtain support for that mission. The time was when I would have gladly accepted the invitation, but that time was past then; and though I labored to secure a deputation, I had resolved not to be on it, when a letter from an influential quarter in America changed my plan; for that letter, in contradiction to the statements of yourself and Dr. Murray, asserted that America would give no welcome and no money to Irish Presbyterian missions, and assigned reasons unfounded and provoking. I wrote to you both, and your answers determined me to go, no matter what the sacrifice. Some, on whom I depended, declined; but if I did too, it would have been a personal insult to friends who showed exceeding kindness, and who were so able to realize the hopes they raised.

"With my brethren I went, and prospered beyond all precedent, upward of six thousand pounds sterling for our mission being only part of the large and varied fruit of that most effective delegation.

"Of our obligations to Dr. Murray and you for our success we spoke truly at our farewell meeting, but far from the sum total of the truth when we said, 'Among the many of highest name and worth who have laid us under deep obligations, we are bound in gratitude to give a distinguished place to Dr. Murray and George Hay Stuart, Esq., not merely because it was chiefly on their invitation and by their advice that we visited your country, but because their time, and talents, and influence, and unceasing anxious labor have been devoted to promote the objects of our mission with an earnestness, wisdom, and success which we have never seen equaled, and which we can neither fully estimate nor describe. To these noble sons of old Ireland, and the influence which their name and character wield in the great new world of their adoption, we chiefly owe the large and triumphant success which has crowned our enterprise.'

"Little did I think, while reading this, amid the splendid hospitalities of Dr. Prime, how soon a precious gem of that shining circle would drop away. Oh! what melancholy would have filled the inmost heart of that great meeting had we known how soon would be verified, in the prophet himself, the prediction uttered by Dr. Murray at the Fulton Street farewell meeting, when, pointing to me, he said, 'You will come to our shores no more. These junior brethren may come to this country again, but we shall not be here. We shall see your faces no more.'

"In the young land of his wife and his children, he shall see their faces no more; but in the old land of his father's and mother's grave he did see them, to rejoice with them, and over them, and to be received by their exulting families with ecstasy and triumph.

"You were our inseparable companion through all our long and most enchanting and successful missionary tour in the centre, south, and west of dear old Ireland, and you can tell how, with open arms, we were every where received—how private carriages were waiting for us every where we stopped—how we were ministered to by the fair, the fascinating, and the good—how crowds flocked from far to welcome and to hear—how the fame of our venerable companion traveled before him—how highly his religious services were prized—how joyous the greetings, and the partings how sad—how deeply he felt poor Ireland's degradation—and how, as at Allan Pollok's and other places, he gloried in her regeneration; and with what hearty, exulting good-will he welcomed and answered genuine Irish wit and humor, even when playing on lips pale and thin with hunger, or flashing in the dark hovels of sordid poverty. You knew him long and well, but you never knew Nicholas Murray, the Romish Irish boy, the eminent Protestant divine, so thoroughly himself, in the length and breadth of his character great and good, as in Dublin, Killarney, Cork, Limerick, Galway, Ballinasloe, and through all the bounds of the Presbytery of Athlone. The Presbytery of Athlone acted nobly, and gave him and you a reception worthy of old hospitable Ireland, and of great America too; and I hope to be long welcome in those parts, on account of the loved companions I once had there, and the amount of happiness and benefit thus brought to their homes. Alas! how little did you or he know that every where you were adding to the burden of a loud Irish cry, and preparing a deeper, wider wail for his early grave.

"Full of honor and of gratification, you returned to my home, but not to rest, for the calls of hospitality, friendship, and, above all, anxiety to hear, dragged you hither and thither, every where welcome, every where applauded, and furnished, on all hands, with large opportunities for good. Your career from Belfast to Derry, with such a succession of enormous admiring crowds, was a triumphant march; but what of that? It was a great series of occasions, happily and successfully improved, for winning souls and honoring their Savior.

"My next and last meeting with him and you was in the centre of London's most neglected throng; and yet, even in that home of infamy and crime, there were that night symptoms of reformation which is spreading so rapidly now. An earnest lad, preaching in one of the vilest streets, had round him a little listening throng; school houses lately opened gave ground for hope; and the innocent gayety of children playing in the street so joyfully amid poverty, ignorance, and crime, seemed to say that neglect and wretchedness would not always be the lot of the London poor.

"He who saw London's dark night then has not lived to see its day. He is now among the increasing evidences of his Savior's triumphs, as one and another of Christ's redeemed join the heavenly throng; and, for aught we know, he has made acquaintance already, in the home of the blessed, with some who were to him that night subjects of deep sympathy and ejaculatory prayer. Dr. Murray is no more, and no thought regarding him presses on my spirit, in American war, like this—'The righteous is taken away from the evil to come.' Ever devotedly yours,

"JOHN EDGAR."

From the Rev. Prof. Gibson, Belfast.

"It was in the summer of 1851 that Dr. Murray, of Elizabethtown, after a long absence, revisited, for the first time, the shores of his native land. He had, in company with other fellow-travelers, been wandering over Continental countries, where he enjoyed the opportunity of studying, with more striking practical developments, the system of the Papacy, against which he had so successfully girded himself to battle, as an intrepid champion of Protestant truth. We had long been familiar with his name and achievements, and rejoiced to welcome him among us as a true-hearted son of Erin, who, by his native genius and force of intellect, had risen to a position of eminence and influence in that great country to which we are allied by so many ties of kindred and of faith. The period at which he visited us was during the sittings of our General Assembly in the metropolis of Ulster, and gladly did we seize the occasion to extend to him the right hand of fellowship. It was at the same meeting that we were favored with the presence of the apostolic Duff, whose overwhelming appeals for the prostrate millions of India have done so much both in America and here to fire the Churches with a portion of his own sublime and sanctified enthusiasm. Before the assembly rose, Dr. Murray was invited to address the house, which he did with characteristic power and eloquence, referring more particularly to the impressions made upon his mind by what he had lately witnessed of the Romish system on the European Continent, and especially in Rome itself. At a public breakfast a few days previously, he and his fellow-traveler, Dr. Breckinridge, then of Louisville, Kentucky, together with Dr. Duff, had been welcomed to Ireland. The greater portion of his time during that brief sojourn was occupied in visiting those parts of the country where Romanism has been in the ascendant, and his impressions in reference to which he gave in a permanent form, on his return, to the American public. While he remained in the North he had frequent opportunities of mingling with us in social intercourse, in which he drew all hearts toward him by those rare qualities which, wherever he went, rendered him one of the most charming companions, whose presence ever brought along with it smiles and sunshine.

"Seven years after, and I had the happiness of renewing my acquaintance with Dr. Murray on the other side of the Atlantic. I had been traveling with my friend and fellow-deputy, Mr. M'Clure, of Derry, from New York to Albany, on my way to Canada, and, sailing up the noble river which connects these cities, had casually been informed that Dr. Murray had a few days before gone to Saratoga, it being the season when the American citizens are in the habit of repairing to that celebrated watering-place. We resolved, accordingly, to make a slight detour off the direct line for the purpose of meeting one from whom we were persuaded, whether at home or elsewhere, we should receive a cordial welcome. Arriving at Saratoga, we came into contact with our friend almost immediately, returning from one of the morning meetings for prayer held daily in the place, as a means, under the Divine blessing, of perpetuating and extending the influence of the great American awakening of the preceding winter. Recognizing us at once in the distance, he hailed us with the affectionate cordiality of a brother, placed himself at our disposal for the day, introduced us to the far-famed Springs, gave us the entree of the hotel at which he had taken up his quarters, and after dinner, and a drive around the neighborhood, accompanied us to the railway station on our onward route, and took his leave in the expectation of our meeting again, as we did some two months after, under his own hospitable roof. In the course of our conversation I had mentioned that my son, a student of theology, was on a visit also in another part of the States, and ere we parted Dr. Murray suggested that, being in the country, he should remain for the sake of prosecuting his studies during the ensuing session at Princeton, offering, in the kindest manner, to introduce him to the professors of that distinguished seminary. I may add that, after giving the matter due consideration, the suggestion was adopted, and I shall ever regard it as a subject of congratulation that my son enjoyed the inestimable advantages of a winter's tuition under those masters in Israel whose praise is in all the Churches. To the student in question, now for two years a minister in the Irish Presbyterian Church, Dr. Murray acted throughout with the considerate attention of a friend and father, introducing him in the ensuing spring to the Presbytery of Elizabethtown, by whom he was licensed to preach the Gospel, and subsequently receiving him into his pulpit, where he delivered his first sermon. The letter which Dr. Murray addressed to myself immediately after is before me as I write, and breathes those sentiments which he knew would be peculiarly grateful to a parent's heart.

"In due time I visited my esteemed friend at his own residence, but not till after having experienced, on two successive public occasions, his kind offices. The Synod of New Jersey had been holding its annual meeting in Trenton, and, through the agency of Dr. Murray, my friend from Ireland and myself were honored with an invitation to attend. With the request we gratefully complied, and had the pleasure of addressing that reverend court and of receiving their fraternal greeting. We also shared, through the same kind instrumentality, the hospitable attentions, of which we shall ever cherish the recollection, of Chief Justice Green, one of the most eminent of the American bench. The other occasion I refer to was in Philadelphia, where, under the auspices of that noble Irishman and true philanthropist, George H. Stuart, Esq., a number of our warm-hearted friends from the 'Old Country,' and others, including Dr. Boardman and several of his brethren of various denominations, held a social meeting in honor of the Irish delegates, and where Dr. Murray delivered one of his raciest addresses on his fellow-countrymen in the Old World and the New.

"In Elizabethtown itself I spent a brief but happy time in that pastoral dwelling, never more, alas! to be enlivened by the radiant countenance of its honored head. I officiated on the Sabbath to the great congregation over which he presided, one of the most influential, as it seemed, which I had addressed. On the following day we proceeded together to New York, where I was introduced by him to Dr. James Alexander, and others, both of the clergy and Christian laity of that city, so desirous was he that the Irish stranger should form the acquaintance of those whom he so highly prized among his adopted countrymen. Of these, both in New York and elsewhere, it is affecting to think that others besides himself have since then fallen in the full maturity of their strength, and passed away forever from the earth! Where shall we look, in any Church, for brethren so beloved as the Alexanders and the Van Rensselaers, whose sun has gone down while it was yet shining in the meridian of its splendor?

"Scarcely two years elapsed until I again met Dr. Murray, not upon Irish or American, but Scottish soil. The Tri-centenary of the Reformation under John Knox had come, and the Free Church of Scotland, the noblest representative of the principles of the great reformer, was occupied in the commemoration of that event, so worthy to be held in undying remembrance by the entire Presbyterian family throughout the world. A discourse had been delivered by the moderator, the Rev. Dr. Buchanan, of Glasgow, and the Assembly having engaged in an exercise of thanksgiving, an opportunity was afforded to brethren from other countries to take part in the proceedings of the auspicious day. As moderator of the Presbyterian Church of Ireland for that year, it was my privilege to be first called on; and after an address, in which I took occasion to refer to the first planting of Presbyterianism in America by ministers from Ulster, and to the Scoto-Irish element as not the least important in the social organization of the United States, Dr. Murray was introduced to the Assembly. His speech was of the genuine 'true blue' Presbyterian character, not unmixed with pleasantries, which unmistakably identified the speaker with the green isle from which he sprung. It was a highly successful effort, and was received with hearty demonstrations of approval from the house.

"In the months of June and July in that year Dr.

Murray again visited his native land. He came at a period of unusual interest; for the breath of the Almighty had breathed upon our churches, and, after the lapse of a twelvemonth since the great revival, we were rejoicing in the wide-spread and happy renovation which had been wrought. Wherever he went, he occupied himself in making inquiry into the character and extent of that spiritual movement which had swept so widely over Ulster, and had abundant opportunities of witnessing its pleasant fruits. From the reports which were submitted to the General Synods and to the Assembly he prepared a digest, which, with the statement of his own experience, was published in the New York Observer, to which, in the midst of his journeyings, he always found time to send a carefully considered contribution. He looked as hale and hearty as when we had seen him ten years before, his step as firm and his eye as bright as ever. Wherever he went, he was received with every demonstration of regard. In the autumn of the year preceding, a deputation from our Church had visited America, and he had laid us under weighty obligations by the generous and effectual aid he rendered in the prosecution of their mission.

"It was on a soft summer evening that he took a final leave of us, and of the land that gave him birth, the moderator of our Assembly, then in session, and other brethren, accompanying him on board the steamer in which he sailed for Liverpool. A minister who was a fellow-passenger, the Rev. J. R. M'Dougall, of Florence, has since informed me that long after those of us who lined the shore had faded from the view, he stood fixed in his place on the vessel, waving his adieus, his eye resting on the receding land, and his heart evidently too full for utterance. He was taking his last fond look of the country from which he went forth, in the noon of life, an unfriended exile, and his attachment to which continued to the end, unabated by time or distance.

"But a few months after, and we were deeply affected by the announcement of strange and unexpected tidings. His course of toil was finished, and he had all at once been taken up and away from those he loved, and entered into his rest. Tenderly did we sympathize with the weeping family and widowed congregation, and universally did we mourn the loss of one of the most devoted friends of our Church and country. We shall see his face no more; but fondly would we cherish the recollection of his genial presence, and revere his name as that of one of the true men of the earth—an honor both to the land of his nativity and to that in which all of him that is mortal reposes until the resurrection of the just."

From Mrs. Duncan, Edinburgh.

"7 India Street, April 20th, 1861.

"MY VERY DEAR FRIEND,—Your most touching note reached me a few days since. It places you, with your mournful and dutiful heart, before me, showing me the tears which you must shed, and the longing to show forth the grace of God as it was displayed in the conversion and the unfailing protection and guidance of your honored husband.

"I can not refuse to write, but I feel that all about him was so right-forward, combining the simplicity of the child with the wisdom and experience of the man, that I can tell nothing which Dr. Prime has not seen and rejoiced in himself.

"The first time I saw Dr. Murray I was a stranger, introduced to your hospitality, scarcely aware whither I was going, by Mrs. Smith, a daughter of Dr. Griffin, and the first characteristic that came forth in lively relief was the *genial spirit* which instantly displayed itself. He went to fetch his little son in his arms, that he might cheer the Scottish minister's widow by showing me his little Thomas Chalmers; and then his parental heart overflowed with hopes that the child might be like the man, with some sly, smile-exciting remarks about the size of his head, which made me feel as if we had been acquainted long before.

"On a more mature acquaintance, his *mild and cheerful demeanor at home* was remarkable. A balmy influence seemed to flow from him which soothed all around. While he trusted all domestic details, as well he might, to the skill and energy of his wife, he was not abstracted, as many men are, the line of whose duties is diverse from their families, but he was ever fully prepared to sympathize in all their interests.

"His *exceeding industry* could not fail to attract notice. He would converse in the circle, and enliven us with his wit, which seemed never exhausted, and in a moment he had entered his study and was plunged in his books and papers, as if the little world he had been smiling on were very far away. This gift of industry, and his power of fixing his mind readily on a new subject, accounts for the facility with which he dashed off papers for the Observer or chastised Bishop Hughes.

"When he was in Liverpool in 1851, by his own request we waited on him to see some of the Romish pictures or images that he had assembled in his travels. The servant said he was at home, but very busy; however, she would tell him. It was curious to see the abstracted countenance with which he entered yield instantly to beaming benevolence, and to hear him mingle the art and drollery of a showman, ridiculing the mummeries he was exhibiting, with the Christian's sigh of sorrow that the Man of Sin had so far ruined the Church of Christ.

"It is not for me, who have heard him rarely, to remark on his Church services. I enjoyed them at Elizabethtown and in Liverpool. But the aspect of his crowded congregation led me to observe it narrowly. I hope those who listened then are enjoying the blessing now. And they were clearly gathered from a wide circle, for I was so struck with the number of vehicles on the green when we left the church that I numbered them, and they amounted to fifty-three.

"Dr. Murray's conversational powers were delightful; and it was pleasing to find his natural buoyancy and wit never led him to utter, or seemingly to imagine, any idea that did not become a Christian; and he was always prepared to gather in his thoughts, and engage on the most solemn subjects and occupations.

"I had the misfortune to be in the States when the Fugitive Slave Law was passed, and to mourn that

Thanksgiving sermons said nothing in defense of the slave. We discussed this painful subject, and Dr. Murray persuaded me, as he had persuaded himself, that slavery would cease. He pointed to four border states, and said in ten years there will not be a slave there. Alas! ten years have passed, and they are in all the woe, and crime, and bondage still. If he and all his brethren had opened their mouths for the dumb, and shown how ill it becomes the man who is called on to love his brother as himself to presume to be the owner of human flesh, these four and other states might ere now have shaken off the shackles, which are more degrading to the usurper than to the bondman.

"When Dr. Murray was in Edinburgh in 1860, we once more seriously discussed this painful subject. He said, with tears in his sincere eyes, 'I have not prayed more earnestly for my own soul, nor for my wife and children, nor for my flock, than I have prayed to be shown my duty on this subject, and also to be shown what to do with the colored race if they were free to-morrow.' And then he told of his dear wife and his departed daughter's exertions to raise the tone of the colored people in their own city. In my heart I believed him in earnest; but still, he and his fellow-laborers have made a convention to let the slave suffer and the owner sin, and to be silent.

"I can not but mention this conversation, which made me part with my honored friend with a heavy heart.

"Let me rather turn to our last interview. Dr. Murray was hurried away, and drove down to take leave early in the morning, when assembled round the breakfast-table were about a dozen of my children and children's children, who had come to Edinburgh for the General Assembly. Hurried though he was, he did not fail to inquire about them and their pursuits, and which were Mary Lundie's children in particular. With a benignant smile he blessed us all, and hurried into the hall to conceal emotion; but he returned with a modest blush, having found in his hat a print of himself. Extending it to me, he said, 'My wife bid me give you that,' and then hastened away. The print was soon suspended in a frame over the dining-room chimney; and often, as I have looked on it, I have remembered the look, as if he was ashamed to be prized, when he presented it to me. And now, till through grace we meet in the better land, the picture is all I have to look upon. But there are many who will honor his memory, and feed on his words, and press after him, I trust, to the presence of Jesus. Doubtless the city misses him as well as the Church, for, apart from his religious influence, he entered into every plan for the promotion of all that could advance the interest of the town with all his large-hearted energy.

"Ah! how mournful is that sentence of death that must pass upon all men, on the public-spirited, the energetic, the loving, and the beloved! My beloved mourner, my heart mourns on every remembrance of you; yet I know you will not be forsaken, and I pray that your children may rise up to call their dear mother blessed. Believe me, as ever, your deeply sympathizing and loving friend, M. G. L. DUNCAN."

From Mrs. Jones.

"Philadelphia, August 19th, 1861.

"My dear Friend,—I have been thinking of your departed husband, and of the memoir in course of preparation, and I have been wishing that I could clothe the impressions his character has made upon my mind in fitting garb for introduction into the volume.

"My recollections of Dr. Murray go back more than thirty years. In my mind he is identified with the Sabbath-school, the Tract Society, and special personal effort for the conversion of a soul. I remember his appearance, in company with another servant of the Lord, also gone up to his reward, at the Sabbath-school which it was my privilege to superintend, at the corner of Arch and Third Streets, in the year 1828; his cheering smile and his encouraging manner are still present with me, and I remember his labors in the Tract cause, how indefatigable his efforts, how systematic in the performance of his duties; and I remember, too, how this department of Christian labor in this city prospered in his hands. I call to mind, with pleasure, his visit to me to enlist my sympathies in the cause, and now, in the life-long friend and strong champion of that blessed institution, I recognize the youthful stranger who in that visit opened up to me, with so much earnestness and engagedness, its importance, and so kindly invited my co-operation. I remember his deep interest in the salvation of the soul, as in a casual meeting on board of a steam-boat he commended to my notice and care the case of a young person just beginning to be interested in the great subject of religion. As my mind goes back to these delightful days of my own early consecration to my Redeemer, and recalls the companionship and the joys of those seasons of Christian fellowship and active duty, when you and I, my friend, walked hand in hand and heart to heart, and contrasts them with these days of buried treasures and widowed households, I should faint by the way were it not for the sure words of prophecy. That is a beautiful scripture, 'Thy dead men shall live; even with my body shall they rise. Awake and sing, ye that dwell in dust; for thy dew is as the dew of herbs, and the earth shall cast out her dead' (Isa., xvi., 19).

"In the autumn of 1831 it was my privilege to enjoy the society of Dr. Murray under his own hospitable roof for the first time. As pastor of the Presbyterian Church at Wilkesbarre, where he then resided, he exerted a very decided and powerful influence for good. If ever a people were divinely directed in the selection of an under-shepherd, it was that people. The state of the parish at that time was such as to require just such unflinching firmness, such energy, such engagedness in his Master's cause, and such a fearless spirit as characterized Dr. Murray. His influence was not confined to his Church nor to the town; the country for miles round felt that a man of God, valiant for the truth and fearless for right, had come among them. Many souls were given to him during his ministry there, some of whom have, no doubt, welcomed him to a participation in their joys. I think the article

'Beasts of Ephesus,' in his work entitled 'Parish Pencilings,' most clearly delineates his character as an energetic and fearless minister of the Gospel. With these traits he combined great tenderness of heart, devoted attachment to his people, a deep personal interest in their welfare, temporal as well as spiritual. He seemed to be almost as well acquainted with the different members of the families of his flock as with the members of his own family. In the intimacy of my acquaintance with him, and in my yearly visits to your happy household, I have been particularly struck with his heart-devotion to his people. Oh, how they ought to love his memory, and all he has left, for his sake! When a little recreation at a distance had been planned, and a member was sick, how he would hesitate and dislike to go, lest the sick one would miss his visits and comforting words; and what messages he would leave, and directions to be sent for, if needed, when he decided to go, and how he loved the young of the flock, and delighted in them! He seemed to me always to have time for every one and every thing, and never to be in a hurry.

"The stranger ever found a welcome at his board; his hospitality knew no bounds, and his table was ever the seat of intelligence, wit, and humor, tempered with the religious. In his gayest and most cheerful moods, if you but touched the spring, you would discover at once the rock upon which he rested, and the fountain from which he drew. He was the life of every circle in which he moved, and seemed to carry away with him the most vivid impressions of all that was passing. His very graphic descriptions of persons and scenes given to the press have charmed many of his friends who never suspected the author. Among these I recall his article on the General Assembly convened in this city in the year 1853, and moderated by Dr. John Young.

"As a servant of the Church, every one knew where to find him; always decided, never vacillating, and more than once, to my knowledge, when a master-spirit was needed, when difficulties had sprung up, he was sent for, to leave his home and take part in the deliberations of the boards of the Church. He loved peace, but he must have it based upon purity; first pure, otherwise he was a man of war. One weapon which he wielded very successfully in debate was ridicule. This is very apparent in his letters to Bishop Hughes. He could deride, satirize, treat with contemptuous merriment, disapprove or condemn the opinions or course of an individual, without affecting his feelings in the smallest degree toward him as a man.

"In all the walks of life, his genial nature flowed out in acts of kindness to his fellow-creatures. The lisping infant hailed him as the companion of his childish sports. How often have I seen him playing ball with my boy of three years old, laughing and shouting as loud as he; and the youth just merging into manhood found himself drawn toward him by the same genial spirit that in playful anecdote gave many a lesson of instruction. So apparent was this kindness of his nature as to attract even a passing stranger. You may not remember the circumstance of the old Quaker lady, who walked up and down the boat, fixing her inquiring eye on the passengers, until she stopped in front of Dr. Murray. 'I have been looking for some one,' said she, 'that I thought would do me a favor, and I have fixed upon thee: I have a very sick and helpless daughter on board; we shall soon arrive at the landing, and I have no one to assist me in getting her to the coach: wilt thou help me?' 'Certainly,' was the reply; and when they arrived, the coaches were immediately filled by those unwilling to be disturbed, and the poor mother and her suffering daughter were unprovided for. Dr. Murray stepped to the coach door, and with his strong manly voice cried out, 'If there's a gentleman here, he'll give up his seat to this mother and her sick daughter.' It was all that was necessary.

"Even the poor maniac felt the influence of his genial nature. In one of his frequent trips to Philadelphia, he met a frantic woman in the cars, whose friends were taking her to the Asylum for the Insane. She was perfectly wild and ungovernable. He stepped up to her friends, strangers as they were to him, and said, 'If you will allow me, I think I can soothe that poor woman.' They consented; he took his seat by her, entered into conversation with her, sympathized with her, saw the difficulties of the case, and that her aversion to her friends was so great that they would not be able to control her but by brute force. In a short time she became as a lamb in his hands; he stopped on his journey, and, with the consent of her friends, took a carriage, and in person conveyed her to the Asylum at Trenton. Having performed this act of the good Samaritan he came to his Philadelphia home, where he was ever a welcome inmate. I have lost a friend in Dr. Murray whose services I could command with as much freedom as if he were my brother, and whose presence was always a beam of sunshine in the family circle. But what is my loss, or the loss to the Church, to the world, or to all earthly friends, compared with the loss to his family? What he was there none can tell as well as the bereaved household. But God has taken him, and He has not left them comfortless.

"In compliance with your request, my beloved friend, I have gathered up some of my recollections of the departed. I am thankful that it was my privilege to enjoy so much of his society, and to share so largely in his confidence and regards. Death only *interrupts* these earthly friendships. Thanks unto God for the believer's hope.

"Your loving friend, ELIZA."

From the Rev. Mr. Reinhart.

"Elizabethport, March 31.

"S. I. PRIME, D.D.:

"DEAR SIR,—I noticed your purpose to publish a memoir of our dear and respected friend, Dr. Murray. I do not know that you will descend to matters so small, but as revelations of the kindness and sympathy of his heart, in individual cases, I send you two extracts from his letters. The first is dated 1844, in the early part of my ministry. As he was the instrument of introducing me into both the Church and the ministry, he took the liberty of giving me this good advice:

"'I hope, my dear friend, that you are laying yourself out to be useful. You have the qualities and talents, if you only improve them, to the full. Close study never omit. Renew it day by day, so that your profiting may appear unto all. Do not think of feeding your people with whipped sillabub. There are many who consider themselves Samsons in the ministry, who, if they slay any, do it with the jaw of an ass. Beware of thinking that doctrine or orthodoxy is the great thing. Mix the milk with the meat of the Word. Do not think all is done when you teach your people to *talk* well. Remember Mr. Talkative, who lived in Prating Row. Do not fear excitements produced by the truth. Remember your Great Master and His apostles produced excitements. They *cried out* that heard them, "What must I do to be saved?" But all this you will consider packing needed to fill up a letter, and sending a sermon in envelope,' etc.

"The second extract is from a note to a lady bereaved of her mother, and dated Dec. 24th, 1860:

"'I assure you that the contents of your note were unexpected and undesired. I felt it to be a duty I owed to the memories of the dead to attend your sainted mother's funeral. It was reward enough to me to gratify your desire, and to know that you *were* gratified rewarded me a thousand fold. Your dear mother has left you a noble legacy in her character and in her recorded prayers on high. Oh, may her children be all like her—may her mantle fall upon *you!* The few returns, like yours, that I have received for such duties, I devote to the spread of the knowledge of Him through whom we hope for the resurrection and the life. God bless you, my friend, and may you be a follower of those who through faith and patience have inherited the promises! Sincerely your friend.'

"My own experience testifies that, in true Christian friendship, Dr. Murray was a model man.

"Yours truly, E. H. REINHART."

From the Rev. Dr. Chickering.

"Portland, April 8th, 1861.

"REV. DR. PRIME:

"DEAR SIR AND BROTHER,—Your request, as to the correspondence or reminiscences of our departed friend Dr. Murray, has brought afresh to my mind some days of pleasant intercourse with him in Switzerland in the summer of 1851.

"We met at Geneva, where also, besides other well-known men from this country and England, was the since departed and lamented Choules, a genial man, whom our brother may already have met in the more glorious scenes and higher companionship of the better land.

"The missionary anniversaries occurring during our stay in the old 'city of Calvin,' Dr. Murray was made the American spokesman at the soirée, held at some public rooms, at which Count St. George presided with a grace that seemed to favor the notion of native aristocracy, at least of manners.

"When our country's turn came to be complimented, our brother rose with his inimitable expression of mingled dignity and archness, and, in a characteristically Irish-American style, spoke through Dr. Merle D'Aubigné, I think, as an interpreter. He greatly interested, and, at times, amused the large assembly of ladies and gentlemen, who needed not to wait for the translation, or to know our language, to appreciate, in some measure, his genial manner and mirth-provoking sallies.

"They were especially amused at the translation, by means of the word '*moulin*,' of his saying that we in this country received thousands of popish immigrants into our great mill, and ground them out good Protestants.

"We traveled together into Savoy, first stopping at Bonneville, where we dined, and saw, to his alternate amusement and indignation, freely expressed, the absurd superstitions and rude military demonstrations connected with the celebration of the *Fête à Dieu*. Our last stage to Chamouni, by the awkward *char-à-banc*, was shortened by his cheerfulness and ready wit, while he fully shared the deep emotion with which we caught the first glimpse of the Glacier de Boissons in the dim evening light, like a sheeted ghost stealing down from the dark forests above.

"During the days we spent together in that charming valley, and in climbing to the different elevations, and in visiting the Mer de Glace, there was much both to call forth his keen sense of the ludicrous and his own powers of wit and humor, which he sometimes practiced on the unfortunate traffickers in minerals, 'Echos,' and other means of begging, greatly to their perplexity and good-natured astonishment, when, without understanding his language, they slowly penetrated his meaning.

"Far more characteristic was his deep enjoyment of the wonders of Nature and works of Nature's God, of which that locality seems to be a grand central repository.

"When he led our social devotions, thoughts too deep for other utterance revealed his heart to ours. And when that pleasant American party of nine broke up at the Hôtel de Londres, some of us to go up the Rhone Valley and thence to Italy, and he to return to Geneva, it was with increased Christian affection, and in the hope, now by him happily realized, of standing on Mount Zion above. May we all be together there!

"As I was his friend, so I remain truly yours,

"J. W. CHICKERING.

"Cottage Manse, Portland, Me., April 20th, 1861."

From the Rev. Dr. Childs.

"Hartford, Ct., April 19, 1861.

"REV. DR. PRIME:

"DEAR SIR,—Dr. Murray came to Hartford on the twelfth of January last, and was my guest during his visit. Although I had known him well for several years, it was at this time that I became more intimately acquainted with him than ever before; and if the experience of others is like my own, it may safely be said, that the better Dr. Murray was known, the more deeply was he respected and loved.

"Perhaps nothing, as he appeared to us, impressed me more strongly than this—the degree to which his unbounded cheerfulness was mingled with true spirituality.

"His interest in children never seen before, and never to be seen again on earth, was remarkable. He had hardly entered the house from a bitterly piercing New England winter's atmosphere before he had them on his knees, in all the glee of his and their youthful sympathies, 'both hearing them and asking them questions;' and from that time forward, while he was with us, they may be said to have been his almost constant companions. To those who knew Dr. Murray only as a preacher and a controversialist, this is an interesting feature of his character. With many others, he had been subject to that judgment which has been proved so manifestly unjust that it ought to be ended, that if a man engages in controversy he must of necessity be of an unhappy or belligerent temper. Dr. Murray certainly was neither of these. Referring to the subject in one of our conversations, he observed that it seemed remarkable to him that he should have been engaged so much in controversy while he had so little of the controversial spirit in him.

"May I venture the suggestion that he had, perhaps, the true spirit for controversy. That spirit is not one which seeks controversy for its own sake; it may, indeed, be very reluctant to it; but when the interests of truth and religion solemnly demand controversy, it does not shrink from the issue. The very reluctance, in such a case, forms one of the elements of success.

"The object of Dr. Murray's visit was to deliver an address before the City Tract Society, in connection with the American Tract Society, New York. This was a service to which he had been previously invited, but which he had not before found it convenient to undertake.

"Sabbath morning, January 13th, he preached for me in the Presbyterian Church. His theme was '*The Church, a Family*' (Eph., iii., 15). The discourse preceded our communion service, and, it is hardly necessary to say, was appropriate and profitable.

"In the service he repeated, with a pathos that has often recurred to me since, the beautiful stanzas of our hymn:

"'One family we dwell in Him—
One Church, above, beneath;
Though now divided by the stream—
The narrow stream of death.

"'One army of the living God,
To His commands we bow:
Part of the host have crossed the flood,
And part are crossing now.'

Yet who of us supposed that *his* feet were even then touching the dark waters—that our next message from him would be that he had 'crossed the flood,' and joined those upon the other shore? It is a touching thought to us that he should have passed from our communion to the marriage supper of the Lamb!

"At a reference to his death in our services the Sabbath after that event, the whole congregation were in tears. It was a striking evidence of the interest his brief visit had awakened.

"In the afternoon he preached, with marked acceptance, at the Pearl Street Congregational Church (Rev. E. R. Beadle's).

"In the evening he fulfilled his engagement for the Tract Society. From circumstances which it is not necessary here to state, it was a difficult and delicate work. He felt the difficulty, and entered upon the work with some anxiety; but he was made competent to it. For an hour he held the large audience that had gathered to hear him with an address of deep interest, of decided power, and of complete success. Whatever differences of judgment there may have been among his hearers as to the object he was advocating, there was probably none as to the success of the advocate. It is only repeating the frequently expressed sentiment of those who heard him, that no man ever succeeded better under similar circumstances, or made a more favorable impression upon the public mind. Nor was this by a cautious withholding of his own views. He avowed them openly. In a manner that rather strengthened than weakened his hold upon the sympathies of his audience, he declared his own religious faith and his denominational preferences. He bore his testimony to what he believed to be the truth and the order of the Gospel, and he lost nothing of respect or of success by his testimony.

"This, I believe, was Dr. Murray's last service for

his Master abroad. Three weeks from the day he left us he fell asleep. I can add nothing to his eulogy. His record is on high.

"Yours fraternally, T. S. CHILDS."

From the Rev. Dr. Janeway.

"MY VERY DEAR FRIEND,—I first saw Dr. Murray at the Society of Inquiry, in the Theological Seminary at Princeton, in the autumn of 1826, and was arrested by an impressive speech in behalf of his countrymen, the Roman Catholics of Ireland, earnestly urging some measures for their relief. Circumstances connected with these projcted missions drew us together, and laid the foundation of a cherished friendship which only death could interrupt. Much together at Princeton, and in constant correspondence when separated, this friendship ripened and became more mellow. We were ordained at the same time, in the bounds of the same Synod, though in different states. We commenced our young ministries with similar views and aspirations; a few years later made us, in God's providence, near neighbors, our congregations touching on the borders, and calling for frequent ministerial communion in our several and contiguous neighborhoods. Personal intercourse increased and became more pleasant, and in the great ecclesiastical troubles which soon thickened upon us we moved together, for we thought alike and felt alike. While a member of the Seminary, Dr. Murray maintained, deservedly, a high standing for breadth of view and known energy of character. His associates were among the foremost and the more earnest, many of whom remain to this day, but some are fallen asleep. His course was interrupted, and for reasons not altogether known to me; he spent part of the time in charge of the Pennsylvania branch of the American Tract Society at Philadelphia. His business habits, his tact, his great energy, soon gained him reputation, and several of the Church boards would gladly have secured his services in their offices. I believe the Board of Education did choose him as associate secretary. While in this city he secured, by his affectionate treatment and genial manners, the love and regard of my sainted and venerated father, who all his life long regarded his young friend with the utmost confidence and greatest esteem. To my father's house he was then and ever a welcome and frequent visitor; all the family loved him, and those who survive cherish his memory and mourn his departure. Dr. Murray reciprocated these feelings, and bore ever and always the highest testimony to the worth and character of his venerable friend.

"His settlement at Wilkesbarre was an era in the history of that Church and region. A new influence went forth, and Wyoming felt his hand in the new and vigorous measures for the spread of Gospel truth. What the Church at Elizabeth continued and became under his earnest and successful ministry, the Church knows by heart; I need not repeat the story. *Si monumentum ejus quæris, circumspice.* Among all churches outside of the cities, it stood in marked and commanding eminence. So far from losing the character it had attained in the eminent pastorates it had enjoyed, it increased under his earnest and energetic labors. The troubles which culminated in the disruption of the Presbyterian Church occurred during his pastorate in Elizabeth. In their whole course I knew his inmost heart. It is doubtful if any other minister so intimately understood his views and feelings. From conscience and conviction he had taken the side of the Old School, and he never faltered; and though his warm Irish heart might have been expected to impel him, in the stormy debates in which he mingled, beyond the rule and line of Christian propriety, I never remember an instance where decorum was violated, and any arrogant disregard of the feelings of those who sympathized in the views of the opposing side. He was too honest, too open to fail in fullest expression of his views; and though he regretted to part with men whose Christian character he respected, he felt that all propriety required a separation, as a peace measure, from men whose views were so divergent. Through these storms he saw our Church escape and pass into untroubled waters. To the belief of the Church's duty, in her ecclesiastical capacity, to conduct all missions—train her young men for the ministry of the Word, he was a full and earnest convert; and yet the Bible and the Tract Society numbered him among their abler advocates to the close of his life; and so he was. A warm and true Presbyterian of the straitest kind, his heart was catholic, and, on the platform of a common faith he gladly stood with brethren of other denominations. In all this was he consistent; he never gave up to party what was meant for mankind. Narrow hearts and bigoted views can not comprehend the coexistence of true denominational zeal with a charity which could stretch its girdle around a world. To the Church of his adoption he was a loving and true child. From his extended pastoral labors, and few men have more, he redeemed time to give a frequent attendance on the meetings of the different boards, and was always heard with respect, and his expressed views frequently shaped the course of action. His known honesty of purpose—his utter freedom from indirection—his acknowledged love for truth, gave him a sway to which few men attain.

"A warmer friend to the Church and her institutions there could not be, and his Church honored him by placing him over most of these, and continuing him to the end of his life. Over our success he rejoiced with exceeding joy, like the joy of harvest. His ardent and comprehending mind marked out a wider field of effort and more expanded movements. Familiar, by reading and reflection, with the vast wastes of our land, he was deeply desirous that our Home Missions should keep abreast of the swelling wants of our great country. He counseled and urged enlargement and expansion when it could be safely done. His heart was wide, and took in a continent and a world. Other and abler pens will reveal these features of his character; mine are the personal reminiscences, the retired creed of his heart, as they came out in the familiar and unrestrained intercourse of our

Christian friendship. His general character, the massive and the genial, will doubtless find other limners; mine is an humbler duty, paid at the demand of his family, and which I could not refuse; the simple effusion of heart, a slight, and, I know, inadequate tribute to his precious memory. His death, in the full prime of an unwasted manhood, came to me with heavy and unexpected force. Few men could be more missed and less spared. His enlarging experience, his wide acquaintance with men on both sides of the Atlantic, his extended correspondence, his views quickened and chastened by this intercourse with evil and good men, all seemed to promise greater usefulness and richer results. God willed otherwise: His will be done; he is not, for God hath taken him. I knew not that my friend was sick until I heard that death had put his seal upon him. The very week he died I had planned, at his request, to meet him at his hospitable home, in consultation on important matters likely to occupy the hearts of those who thought alike on the interests somewhat complicating the institutions of the Church so dear to both of us. We had often had these familiar and friendly interviews, and in perfect and unrestrained confidence we were wont to discuss and agree on plans to be submitted; but the grave closed on them all, and I went to bury my friend and mingle amid the tears of the vast assembly who gathered around his coffin. That his end was peace I was well prepared to hear.

"In a visit of a night I paid him after his return from Europe, I was impressed with his increased spirituality. I was struck with the soberness of his conversation, and the growing fervor of his personal religion. He was, as ever, cheerful; his genial wit sparkled as before, but it was held in check. It was manifest he had grown in grace, and his European tour and the marvels of Divine Love which he witnessed in the revivals abroad had been greatly sanctified. I now see God was preparing his servant for his great reward. I must cease. I have uttered too much, perhaps, my personal feelings; if so, it was at the command of one who survives, and whose wishes I shall ever find pleasure, for his sake also, in consulting. I know other hands will rear more fitting memorials of my friend. The kind partiality of his surviving family requested this tribute of a long friendship, interrupted by the grave, to be renewed, I trust, in Heaven.

"Yours, in Christian friendship,

"THOMAS L. JANEWAY.

"Mission Rooms, Philadelphia, February, 1862."

From the Rev. Dr. Schenck.

"My first recollection of Dr. Murray is of hearing him preach, in the year 1836, in the First Presbyterian Church in Princeton, of which the Rev. Benjamin H. Rice, D.D., was at that time the pastor. I was then a mere boy, a member of the Sophomore Class in the college; but I remember the whole scene, the sermon, and the preacher's appearance as if it were yesterday. Dr. Murray was then in his matured, but his early and vigorous manhood. There was not yet a gray hair upon his head or a furrow upon his brow. His form was robust, but not so full as in later years. His sparkling eye, and his vivacious and energetic delivery, at once fixed my attention. His text was, Lamentations, iii., 27: 'It is good for a man that he bear the yoke in his youth.' Peculiar circumstances of difficulty and trial through which I had recently been passing caused my attention to be riveted to the discourse, although I had at that time few and superficial thoughts upon eternal things. I well remember now how earnestly he expatiated upon his theme, and exhibited the benefits the young man might derive from an early training of trial. I then knew nothing of Dr. Murray's previous history, but I felt that he was speaking from his own experience and consciousness. I never lost my special interest in Dr. Murray from that hour. Although years passed before we became acquainted, I always felt drawn toward him by some secret sympathetic attraction. Nor was his sermon ever forgotten. In after years its cheering truths often rose before my mind, and encouraged me in many an hour of struggle when tempted to despond. I have always felt that it had been to me a source of unspeakable benefit. Not more than a year before his death, when chatting freely with Dr. Murray in his study, I mentioned these facts. He seemed deeply affected. Tears rose to his eyes, and he exclaimed, with emotion, 'My dear brother, how much more faith we ought always to have when we preach. I am meeting such incidents every now and then along my way in the ministry. We preach, and then forget what we have done, and often think we have done no good at all. I am more and more convinced that a minister never preaches a sermon after true prayer to God, and in humble dependence on God's Spirit, without that sermon doing good somewhere and somehow. What a pure and constant source of delight will it be in Heaven to every true minister of the Gospel to have the long-hidden results of his preaching revealed to him, to follow his sermons one by one, and every one, as he sees them accomplishing the infinitely good and wise purposes of God!'

"I became acquainted with Dr. Murray while I was a student in the Theological Seminary. Toward young men his manner was always unreserved, genial, captivating. He was never stiff, patronizing, condescending in his intercourse with them. Hence, in fact, he was always beloved and confided in by young men. For myself, I felt from my first talk with him that he was my friend. And so he was. All our intercourse in after years only helped to ripen that friendship, and assured me of its entire reliability. The same frank, genial, affectionate manner every year attached to him a new circle of younger friends.

"During the last eighteen years I have seen Dr. Murray often, and in every variety of circumstances, and in his study, in his family, in the house of his parishioner, in the Synod and General Assembly, in the pulpit, every where, he was the same. There were no two sides to his character. It was not a faultless character, but it was admirable, and it was every where consistent, impressive, and Christian. Those who were favored with unrestrained social conversations with Dr. Murray in his study will never cease to count such opportunities as memorable privileges. What rare and genuine humor curled his lip and sparkled in his eye, accompanying some witty utterance; and anon how sweet and tender were his manner and his tone, as some elevated and pious sentiment fell from his lips! For each of the last eight years I had the privilege of spending a Sabbath with him at Elizabethtown, usually in the month of February, and I look back upon those days as days to be specially marked with a white stone—days rich in enjoyment, and precious in the remembrance.

"Others will draw the mental, religious, and ministerial portrait of Dr. Murray. It is not my purpose to attempt any such delineation.

"It was my melancholy privilege to spend in his house the last Sabbath of his life, February 3d, 1861. It had been understood between us that he was to spend that Sabbath with his beloved friend, the Rev. Dr. Sprague, at Albany. On arriving at Elizabethtown on Saturday I learned that, after having made all his preparations to go, he had only that morning felt compelled to abandon his intention through indisposition. Still, he conversed cheerfully, and late in the evening expressed the hope that he would be well enough to attend at church next day and hear me preach. That hope was not realized. On the next day he was worse, having occasional spells of violent pain about his chest. In the intervals of service on that Lord's day I was much with him in his room. He conversed cheerfully between the times of pain.

Twice in the course of the day he asked me to pray with him and for him, and his thoughts appeared to be much on things spiritual and heavenly. He conversed much upon the state of our Church, whose continued unity began to be threatened by the growth of our fearful national troubles. His heart was deeply moved upon this subject. The welfare of our beloved Zion seemed to be continually upon his mind. He expressed his views in strong terms in regard to the responsibility and wickedness of those who were laboring to accomplish the disunion either of the Church or of the nation.

"While conversing, I picked up a daguerreotype of his daughter Elizabeth. 'Ah! what a good and noble child she was!' he exclaimed. 'No one can tell what bitter pangs it cost me to part with that dear girl. But God was pleased to take her to Himself, and among my sweetest hopes and anticipations is that of meeting her in the heavenly mansions. You have never lost a child.'

"'No,' I replied, 'I have been mercifully spared that trial; but I have been called to endure another, which seemed to darken this whole world.'

"'Ah! yes,' said he, 'I know to what you allude. That was, indeed, the cutting of the main artery. And yet, in every bitter cup our heavenly Father calls on us to drink, we may find a precious medicine; and, however bitter that cup may be, we can always look around and see some who have had yet more bitter ones put to their lips; and we can always see how much more bitter our own might have been made but for God's wondrous mercy.'

"On Monday morning he was still no better. During the night he had suffered occasional spasms of intense pain, yet in the intervals he was cheerful, and no one felt alarmed. About ten o'clock I had my last interview with him. He spoke again of the state of the Church, and of his anxieties in regard to the approaching General Assembly, and gave me some messages in regard to it to bear to the ministers at Princeton. He did not know whether his Presbytery would see fit to send him as a commissioner. He had no desire to go; but if they did, he would feel it a very solemn duty to attend. Little did any of us who stood around his bedside think he was so soon—so very soon—to ascend to the General Assembly and Church of the First-born on high. He made some very kindly reference to my visit and the pleasure it had given him; also to the services of the Sabbath, and hoped I might often visit Elizabethtown. And then I bade him farewell, no one of us supposing him to be seriously ill. Within twenty-four hours I heard in Brooklyn of his death; and the next time I saw that loved and venerated form it was occupying the 'narrow house,' and prepared for burial. 'My work is done!' he exclaimed when dying. 'Yes, and well done,' we may all say, as we think of his useful and unintermitting labors. Long will his memory be dear and fragrant to all who knew him, and most so to those who knew him best. WILLIAM E. SCHENCK."

THE END.

Harper's Catalogue.

A New Descriptive Catalogue of Harper & Brothers' Publications, with an Index and Classified Table of Contents, is now ready for Distribution, and may be obtained gratuitously on application to the Publishers personally, or by letter inclosing Six Cents in Postage Stamps.

The attention of gentlemen, in town or country, designing to form Libraries or enrich their Literary Collections, is respectfully invited to this Catalogue, which will be found to comprise a large proportion of the standard and most esteemed works in English Literature —comprehending more than two thousand volumes — which are offered, in most instances, at less than one half the cost of similar productions in England.

To Librarians and others connected with Colleges, Schools, &c., who may not have access to a reliable guide in forming the true estimate of literary productions, it is believed this Catalogue will prove especially valuable as a manual of reference.

To prevent disappointment, it is suggested that, whenever books can not be obtained through any bookseller or local agent, applications with remittance should be addressed direct to the Publishers, which will be promptly attended to.

www.ingramcontent.com/pod-product-compliance
Lightning Source LLC
LaVergne TN
LVHW021138110826
845150LV00005B/1061

* 9 7 8 1 4 2 5 5 4 9 6 8 8 *